The Making of an
Orphan

Leslie T. Dean

Cover image © Shutterstock.com
Interior images are from the authors family archives.

www.innovativeinkpublishing.com
Send all inquiries to:
4050 Westmark Drive
Dubuque, IA 52004-1840

ISBN: 9-798-7657-4560-1

Published in the United States of America

Dedication

To Karin.
You have finally been heard.
You are finally safe.
You are finally free.

To Ellie and Esme.
Mimi loves you so much.
Let the buck stop with you.

To Ariana, my adopted granddaughter.
Mimi loves you.
This book is your example.
Tell Aria's story.

Table of Contents

Foreword

After having read Leslie Dean's first book *Forgiven Much* I was very excited to hear she was writing another. Her first book offered insight into what happens to a person as they live through abandonment, rejection, and pain. It explored how mental health and substance abuse issues develop as a way to cope in an unhealthy way with the emotional trauma.

As expected, the second book, *The Making of an Orphan*, did not disappoint, but goes even further to explore intergenerational trauma and its impact on future generations. Leslie writes from her own generational trauma in a vulnerable way that readers can connect to in their own lives. She opens her heart and story so others can benefit from her pain. But not only that, she does it so others can benefit from understanding redemption is possible.

Now is the time for this book as we are becoming a society that is acknowledging generational trauma. It can be difficult to connect the dots, and this story is not about finding blame or fault. It is about recognizing the hurt and pain from past generations, while taking responsibility for future generations. As a licensed professional counselor, I have referred clients to *Forgiven Much* and am confident I will also refer *The Making of an Orphan* as a resource for their healing."

Patricia Boyce, PsyD, LPCMH, NCC

Acknowledgments

There are so many I wish to thank for their faithful efforts to assist me in the writing of this book. Their patience and the time they donated to me, in lieu of their own busy lives, will be forever treasured in my heart. Their prayers, moral support, financial assistance, and constant encouragement made this work possible. Each gave selflessly and with great love. I love them dearly and want to thank each of them.

Lynette Wright—Well, we did it again. You have been my mentor for 30+ years and have never failed to be my cheerleader. Thank you again for the endless hours of helping me re-think, re-word, and re-write till I got it right. Thank you for listening to the angry rants and the crying jags, as these decades-old memories raised their ugly heads and were given the light of truth, the permission to be healed, and a final "good riddance" . . . at last. I think you may have learned a few new things about me in this book! And you know I will be depending on you for the sequel as well. There are no words to express my gratitude for standing by me through it all. I love you.

Patsy Boyce—You have always been my role-model as the type of counselor I aspire to be. I have admired your honesty and integrity for years and am certain every client you have is aware how blessed they are to have you. I am so appreciative of your help with this writing and am immensely grateful for your support over the years. Your encouragement with my first novel, *Forgiven Much*, has always been gold to me. Thank you.

Jeanette Hazel—Getting to know you has been such a blessing. When you agreed to peer review for me, I was thrilled to add your knowledge and experience to my list of people who I knew would be honest and forthcoming, and would help me stay focused on the One who was truly guiding this work. Most of all, without you, this work would not have moved forward as quickly as it did. Your generosity was God's provision. You are another whose encouragement with *Forgiven Much* helped me believe I could write another book. Thank you for all you are.

Dawn Robyn—What a blessing it was to meet you at Sulphur Springs and experience your beautiful retreat center! I was so blessed to see *Forgiven Much* sold in your bookstore. When I reached a writer's block, and needed to get into a different environment, I knew the place that spoke to my soul. Mountains, horses, and complete quiet and peace are what I had found in Sulphur Springs. And you provided a whole week of exactly that. I broke through some very tough memories I had failed to confront, and the book went forward. I am forever grateful for your kindness and generosity.

Colleen Morris—My girl! Your prayers and encouragement have been God's hand on my life in those times of wanting to give up. You have allowed me to be candid with you about some painful pieces I found hard to share. Your faith in me, and for this project, has been a light to keep me focused on the prize. Your relentless and faithful desire to help me with the technical issues involved in its preparation has been my blessing. You are my girl. Thank you so much for believing in me.

Jackie Seldon—My pro-life partner and boss, but most of all, my friend and prayer warrior. You have consistently reminded me that through my pain and transparency, many would be led to the foot of the cross to finally heal their wounds. That has been my driving force. Thank you so much.

Nicole Theis—Thank you for your prayers, your partnership, and your support . . . in so many ways. You have a beautiful gift of knowing exactly what someone needs when they need it. You have done that numerous times as I have traversed through this work. Texted an encouraging word, called just to see how I was, or dropped off the perfect gift—unannounced and unsolicited—when the need was there to just feel special. You are a blessing.

Wallace Rumbarger—Without your provision of a computer, one I could rely on, this book would not have been written. Your desire to help me make that happen, then supplying me with just the right one to accomplish it, has been another blessing from the Father's hand. Thank you from the bottom of my heart for all you do.

Introduction

This book was not written to blame anyone. Nor to impose guilt. It wasn't written to request an apology, ask forgiveness or seek forgiveness. It wasn't written to impose accountability nor to negate responsibility. It wasn't written to embarrass, shame or deny.

This book was written to share truth. The truth about intergenerational trauma. The truth about how abuse, neglect, abandonment, and rejection shape a person's thinking, feelings, and behaviors. And how, in the absence of good counsel and therapy, these are passed down from one family to the next, one generation to the next.

It doesn't happen because you want it to. It happens because you don't even realize there is a problem. There is a complete lack of recognition of the symptoms. You have not been educated to the fact you need a paradigm shift—a reframing of what you believe to be true replaced with what IS true. A wake-up call to understand why the life you're living isn't the life you wanted—and how you can change it—or even believe change is possible.

The sad part is, when too much time has passed, the wall of deception becomes thicker. You don't want to know the facts, because how you live your life has become your comfort zone, and no matter how bad it is, it's more comfortable than the changes that truth would bring. The reality of knowing you have thought one way your whole life, then learned it was based in a lie, can be very disconcerting. It's as if your whole world is turned upside down. Like you are walking one way and unexpectedly you do a 180. That can be a scary premise and can play incredible games with your head. So, you stay in denial.

To be healed—truly healed—a person must be willing to replace what they have believed to be the "truth"—either as it appeared to them, or as it was told to them—with the facts. They must be willing to accept how painful hearing them or remembering them might be. Because no one can change how they think, feel, or behave until they realize there is a problem. A problem where misinformation has been fed to them. Or the truth, the whole truth, and nothing but the truth has been omitted.

This book is about healing. About offering hope. From someone who has walked the road of denial and bought the misinformation as if it were fact.

Who existed in the belief that her worth and value were defined by how she looked or how others treated her. Someone whose world was turned upside down when the truth was revealed. Yes, I can offer you hope because I learned that no matter how painful the facts can be, they are still better than living a lie. I did that 180. I had my life reframed. It was hard and painful work. But the freedom on the other side was golden. And best of all, I discovered I never had to live there again. I want that for you, too.

This book is about finding truth. Real, solid, black-and-white truth. The truth that has no gray areas. The truth that is hard to look at because it involves people who were supposed to love and protect you. I have had to share some very hard truths—some ugly truths. About my parents, myself, and those involved in the unhealthy life I was trying to navigate. The purpose is not to make them look bad, but to get to the bottom of what made me tick. And why my ticker needed adjusting. It took exhaustive research, and the outcome was to finally see my family through a different lens. Through Jesus' lens. And to realize nothing—absolutely nothing—is beyond the redemptive blood of Jesus Christ. Because only two things bring about the healing of intergenerational trauma:

The truth . . . And the One who will lead you to it. The One who is defined as *The Truth*.

Part One:

The Lost Years

1

In the beginning . . .

Webster's Dictionary defines *orphan* as "a child deprived—by death—of one, or usually both parents." But they have a second definition I find much more appropriate for the purposes of my story. "*One deprived of some protection or advantage.*" Because I would contend, one can have both parents present, and still be an orphan. Orphaned of love, adoration, compassion, protection, and the advantages that wholeness and a healthy mind can provide. The absence of these can leave a child much more orphaned than the presence of a warm body.

And, so, begins my story . . .

To gain understanding of "how" my story could take place, one must understand the "who, what, where, and why" leading up to it. We will cover all of those. For now, my tale begins, in the middle of January, in the year 1955.

As the story goes, my father was stationed in Alaska on a survey ship. In his absence, my mother was staying with her family, in Crisfield, MD. They shared a home her father had built for them in 1917. Besides her mother, my mom's aunt and younger brother lived there, and this was her safe place as she approached her final days of pregnancy. At her last doctor's visit, she was told it would only be a few more days, and she was given instructions on when to come to the hospital. She immediately sent word to my dad and asked him to come home as soon as he could. He was 4500 miles away. He said he would get there.

Now, I have heard my father share this story many times as to his adventures to get to my mom for my birth. Unfortunately, none of them impressed her very much. Because of the winter weather, the only way he could get to

Annapolis Naval Academy was in the bomb bay of a military prop plane. He said he was "close to frozen" the whole time, and he only got to warm up once, when they stopped to refuel at an Air Force base in Colorado. He said his fingers and toes had been blue, and he had icicles hanging from his uniform hat. After arriving in Annapolis late at night, he had no luck finding a ride. So, the next day, he had to hitchhike the 125 miles to my mother's hometown of Crisfield. No easy feat since we are talking all rural country. Consequently, he arrived a day after my birth.

My mother had gone into the local hospital in the midst of a snowstorm, on the eve of January 17, and she labored hard until my birth on the morning of the 19th. Remember these were the days before IV Pitocin, now used to augment labor. Except for the doctor, she was alone at my birth. The snow prevented her family from being there, so she was hurt and angry. There was no one in which to show off her new little baby girl, or with whom to share her happiness.

The nurses asked her what name to give me, and she requested time to wait for my dad to arrive. There had only been one name they had discussed together. My dad had become friends with a CPO (Chief Petty Officer) aboard their ship. He was Swedish, and told my dad if I was a girl, he should name me Karin (Swedish pronunciation is Car-in) because it meant "little princess." My parents decided they would use it.

By the next morning, the nurses told my mom she had to give me a name, since no one knew when my dad was arriving (no cell phones—not even many landlines back then!). This only added to my mother's stress—and mounting anger with my dad. So, she complied, and I was named Leslie Karin Taylor. Mom honored the CPO's request, but assigned my first name as a constant reminder to my dad of his absence at my birth—Leslie had been the name of one of her past boyfriends. So, by the time my dad arrived late that night, the name was on the birth certificate.

I don't know what my dad expected when he got there. I don't know what my mom expected either. Healthy people would have done away with their personal issues and shared in the joy of their new daughter. But there were no healthy people present, so when my dad walked in, and found my mom feeding me, the first thing out of his mouth was, "She can't be mine! Look at that nose! She looks like a parrot!" If you knew my dad, you would know this is not outside his sense of humor, and much canned laughter might have been heard in the background had this been a sitcom. But whether he meant it or not, his timing was way off, and a nuclear war began in that small, isolated hospital room.

So that is how my life began. What was meant to be two parents sharing the joy of their baby's birth, became a war. Where there was to be love, adoration, compassion, and protection, instead there was vengeance, ridicule and unforgiveness. Love tanks were running on empty. What was to be the first day of the rest of my life, became my first day of being orphaned. And it would not be my last.

2

Hawaii

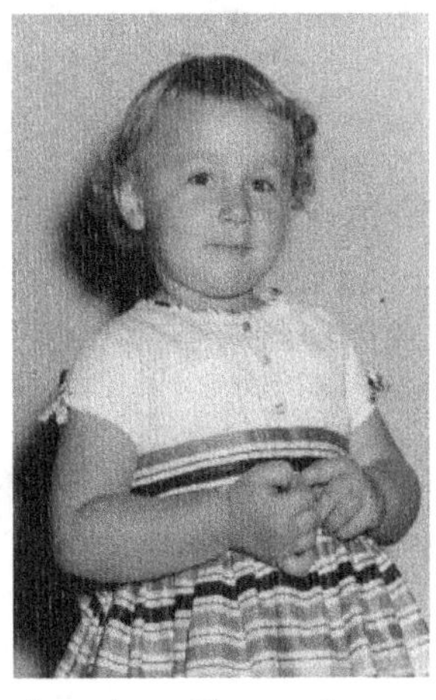

My memories as a young person, were usually based in where we lived. We moved so frequently, this seemed to be the way I kept track of the events in my life, and so I have presented my stories accordingly. The first experiences I recall came somewhere between the ages of 2-3 years old. I remember living in an apartment at the top of many, many steps. I only remember my mom and I being there, and I recall her crying . . . a lot. I remember one occasion when my dad came to visit, and he was wearing his uniform. He hugged me, then started tickling me and I yelled, "I hate you" right in his face.

Now, I don't recall that we had TV, so I must wonder where I learned to say this, but on that particular day, it made no difference. All I remember after that was my mom grabbing her hairbrush and beating me with it. I didn't know why I was getting punished; what had I done wrong?

At some point that day, they talked about having to move, and Dad telling Mom it was pretty far away. I don't remember much after that, except the screaming and crying that followed. Mom was very angry with him, and I remember wondering if Dad was going to get a beating with the hairbrush, like I had. After Dad left, I do remember trying to hug her because she was crying so hard and being pushed away and told to go to bed. She wasn't the only one who cried herself to sleep that night.

In later years, I learned we had been living in San Francisco at that time, and Dad had just gotten orders to transfer to Hawaii. Yep, it was a long way away. Remember this was the 1950's, and there were no Boeing jets. Just prop planes and very, large ships that took you that far across the ocean. Yes, Mom would be extremely far from her small hometown, and her family

. . . her safe place. I guess you can feel orphaned at any age.

***

Hawaii. I have a few memories of this place. I would like to say they were good, considering the beauty there. But I was beginning to learn, even at this tender age, being happy was a relative thing. No matter how beautiful your surroundings, if you are around miserable people, it is hard to be happy yourself. Especially when you get blamed for their despair. It's when a child begins to believe she has the power to somehow control their feelings . . . to make them happy . . . if she just tries hard enough. *More on that later.*

So, my first experience in Hawaii, that I recall, was playing tag with some kids who were visiting. Our dads worked together, and so our mothers were friends. This was back in the days when moms used to visit each other, have coffee, and the kids were sent outside to play.

We had gotten bored playing outside, so we started chasing each other by running in the front door and out the back door. My mother had an old utility table that sat by the kitchen door. This is a piece of equipment most everyone had in their homes in those days. It was made of metal, with three shelves, and people stored their electrical appliances on it—like blenders, toasters, etc. Mostly it was for convenience.

Well, I was running full-tilt boogie through the kitchen, slipped on the scatter rug by the backdoor, and fell. My left foot slid under the utility table. I was in such a hurry to get up and keep running after my friends, I am sure what happened next took less than five seconds. To this day, I can remember my little 3-year-old mind thinking, "Should I pull it out heel up or ankle up?" Heel up it was, and I yanked it out as hard as I could, leaving a chunk of my heel, and a severed Achilles tendon behind. I don't remember a lot after that except my mom's friend holding me while trying to help my mom calm down. She was yelling at me for ruining her day.

It took a lot of stitches to put me back together, and I went home on crutches, with a cast up to my groin. Years later, Mom told me she could hear me screaming from where she was on the first floor of the hospital. These were the days before air conditioning, so I guess the operating room window was open. The doctor had told her I was too young to be put to sleep, so I didn't receive any anesthesia. He also told her I would never walk without a limp, because there would probably be a  difference in the length of my left leg. I don't remember my accident being something awful for me. It was just an event that was inconvenient for everyone. I walked with crutches for four months.

The only other memories I have in Hawaii, both involved my mother blowing up at Dad. One was when he took me with him to the beach while he went surfing. He thought it would be fun for me to ride some waves with him, and when she found out, it wasn't good. Honestly, if I found out one of my kids was taken to the ocean at 3 years old to ride a surfboard, I probably would have lost it too. Dad was not really providing much protection for my little self. But, as time will show, that became a common theme.

The other memory plays back like a movie in slow motion. And, oh my goodness, there was so much more to it than I would remember . . . for many, many years. The picture begins with me standing behind my mom, her screaming at my dad, throwing dishes at him, and him running out the front door. Again, I vividly remember him being in his uniform, calling her crazy, as he dashed through the door, quickly slamming it shut as the last dish exploded on impact behind him. *We will be visiting that scene again, as it became a huge factor in my life—and my healing—decades later.*

So, let's look at some things. Children this young, have memories about things that are a lot of fun, and things that make them happy. Going to Disney World, a special Christmas present, sitting on a parent's lap while being read to, or being tucked in at night. These are all events that release dopamine, oxytocin and endorphins—all hormones that make us feel good and enhance our experiences. Kids also recall what was sad—like the death of a loved one, the loss of a dear pet, divorce, or even moving and having to leave what was familiar to them. These could be considered traumatic events for a child, depending on how the situation was handled by their caregivers. Trauma is accompanied by adrenalin—the fight or flight hormone, CRH—the master stress hormone, and cortisol—another stress hormone. Sometimes children who live in un-healthy environments experience these stress hormones so frequently, they begin to believe its normal. The feelings that are produced by them—how their body feels—becomes second-nature. Symptoms of anxiety are often seen, and sometimes they may even get misdiagnosed as ADD or ADHD.

Examples of this could be involvement in an accident, and being blamed for it, as if it was a plan to harm the parents. Or an abuse of some sort, like get-ting spanked with a hairbrush for repeating what they had heard their mother say, or maybe listening to their mother cry every night because their father is "never home," and when they try to console her, they are pushed away and told to go to bed. These are acts that confuse a child. Makes them begin to define truth as relative to the situation. Makes them feel rejected. Abandoned. And where the faith in who is supposed to be their most trusted protector, begins to waiver. This is where a shaky foundation begins forming—one that will even-tually lead to unhealthy behaviors and feelings of worthlessness later in life. One that will set up a child to people-please, to gain attention and affirmation. The foundation for codependency.

So, back to the story. The last thing I remember about Hawaii was leaving it! We were on a huge ship. I don't know how long it took, I only remember seeing my mom happy and that felt really good. When she was happy, I got hugs. I got smiles. And I felt loved.

Next stop was her hometown . . .and my Granny's house.

3

Crisfield

I loved going to my mom's home! Crisfield is found on a small peninsula in the Chesapeake Bay, and once-upon-a-time it was known as the "Seafood Capital of the World." Crabbing, oyster tonging, fishing, and clamming were the trades of many who lived there. It was country—lots of open land, lots of trees to climb, and my cousin, who was my age, only lived a few houses away. My Aunt Ruby (my grandmother's youngest sister) and my mom's younger brother, Junie, lived there as well.

As soon as we arrived, they didn't stop hugging me and telling me how much I had grown! I didn't realize it then, but we had been gone fifteen months. I was now almost 5. They just kept hugging me and putting me on their laps, so they could keep hugging me. I felt so loved . . . and THAT felt so good. Ahh, if hugs and kisses could metaphorically be called food—I was stuffed! *We will unpack that comment a little more later.*

Now, my dad was not with us, and I couldn't tell you where he was, but I can say that was the norm during most of my young life. There was constant arguing between my parents because he was "always going somewhere." They argued, my mom cried, and I was sent to my room—or anywhere out of her sight. So, I wasn't terribly sad that Dad was not here. Half of the problem was missing. All I knew was Mom was smiling . . . and smiling A LOT! And that felt wonderful for me!

My mom changed so much when she was with her family. You could almost say she became a different person. She laughed a lot, smiled a lot, and most of all, she wasn't ignoring me. She actually seemed to want me around! Even though it was my Granny, Aunt Ruby and Uncle Junie who spent the

most time with me, I still enjoyed hearing my mom singing, laughing, and having fun with her family. Almost every night, we sat on the back porch, sipped iced tea, and talked—just staring out at the corn fields across the street, and watching the cars drive by. And sometimes, no one said anything at all! Just listened to the frogs, the locusts, and the peace and quiet. These were good times.

Almost every day, my uncle would come home from work at lunch, pick me up, and take me to the little store where Aunt Ruby worked so we could get a "zip." She would take milk, add some flavor to it—chocolate or cherry—then some soda water and ice. It was delicious! Sometimes I would stay there with her and help her make ice cream cones for the fisherman who came in after work. Or sometimes, she would put me up on a chair and let me flip the burgers, while she got the rest of the sandwiches ready. Crisfield was a fishing town, more specifically, a crabbing town. There were a couple places where they all stopped when they got off their boats to grab a snack, or just take a rest. And it was either where Aunt Ruby worked, called "Kirk's" or the place just down a few doors, called "Gordon's." Both were named after the owners. There was no real competition. The fishermen just picked their preferred spot, and they were loyal to it.

My favorite part about going there to see Aunt Ruby was helping her cook and make soft drinks. Back then, you mixed your own. First, I put some ice in the glass, followed by the cola syrup, then soda water, and stir! That summer, Kirk let me come in with Aunt Ruby almost every day to help out! I felt very grown up doing this since Mom rarely let me help in her kitchen. After all, I was almost 5 years old now! And my other favorite thing? Looking at the comic books. I loved, loved, loved, the comic books!

Coming home was fun, too. If Uncle Junie brought me back early, I got to play with my cousin, out in our yard, or best yet—I got to help my Granny make biscuit animals out of yeast dough—watch them rise, and then bake them! They were the best! If I came home with Aunt Ruby, dinner was already on the table, and we all ate together. Lots of stories, lots of laughs and lots of good food! Best of all was bedtime! If Aunt Ruby was working night shift, Granny took me up to bed and laid down with me till I went to sleep. She always had her apron on, and in her apron were always a handful of saltines. Every night she would whisper, "Now, Karin, don't tell your mom I gave these to you." I never did. On nights when Aunt Ruby was home, she would take me to bed, and she always had a new comic book to read to me. I loved that! Superman. Supergirl. Batman and Robin. Aquaman. Green Lantern! I loved them all! On those nights, I slept with her. My life had changed so much since I had come here. I was smiling all the time!

So, let's look at some more things. Have you noticed none of these memories include much of my mom? She was there, some of the time. Did she leave to go visit my dad? I am fairly sure that was the case. But I honestly don't know. I loved my mom, but, as I shared earlier regarding my dad, I was not all that upset when they weren't around. Not when I was here with these three awesome people. People who never pushed me away. Never ignored me. Always loved me. Complimented me. Included me. A child is supposed to feel all these things with her parents. More with them than anyone else on the planet. Parents are supposed to supply your emotional needs. Protect you from harm. Provide a safe and loving environment. But I didn't have that. And truth to tell? I never did have that with them.

If I were to ask you, "What is the opposite of love?" What would your answer be? Most people would reply "hate." But that's not true. Because when you hate someone, you are still responding to them. Still putting forth an effort. Even though a negative one. In your emotions. In your actions. You are still putting out energy. No, the opposite of love is being disregarded. Discounted. Ignored. And at my young, tender age, I already knew what those felt like. Except when I was here. I felt good at Granny's, and it didn't matter to me who helped me feel that way. My comment earlier about hugs and kisses being metaphorical food? When I was not here, and was not "fed" those things, it did feel like I was starving. And I learned at a very young age to substitute food for the love I craved so desperately. It was unavailable from my parents. This would haunt me most of my life.

By the way, before I leave this subject— did you notice my grandmother calling me Karin? Yep, after that faux pas at my birth, my dad never allowed me to be called Leslie. To all who knew me, on both sides of the family, I was Karin (but pronounced Karen). However, that would change, and in the not-so-distant-future. *To be continued . . .*

My wonderful summer ended. It had been full of fun times, and warm memories. My mom told me I was going to kindergarten in a few weeks, and it would be here in Crisfield. My dad was apparently away on a "ship at sea" and both of us would be living with Granny! Now, I don't have a lot of memories of this kindergarten year that differ much from what I have already shared, with a few exceptions.

This was when my granny got a phone. You picked it up and asked a lady, "Please give me 8-9-1" (or whatever number you were seeking) and then you could talk to someone else at their house without going there! I thought it was so cool! The lady's name was Myrna, and I sometimes picked up the phone just to say "hi" to her. She was also my Uncle Junie's girlfriend.

This was also the year of the first Christmas I can remember. I went with Uncle Junie, and it was so cool to cut down our own tree, bring it in the house and decorate it! I also remember getting the doll for Christmas that I really wanted. Mom was very quiet and stayed in her room a lot, maybe because my dad was not there. She got presents, including something I had made her at school, but she didn't seem happy opening any of them. My uncle told her to "cheer up" and she told him to "shut up" and she went upstairs. Everyone got quiet after that, and then I went in the kitchen to help Granny make biscuits. Uncle Junie turned on the TV and then Mom came downstairs and sat with him. Like nothing had happened. *That is a snapshot of something we will visit again . . .many times.*

A couple more things happened. The first was my mom started taking me to church with her. I went to a Sunday school class with a sweet older lady named, Miss Clara. She gave lots of hugs. The end of her class was our favorite part! We all got candy! We did fun stuff in her class like color, sing songs, and we learned about a man named Jesus. I learned a new song called "Jesus Loves Me" and Miss Clara promised us He did. I wasn't sure how someone could love you if he had never met you, but I believed her . . . mostly. Mom went to the bigger part of the church while I was in Sunday School. It was really the only thing I remember just the two of us doing together that year.

The other new thing that happened, was going to the store with my mom and Granny. It was a big store called Grant's, and I loved going because they had live animals. As soon as we got there, I would head to the pet department. They had parakeets, finches, goldfish, and tiny turtles. There was one special parakeet I became attached to. She was golden in color, and she was special because she had a broken wing that hung down, so she couldn't fly.

After several visits, the lady who worked there took her out of the cage and let her sit on my finger. She seemed to know me! I started calling her Goldie. Once, I asked my mom if we could buy her, maybe for my birthday, but she said she would end up caring for the bird, so it wasn't going to happen. I looked forward to those store visits, no matter how far apart they were. And every time I realized Goldie was still there, my heart would sing.

At the end of the school year, my kindergarten teacher asked me if I would like to sing a song at the graduation. I loved to sing, so I agreed, and she picked the song, "Love and Marriage." To this day, the only lyrics I can remember are "Love and marriage, love and marriage go together like a horse and carriage." But on graduation day, my little 6-year-old self, did not miss a lyric, and I got a loud applause when I finished! It was a great day, but it would get even better!

My mom, Granny and Aunt Ruby were there to see me, and when it was over, Aunt Ruby went back to work, and my mom took me and Granny to Grant's. I did what I always did and ran straight for the pet department. I was holding Goldie when I noticed my granny walking up beside me. She said, "Would you like to take Goldie home?" I could not believe my ears! I asked her if she was serious, and when she nodded her head, I started crying! This was the happiest day of my life. Granny bought me the cage and all the accessories, and I held her in my hands the whole way home. I kept her cage in the living room, but she spent most of her time on my shoulder. We were best friends!

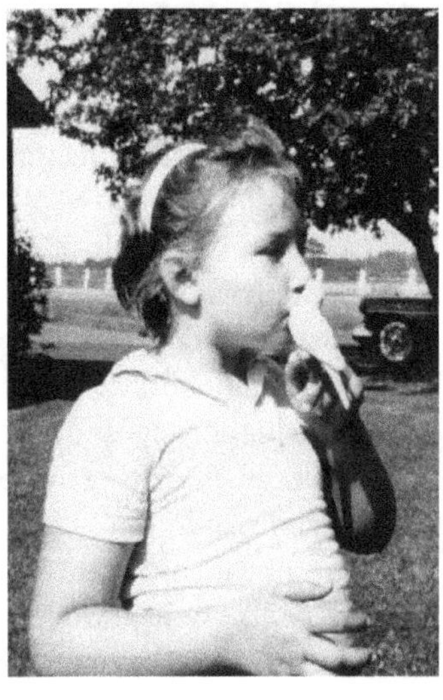

That summer, I remember Dad coming to visit, and it was a little awkward. Uncle Junie had become the person I looked to as a father image. Of course, I didn't realize that at the time. I just remember feeling uncomfortable with Dad, but before it could become problematic, he was gone again. Before he left, he announced we would be leaving Crisfield and living in a new place called Norfolk. Mom stayed in her room for a few days after that. She didn't come down for anything. Not even to eat.

When that passed, she started something new at mealtime she had not done before: "Eat everything on your plate, Karin! There are children starving in Korea who would love to eat the food you are wasting." There were some nights she would get angry with me if I told her I was not hungry. I had to sit there, no matter how long it took, until I finished every last bite. Once, Uncle Junie had taken me for a zip, and I was already kind of full, but she made me eat everything anyway. I threw up from being so full. This replicated another behavior that deeply affected my life in my teenage years. *Another subject for later discussion . . .*

Did you notice something here? Dad comes. Dad makes a big announcement about moving. Dad leaves. Mom has no control of what he does. But, alas, she has control of me. And what I eat has become something she CAN control. As I said earlier, this would profoundly affect my life in the future.

Lastly, before we leave Crisfield, there are two things I want to share from my memory bank about that summer. Both are incidents that happened with my cousin. As I said before, we were the same age, and he was my constant play partner. There was a public pool that we went to about once a week. It was probably the fifth or sixth time we had been that summer, and he and I were both adventurers. When we were not looking for bones in grave crypts, we were jumping our bikes over ditches. On this day, my cousin wanted to go explore an old shed at the top of the hill behind the pool. I was game!

So, we climbed up the hill, and he pushed the dilapidated door open as far as he could and went inside. My cousin was very skinny, and though he had just slid in, I was struggling. I pushed as hard as I could and then put my right hand inside the doorframe to get more leverage. Instantly, I felt sharp burning pain! My hand felt like it was on fire! I yanked it out, and it was completely covered with hornets and in a frenzy, they started attaching themselves to my chest and upper arm. I realized I must have put my hand on a nest! The pain was horrible, and I ran as fast as I could down the hill and jumped in the pool. When I came up out of the water, people were scattering and screaming. I held up my hand, and the hornets were gone, but what remained looked like a mass of red welts. I was crying so hard, and that was the last thing I remembered until we were in the doctor's office.

My hand looked like a giant balloon with little projectiles coming out from the top—my fingers. There were some welts on my chest, as well, and I realized the pain had mostly gone. I felt like I was floating, not quite normal. The doctor told my aunt he had given me a few shots, one to reduce the swelling, and one for pain. He gave her some prescriptions and told her it was especially important to give me the medication on time. When we got home, my mom let me know I had ruined her week, and then didn't speak to me anymore the rest of the day (and that silence lasted several days). This time it was alright, because I had Aunt Ruby and Uncle Junie taking care of me. Granny was there too, but lately, even though she was not as active as she used to be, I still sat in her lap to watch TV. I didn't know why my mom seemed so angry with me, but I stayed out of her way. This scenario would become a frequent flier in my life.

The other incident was a month or so later. Most of the morning, my cousin and I had been catching minnows in the ditch next to my house. He said he wanted to do something else and suggested we go play in the woods between our homes. When we got there, he asked if I wanted to "see mine, and show me yours." Now, as an adult, I know this is not abnormal behavior for 5 to 6-year-olds, and, honestly, I had been curious, too. So, he quickly pulled down his pants, and just as quickly pulled them back up again. I, however, felt I need-ed to completely remove my shorts, lay down, and reveal all. He didn't stick around and ran home, so I got myself dressed, and went home, too. I didn't understand why he left so suddenly. We didn't play together for a few days after that, and when we did get together again, what had happened was never spoken of . . . but we never got "curious" again.

So, here's a question for you. Where does a little girl learn that kind of behavior? This is not a natural thing to do. Remember, TV was G-rated back then. No movies, no porn magazines, no videos to rent. Where would such atypical behavior come from? Another frequent flier in the years to come. *Ahh, and another subject to be explained later . . .*

4

Norfolk

So that summer ended, and the next thing I knew, we were moving to Norfolk, VA. We had a one-level home, on a very busy street. It was a big house and my mom seemed to really like it. I had a nice room, and Goldie's cage was right next to my bed. It was comforting having her nearby. She reminded me of my Granny, and my fun days in Crisfield.

My first-grade year started in a school named Mary C. Rice Private School. It was small, with small classrooms, and I remember learning to read *Fun with Dick and Jane*. I guess this was the book all first graders initially used when learning to read. We also had a Spanish class, and I remember picking up quite a bit in the few months I attended. There are only a few tangible memories I have from that school. One that sticks out was being on the playground, waiting to get onto the slide, when I heard the girl who had gone up the steps ahead of me let out a scream. I looked up just in time to see her falling backwards, and I had this intense impression, I needed to "save her life" and attempted to catch her. She fell on top of me, and she ended up being ok, but I had a huge gash in my knee from a rock I had fallen on. Remind you, I was 6 years old.

I knew the cut was bad, because it was deep, and it hurt a lot. The nurse called my mom to pick me up, and told her I needed to be seen by a doctor, but she did not take me. I don't remember much else about that incident, except I really wished Aunt Ruby or Granny were there. Years later, due to the scar it left behind, I now know that it needed several stitches. Not getting to the doctor when needed would become a common theme in my young life.

Another memory I had was being picked for what the teacher called "a really big responsibility, for a very special person." We were getting ready for the Christmas program, and I was picked as that special person! I was asked to recite "The Night Before Christmas" for the program. It was so long, and a lot of work! My teacher asked if my parents could help me with memorizing it, but I knew I wouldn't ask them. I worked hard to do my best, and I remember wanting to do as good a job as I had with my song in kindergarten. I don't remember making any mistakes, and my teachers were proud of me! I had wanted to make my parents proud, too. But I can't remember them being there.

Mom had started spending weekends away and leaving me in Norfolk with Dad. She said she was going to Crisfield to see her mom, and I wanted to go with her, but for whatever reason, she didn't take me. Mom seemed sad most of the time lately. And when Dad was home, they pretty much spent most of their time together, sometimes bickering. I don't even remember Christmas that year, or where we spent it.

On those weekends, Dad would take me out sometimes. We went to a carnival once, and I won a Bingo game. When the man asked me what prize I wanted, I looked over all the things he had. He showed me a doll, a game, and a jump rope, but I ended up picking the set of towels, thinking it would make Mom happy . . . and maybe, just maybe, she would like me more. Maybe, take me with her to Crisfield. When I gave them to her, she hugged me really tight and had tears in her eyes. I felt good inside and learned a valuable lesson that day. Maybe not a healthy one, but a valuable one. Getting my mom presents was a way I could make her happy, and I would feel she loved me.

I really missed my mom being home all the time because she read me the Disney version of Peter Pan, with pictures from the movie. Dad never did that. He did play games with me though, and that was fun. We would play "invisible" where I would hide, and he would try to find me, and sometimes look right at me, but not see me! And sometimes he would play music, and I would stand on his feet and dance with him. I liked that a lot.

One weekend, he took me to a pond across the street from our house. There were a bunch of kids there, ice skating. I didn't have skates, just some rubber boots that slipped on over my shoes. But I wanted to go out on the ice, so Dad let me. I was not too keen on keeping my balance, and fell a few times, but was determined to do some of the things the other kids were doing. So, I tried to spin around in a circle, and the next thing I knew, I woke up on the ice. Dad was holding my head, and everyone was standing over me, staring at me. Dad said I fell and hit my head and was knocked out. All I knew was I had a whopper of a headache. So, he took me home. No hospital visits. No doctor notified. I watched some TV and hoped Mom would call so I could tell her, but she didn't. It felt like her weekends were getting longer and longer.

I have two more memories to share before I close our time in Norfolk. And both are uncomfortable. One night, I had gone into my parents' room to get my Peter Pan book. Dad was in the bathroom, door open, shaving . . . and completely naked. I felt so embarrassed and hurriedly grabbed the book by the side of the bed. He looked at me, and grinned, and continued shaving. I left and went to my room. My heart was pounding! I looked at the pictures in my book until my heart slowed down, then turned out my light. I talked to Goldie for a little while. Sleep came slowly due to feelings I didn't understand.

On another night I was taking a bath. I would often talk out loud while bathing. In my playtime, I was asking someone if they wanted me to open my legs and show them—like I had done with my cousin—and at that exact moment, my dad threw open the door and took a picture! It was the old days, so it had a big flash bulb, and very bright. He immediately shut the door, and I was left there—so embarrassed. Why did he do that? How did he know the exact time to open the door? It took several minutes for my eyes to adjust to the room light. I did not even want to come out because I would have to see him. I put my robe on, and finally got brave enough to run to my room. I lay in my bed a long time talking to Goldie. More feelings I didn't understand. I hoped Mom would come home soon.

And the next day she did. Mom and Dad argued a long time. All I could make out of their argument was how bad it was for me to be taken out of school. Mom said she didn't care because she was "needed" in Crisfield. And she packed my clothes, grabbed Goldie's cage, and we drove to the ferry that took us to Granny's. I never told her about either of those incidents. I never told anyone for several decades.

5

Return to Crisfield

Granny was very sick. She was sleeping on the daybed in her living room, instead of in her room upstairs. Her color was funny looking; her skin was kind of yellow. Aunt Ruby and Uncle Junie were not working as much as they usually did. And Mom cried . . . a lot. It didn't feel like the last time I was in Crisfield. It felt sad. All the time. And no one would tell me what was wrong. I started school a few days after we got there, and I was glad. It was good to see people smile and go outside to play with other kids. I began dreading going home on the bus at the end of the day.

We celebrated my seventh birthday on January 19. After the cake and ice cream, my granny let me get on the bed with her and snuggle. I could tell Mom didn't like it. She kept asking if I was hurting her, and finally Granny told Mom to "hesh-up and leave us alone." I slept there all night. When I woke up the next morning, the doctor had come, and Mom made me go in the kitchen with Aunt Ruby. I heard crying, and then Aunt Ruby started crying. I asked what was wrong but got no answers. However, my gut was twisted, and I knew something really bad was going on with Granny. After the doctor left, I took Goldie from her cage and went in to see her. She smiled, but it wasn't her normal smile. She had tears in her eyes too. She hugged me tighter than I could ever remember.

Another month passed, and each day Granny talked to me less and less, and Mom cried more and more. Aunt Ruby did, too. I felt funny inside, and one night I wanted to just lay with Granny. This time, Mom let me. I stayed there for a long time, with Granny rubbing my head, before Mom put me to bed.

The next day was George Washington's birthday, and my teacher had some fun things planned for us. Mom got me ready for school, and I gave Granny a kiss. She hugged me so tight as she stroked my hair and whispered, "Karin, I love you so much, and don't ever forget it." I told her I loved her, too, and got my books and started out the door, but something didn't feel right. I turned around and looked at her again . . . and waved. She waved back. Then I went out to the bus. School dragged on, even though we had special treats and activities that day. I wanted it to be over, so I could get home and see Granny. I just knew I needed to hug her as tight as she had hugged me this morning. Finally, the last bell rang, and I got on the bus and headed for home.

When we got to my house, there were a lot of cars in our driveway. Before I had even gotten down the steps of the bus, Mom came out the front door and was running towards me. When she got to me, I could see something was wrong— her face was red, and her eyes were swollen. She had been crying—a lot. She kept telling me she loved me as we walked toward the house. When I came in the kitchen door, Uncle Junie was sitting at the kitchen table, with his head down, sobbing. Aunt Ruby came in, picked me up and hugged me. There were a bunch of people in the living room with Granny. I told Aunt Ruby I wanted to see her, but she said I couldn't, and took me to the dining room. And there she told me Granny was gone. "Angels came to take her to Heaven. And she is happy now." I really didn't understand any of it. I just wanted to see her. They made me stay with Aunt Ruby while some of the people who were there took Granny out. I didn't get to say goodbye.

The next few days are missing for me. I don't remember anything else until we went to a big house where Granny was lying in a box, and we all walked by her and looked at her. She didn't look real to me. I thought she looked like she was made of wax, like the people I had seen when my parents took me to a wax museum. I automatically reached up and touched her. She was hard and cold. I didn't like it. I didn't think it was really her because Granny was always warm and cuddly. Then we went to the graveyard, and they put the big box with Granny in it in the ground. I didn't like that either. I decided right there, it really wasn't Granny in that box. The real Granny was with the angels. And I would never see her again.

Those several months, from February 1962, till the following school year, are lost. I only have one memory of that summer in between. My Uncle Junie and his girlfriend took me to the "city" to see a movie! Going thirty miles to a place called Salisbury, was a huge adventure for all of us! For Uncle Junie and Teeny it was like a trip to New York City!

We went to see a movie called "King of Kings" and it was about the man my Sunday School teacher had taught me about—Jesus. It was the story of his whole life, and even how he died. A really bad man named Judas, whom Jesus thought was his friend, betrayed him. Turned him over to mean people who beat him and killed him on a cross. I thought it was terrible, and my stomach felt kind of sick. It was the first time I had heard the whole story of Jesus. And I didn't like that he was killed. But I thought it was pretty cool that he came back to life. I didn't know people could do that. On the way home, I asked about this, and my uncle explained that will happen to all of us someday. I didn't really understand that. My granny had not come back to life. I didn't ask any more questions.

I literally have no memories of anything other than that. How the school year went, the rest of the summer, or why we never went back to Norfolk (though that was alright with me). I can't even really remember when we moved to Aberdeen, MD, though I know we did, because that is where I started second grade. I can speculate as an adult, with the knowledge I now have of how our psyche works, these were probably some pretty, rough times.

What I learned as an older teen and adult, was my mom had a great deal of difficulty with loss. Grieving was long, and arduous. It was almost as if the death was a personal assault on her. No one could be as hurt as she was by the loss. Couple that with the fact that I have no memory of my dad being at the funeral (and I am not saying he wasn't) but if that were the case, a war would have begun between my parents. She would have blamed him for moving her to Norfolk, and away from her mom. I know that because it happened every time we moved in the future years. These are all possibilities for my loss of time. Potential traumatic events.

You see, God created a gift for children who suffer trauma, known as dissociation, so when things get too bad for them, they just check out. Not everyone would consider this a gift. But I believe it is. During these times, life goes on, but the memories of it go missing. And sometimes the good stuff gets lost, too. It is not a conscious decision, it just happens. It's a defense mechanism. Protection. And it's not just a gift for children.

Honestly, between you, me and the fencepost, plenty of stuff was getting ready to happen in Aberdeen, I sure wish I didn't have to remember.

Nope. Not one little bit.

6

Aberdeen

Our house in Aberdeen was a split level. Classic 1950-1960's home. Three bedrooms and a bath on the top floor, living room, dining room, and kitchen on the main floor, and a big family room, half bath, and laundry room on the first floor. I loved the family room because it was where I could play and watch TV, and its where my mom kept her sewing machine, so I got to spend time with her, even when she was busy sewing. She used to make a lot of my clothes because she said dad always had her on an "allowance." I didn't know what that meant yet, but I could tell it ticked her off. She even made the clothes for my Barbie and Ken! I thought that was pretty cool!

Dad wasn't home much, but when he was, he would take me with him to the Aberdeen Proving Ground, and we would go inside the little round buildings where a big camera was. I didn't understand all the stuff Dad was doing, but he explained he was tracking the first weather satellites, Echo and Anna. The work he did was called "geodesy" and his job was to triangulate the whole Earth with tracking stations at each point of the triangle. It was cool to watch the satellites cross over. This was one of only a few times I remember spending with Dad while in Aberdeen.

So, Aberdeen was where I made my first real friend, Linda. She lived next door with her older sister, younger brother, and mom and dad. We met over the backyard fence when she waved to me while I was cutting grass. I had chores every Saturday that started with cutting the grass with the old-fashioned push mower that had no motor. It took FOREVER! And then I had to go through the yard and pull all the dandelions with a tool that looked like a giant meat fork. Then it all had to be raked. I was so eager to talk with this new girl, and just wanted to get everything done. I took a couple breaks and introduced myself—and she seemed really nice! She waited for me to get done, then came over to visit. I found out she was a couple years older than me, but she liked to play dolls and listen to music, so I didn't care how old she was. I had an old record player that played 45's and sometimes we would dance. It was fun!

Eventually, I met her mom, Ms. Elsie—she was from Germany, and I loved to listen to her talk—she had a cool accent. Linda's dad was retired Army, so I knew he and my dad would get along well. Ms. Elsie ended up babysitting for me whenever mom and dad went out. Not that often, because Dad was now traveling more than ever.

I was in second grade and attending Bakersfield Elementary. My teacher's name was Mrs. Bowen, and I remember she was nice, but very tough. You didn't get away with much, and you didn't want to try. Dad had enrolled me over the summer, and I guess no one had told the school I was known as Karin. So, when Mrs. Bowen called roll, she used my first name—Leslie. I was too shy to correct her, and this is when I began to be known by my first name. By the time Mom and Dad found out on my first report card, they tried to change it back, but everyone at the school felt it would be too confusing. So, I was now "Leslie" to all of those at school but was still "Karin" with all my family.

In class, we said the Lord's Prayer every morning, and Mrs., Bowen always picked one of us to lead in the Pledge of Allegiance. When it was getting close to Christmas, we were all going to be in a Christmas play with the third grad-ers. That was great for me because one of the third-grade teachers was Judy, the wife of my dad's best friend. She was so nice and always found me on the playground to say "hi" because I was new to the school.

Well, much to my surprise, Mrs. Bowen wanted me to take the role of narrator for the whole Christmas play! I didn't want to because I had gained some weight, and I was self-conscious of how I looked. But you never said "no" to Mrs. Bowen. The third practice we had, I was saying some of my lines, and she yelled "stop" and began yelling at me for not having more emotion in my telling of the story of baby Jesus. I was so embarrassed, but after that, I got it right, and I didn't dare make any more mistakes.

I was so excited for Mom and Dad to see me in the play, but Dad left two days before, and they had a big fight because he was going "overseas" and mom said he didn't care "two bits" for his family (actually, bits isn't the word she used, but it rhymes, and it will suffice.) The night of the show, she helped me get dressed, and one of the other moms picked me up. Mom said she would come later. Every time I went on stage, I searched the audience for her face, but never found it. With each search, my tummy hurt more. Didn't she want to see me? Did she have an accident? All the other moms were there. Afterwards, there was a little reception, that included all the home cooked goodies many of the moms had brought. I have no memories of how I got home that night.

I don't remember what Mom and I did for Christmas that year. It is another lost memory. I am betting we went to Crisfield. What I did know is that Dad was not with us. And wouldn't be for many months. And that made me very sad.

After returning to school from Christmas break, we got back into the daily routine. We had just finished saying the Pledge of Allegiance, and the Lord's Prayer. The first subject of the day was arithmetic, and our teacher asked us to take out our rulers. These were the old-fashioned wooden ones—the ones with the metal strip down the side to form a straight edge. The girl who sat next to me, shared the same name, and could not find hers. I had taken mine out, and she pulled it off my desk, laughing as she did. When I went to take it, she jumped back and said, "Its mine! See it says Leslie on it." I laughed and grabbed it, pulling it from her hand. She let out a yelp and droplets of blood were forming down the middle of her palm, and I realized I had cut her when I yanked the ruler from her.

We both began to cry, and Mrs. Bowen came to us and said my friend would have to go down to the nurse. I kept telling her how sorry I was and crying more than the girl who was hurt. The teacher hunkered down and wiped my tears and said, "Honey, it was just an accident. You shouldn't have been playing around, but you didn't mean to do it!" She gave me a hug and assured me it was okay and explained that our parents would need to be called. Dad was still out of town, and all I can remember is dreading to go home. I had a lump in my throat the rest of the day.

When I got off the bus, I walked slowly, not really wanting to face what I expected. I remember hoping Dad would come home soon, but that would never happen. When I came through the front door, I knew immediately, it was going to be bad. Mom just looked at me, and said, "How could you have done something so embarrassing? Do you know how much you humiliated me? You aren't MY child!"

There was no afternoon snack waiting for me. No asking how my day was. Nothing. She went down to the family room and sat down on the couch and continued to watch her TV show. I wanted to make things ok between us, and gingerly walked down the steps, and peeked around the corner, trying to discern her mood. I decided to go for it and ran to the couch and told her how sorry I was and kissed her on the cheek. She wiped her face, looked at me and said, "Judas kisses!" The look on her face made me feel like she hated me, and she told me to go to my room until dinner was ready.

Now I had heard her say this before when she was angry, and I had not understood what it meant . . . not prior to last summer when I saw the movie with my uncle. As I sat in my room alone, those words took on a whole new meaning. I had learned in that movie, *King of Kings*, Judas betrayed Jesus with a kiss. And Jesus died because of it. And now my mom was calling my kisses "Judas kisses." It would be many, many years before I would understand what those words did to me emotionally or how they affected my young brain. *Another area we will visit later.* Suffice it to say, it was not even close to being the last time I heard them.

It seemed like forever before she called me for dinner, and when I went downstairs to the kitchen, only one plate was on the table. I ate alone, and she told me to go to bed. No bath. No tucking me in. No goodnight kisses. I cried myself to sleep. The next day, my clothes were laid out, but she was locked in her room. I got dressed and went down to the kitchen. My cereal was on the table. I ate and left for the bus. This went on for three days, without her saying a word to me. And each night I laid in my bed, crying, completely believing my mom didn't love me anymore. I wondered every night what was wrong with me.

Now you must understand, these thoughts are not the way an adult would think them. As a child receives these messages, their thoughts are all consuming—most everything that is wrong must be their fault. They spend time thinking of ways to make the parent happy again. They believe it's within their power to control or change their parents' feelings. Feelings they have no ability to control, but will go to any lengths to feel loved again. This is what I did as I washed dishes, swept the floor, dusted the furniture, and anything else I thought would make her happy. More codependent bricks cemented into my foundation.

But she stayed in her room, not responding to my knocks on the door. Not responding to my pleas. Not responding, period. The only time she came out of her room was to cook a meal she would leave for me, or wash clothes. I did my homework, played in my room, and continued to hope Dad would come home. I just wanted someone to talk to me.

In school, Mrs. Bowen pulled me aside a few times, asking me if I was okay. She would hug me, and it felt so good. I wanted to tell her, but I knew how angry both my parents would be if I shared anything that went on at home. Family secrets. I have often wondered, as an adult, if that teacher made a phone call to my mom, because on the fourth night, I woke up with her kneeling by my bed, crying, and saying she was sorry. I threw my arms around her neck and hugged her so tight! We both cried, and I finally felt loved again. At least for a little while.

I turned eight years old in this house, and I thought I had been given a birthday party because I had seen a picture and Linda and her family were in it. But I have no memory of it. Maybe it wasn't even my party, but Linda's birthday, and I just happened to get a picture. I never really considered that option until recently when I came across the picture again while working on a scrapbook. Everyone had clothes with short sleeves. I am a January baby. Hmmm. I think I liked it better when I thought it was MY birthday picture.

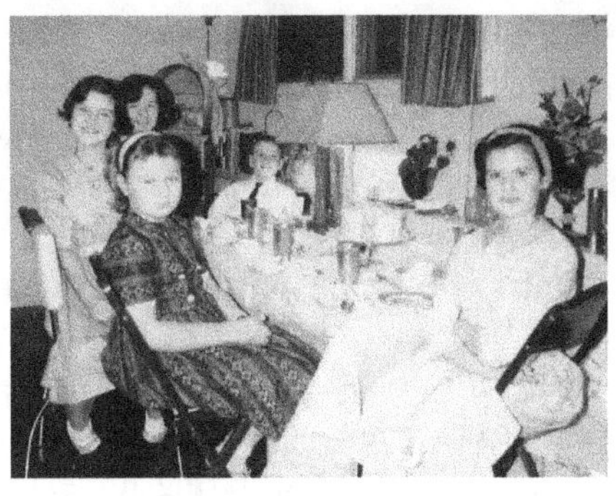

So, as I mentioned before, I had a lot of bad memories in this house. I am going to try to recount them as best I can. The first was a party my parents had during one of the few times Dad was home. Those who came were people Dad worked with, and their wives. I was put to bed early, but sleep alluded me because it was loud downstairs. I snuck out of my room at one point and peeked down into the rec room. They were all doing the limbo! For those of you who may not know what that is, it was a game played while listening to a song performed by Chubby Checker, and it became all the rage in the 1960's. There were even "limbo" competitions on TV! "How low can you go?" was the essence of the game. You had to bend over backward while you tried walking under a limbo pole. Each round, the pole went lower, and the winner was the person who could bend backwards better than anyone else.

My friends and I loved to play this game! It looked like my parent's friends were enjoying it too! And they had a little help from Dad's bar. I saw all the bottles out that mom usually kept in a cabinet. She did not drink and really hated being around drinking, but that was always part of Dad's parties. She did not like it when Dad drank, either, but he did it anyway, (not a lot, just a few each night) even when there was not a party. Anyway, it looked like everyone was having fun! I went back to bed.

I finally fell asleep, but woke up to my mom screaming, "Stop! Put me down! Gene, make him put me down!" I jumped out of bed and ran down the steps to the rec room. A man had my mom thrown over his shoulder and slapping her on her bottom as he walked around the room. He was laughing hysterically, as most everyone was, including Dad. But Mom wasn't laughing. She was crying and fighting to get off this man's shoulder. I couldn't understand why no one was helping her. Dad saw me standing there and told me to go back to bed. He was still smiling, and didn't seem angry, but was firm about me going back to my room. He was acting funny and had that smell on his breath. I tried to ask why no one was helping mom, but he hushed me and said very firmly, "Just go to bed!"

I waited a little while. I wanted to see if my mom was alright. I went to my room, but the party was still going strong. Then I heard a door slam shut. Then I heard a lady's voice asking if mom was ok, but mom asked her to "go away." I decided she would probably say the same thing to me, so I shut my door tight to keep the noise out, and tried to go to sleep. I slept with about ten different stuffed animals and after placing them all around me, I finally drifted off.

I don't know how long I was asleep, but I woke one more time that night. My door was open about halfway. There was a man standing in the doorway, and he was smoking a cigarette. He didn't move except to take a drag on his cigarette. He was just staring at me. I couldn't tell who it was, because the hall light was behind him, and all I saw was his shape. I can't tell you why, but I pulled all my stuffed animals closer around me, and just as I thought he was taking a step into my room, I heard a woman calling. I could not make out what she said, but he turned, and shut the door.

I heard some muffled voices, like people were leaving, and then the front door shutting. I lay there for a while, trying to calm down and I realized I needed to go to the bathroom. I jumped out of bed and went down the hall. I heard Dad taking things into the kitchen, so I hurried to the bathroom. Back in bed, I snuggled in with all my animals, and then heard dad in the hall. The bedroom door must have been locked because he started knocking. He kept calling to my mom, and then he got angry. "You're being ridiculous!" He banged a few more times, and then I heard him go downstairs. This was going to be a bad one. I didn't want to be around the next day.

And it was. Mom did not come out of her room, and when she did come down to get food, she spoke to no one. Dad tried, but it was a failure. So, he asked if I wanted to go to the movies. And we did. This became a maneuver Dad used frequently. This thing called "triangulation." *Let's look at that in a bit.*

Mom didn't come out of her room until after Dad left to go away again. He drove me to school Monday morning and told me he would see me in a few weeks. He was going to Europe. When I came home from school that day, she acted like nothing had happened. Things were never discussed. She just acted oblivious to it. If this was denial or dissociative behavior, I will never know, but as a kid, I didn't dare ask about anything.

I don't remember how long Dad was gone, but it felt like a long time. Mom and I went to Crisfield on two different weekends while he was gone. Gosh, I wanted to stay there so bad. I cried every time we left. Aunt Ruby was getting ready to move into her parent's old house, because Uncle Junie was dating someone, and I wanted to stay and help her. Mom said we would come back over the summer.

During Dad's absence, Mom seemed to soften. We got two more parakeets, Angel, who was white, and Chitter, who was bright green. They would keep Goldie company. She also bought me a hamster. Mom really wanted a dog, and she had talked to her cousin's husband, who was a state trooper, about keeping a watch for one that may come through their dog training program. Dad was not a big animal fan. He was not even thrilled I had Goldie, but I don't think he was considered when we got all the new ones. I did believe Goldie was happier now, and that made me happy. Mom and I got along better than we had before, and I would sit with her and watch her sew clothes for my dolls, or make something for me. She taught me how to knit and embroider, and bought me kits so I could make my own things. I enjoyed these times. She was more like she had been in Crisfield.

There are some other bad memories of things that happened with my dad. Things I really wouldn't understand the impact of until many years later, but they are burned in my memory. One incident happened after Dad had been home for a few weeks. My friend Linda had gotten a new bike and she offered to let me ride it. I was pretty confident because I had been riding a two-wheeler for a while and was sure I could handle it.

We lived on a little bit of a hill, and as I started gaining speed, I got scared and lost control. I ended up losing my balance and went down. I fell off, and the bike slid a few yards past me. I was crying because both my knees were bleeding, and I had hit my head too. Mostly I was scared. Linda and her mom came running, and my dad was outside and saw it happen. I had my arms outstretched to grab him, expecting him to pick me up. He got there first, and instead of stopping, he ran past me and picked up the bike, looking over it carefully. "I hope you didn't mess anything up, Karin!" His face was contorted and red.

Ms. Elsie got to me and pulled me into her lap. Dad was apologizing and telling her he was so sorry, and he would fix anything damaged. Ms. Elsie just pulled me tighter, and asked me if I was ok, and told Dad she wasn't worried about the bike, she was worried about me. That seemed to change his focus, and suddenly he was asking me if I was hurt. He reached his arms out to take me, but I didn't want him to. I wanted to stay with Ms. Elsie. Mom wasn't home, so she offered to take me to her house and fix up my knees and put some ice on my head. Dad said he would check out the bike to see if it was damaged. I saw Ms. Elsie look at Linda and roll her eyes, and then she walked me back to her house. I stayed there all afternoon. She was so gentle and kind as she cleaned out my scrapes, and then bandaged me up.

Ms. Elsie wasn't the only kind person I knew. There was another couple my parents were friends with, Kay and Guy, and they were both very sweet to me. Kay was beautiful—like a movie star! Mom was at her house one day for coffee, and I was with her. They had this cute little poodle that I played with while they visited. We were playing fetch with a rubber ball, and I threw it too hard and broke a vase that was on Ms. Kay's dining room table. I was crying and apologizing profusely. I could tell Mom was upset, but it was Kay who just kept saying it was "no big deal" and telling Mom, "It's just a vase." She hugged me and told me not to worry about it—at all! But I was worried. I was worried about going home.

She and mom cleaned up the glass and went back to talking. I was afraid to play with the dog anymore, so asked if I could watch TV. I hardly know what I watched because I dreaded the ride home so much, but to my surprise, Mom was in a great mood! She said Ms. Kay had asked if I could go camping with them that coming weekend. They were going crabbing in Ocean City and camping in Assateague. Mom said they didn't have any kids and was sure that was why she wanted to take me with them. I was super excited to go! I had never been camping and I had a great time with them!

Assateague is just a few miles from Ocean City, MD, and it was known for the wild ponies that lived there. I had read a book written about it called *Misty*. Every year men come to Assateague to round up some of the ponies, then herd them up to swim across the bay to Chincoteague. Then they have a "Pony Penning," where they auction the ponies and people can buy them.

We camped right on the beach, and caught lots of crabs. We had bought a big metal trash can, and the men filled it with the hot rocks that had been in a fire. They put a metal grate over the rocks, dumped in the crabs, and put the can over the open fire, before adding water to it. I didn't eat any, but it was fun to watch! I didn't want the weekend to end.

So, let's look at a couple things. What messages are being sent to this kid? First, she sees that no one responded to her mother's cries for help. Not her dad, or anyone else at the party. And, when she saw a man standing in her doorway, she did nothing. Why would she not call for help? And to add a little more to the lack-of-protection connection, what kind of message did she receive when her father ran past her to see if the bike was harmed? What is her measurement of self-worth? There were many nights, going forward, when she wished, from the depths of heart, for a mom like Ms. Elsie.

. . . and the triangulation game I mentioned. Over the years, I learned Dad was a pro at triangulation. Mom did her share as well. Pitting one person against another. Sharing all the dirty laundry of the second person with the third person. Surreptitiously. Making the second person out to be the "bad guy." Dad did this a lot. And my young, impressionable mind took it in as fact. It began a long journey of looking at my mom with the tinted glasses my dad had colored for me. It ended in that place I talked about in the prologue, where when faced with the truth, you feel like your whole world has been turned upside down. Like you have lived your whole life in a lie. It's very unsettling.

. . . my mom's silent treatments. My mother's "silent treatment" was her tool to punish people, and it became more frequent and more hurtful as time went on. Known as "cold anger," it's a tool some people use to punish, ignore, control, and even terrorize. It was certainly terrifying for me. This happened with my mom for most of my life—even at my own wedding—until I learned about boundaries, and my mom received some healing as well. Unfortunately, so much time had passed, it left little time for us to enjoy the relationship for which we both longed.

So, now, back to the stories, and for my final tale about Aberdeen. I saved the worst for last (well, up to this point, anyway.)

I could not tell you where we were going on this occasion, but Dad had started giving me spankings "just in case I did something wrong." Yes, read that again. I had not done anything, but sometimes when we were going out—JUST IN CASE—I got a spanking in advance. Again, I don't know the occasion, and it's not even important, but Dad felt I should get one of my "just in case" spankings. Except this time, he wanted to pull my pants down to do it. I cried because I felt humiliated at the thought. But that didn't matter. Mom was there and said nothing. I fought as hard as I could, but he did it anyway. Pulled everything down to my bare bottom. I was hysterical. Fighting and crying for him to stop. But he was smiling, almost chuckling. And when I looked at Mom, she was trying to hide a smile as well.

I felt completely helpless. Unprotected. Betrayed. I wish I could say this only happened once. I wish I could say those feelings were only a one-shot deal. But that would be a lie. Those feelings would soon define my life.

7

Wheaton

Moving to Wheaton in the summer of 1964 seemed to be a good thing, especially for Mom. Wheaton is in Maryland, and is a suburb of Washington, DC. You can find it wedged between Silver Spring and Rockville with Connecticut and Georgia Avenues running through it, both of which end up in the heart of the District. Apparently, Dad had rented the house from another military family, and we were supposed to be able to stay there for three years, a lot longer than anywhere else we had lived, so far. Mom hated to move, so this was a good thing, and she was only three hours from Crisfield, and that was icing on the cake. Dad was still traveling quite a bit, and was mostly in Europe. I started keeping a scrapbook of all the postcards he sent me from places he visited. Mom never went with him.

Our house was situated directly across the street from an elementary school, Connecticut Park. I thought this would be awesome to have such a short walk to school. And I also was beginning to branch out, making friends in the neighborhood, and being more autonomous. The friends I had were all going to Connecticut Park, so I would know some people when I started school, and that was a good thing. But Dad had other plans for me.

About a mile away was a round shaped school called Bushey Drive. Dad informed me he had enrolled me there because it was a "progressive" school. They didn't have grades, per se, but a child was placed where they could best excel. I was going into fourth grade, and my dad said I would be tested to see where I would be placed. There was no bus for this school, so the walk was a bit long, but I did it, each morning and afternoon. And because school lunches were not in our budget, I walked home for lunch, too. And yes, when I complained, I heard the story of how they both walked to school—for miles, uphill both ways, in the snow.

I was already nervous about starting a new school, and needing to make new friends, because the friends I had made over the summer, went to Connecticut Park. I was also nervous because I had started to really put on weight. When my mom took me for my 9-year physical, I was weighing in at 152 pounds. The doctor told her it was important I get the weight off, and handed her a 1200 calorie diet. This was a new challenge for all of us. No more "starving kids in Korea" stories. However, the diet never got started. It may be because my mom had a miscarriage around this time. I didn't understand a lot of what that meant, but the fighting between my parents was pretty clear. She blamed Dad because he was never home, and she had too much to do on her own. My young brain concluded that if Dad was home more often, I would have had a little brother or sister. And I did want one. For many reasons.

A good thing that happened for Mom after this traumatic time for her, was her cousin's husband finding a dog. She had always wanted a German Shepherd and that is what she got. His name was Brutus, and he was really pretty. Where most Shepherds are brown and black, he was silver and black. He had been trained at the dog academy and was very smart and obedient. This was a gift that seemed to bring Mom out of her room, and spending more time with Aunt Ruby and me. She took him for long walks in the evening and it was good for me to see her smiling again.

When Aunt Ruby came to live with us, she became the person in charge of my diet. It was a long walk at lunch, and I only had a little time, but Aunt Ruby always had my open-face cheese sandwich, or tuna on lettuce, or chicken salad in a tomato—and her chicken salad was the best—so I never felt I was deprived. In the winter months, she added some type of soup, and it was always good. I dreaded the day when she would go home for the summer.

I lost some weight, and I remember going back to the doctor, and weighed in at 123. I was so proud, but he was surprised. I heard him tell Mom I should have lost more by that time, and that he wanted to keep an eye on me. He wanted to see me every two weeks, but that never happened. You see, my dad was the penny-pincher of penny-pinchers. When Mom drove us all the way into DC to the Department of Health for our check-ups, it didn't cost him a penny— "and a penny saved, is a penny earned!" But that was way too far for her to drive on a regular basis. I don't remember going back to see that doctor at all. At my 10-year-old physical, I saw a different doctor, one who didn't seem too concerned about what I weighed.

My dad definitely knew how to pinch pennies, but neither of them knew much about how to care for their child's health.

An interesting thing came out of this weight loss. I remember getting dressed to go to a birthday party—Mom had bought me new pants, two sizes smaller than I used to wear—and she took me down to the family room to "show me off" to my dad. He was reading a newspaper, and mom asked him to look at how much weight I had lost. I had to pirouette for him, and he told me he was proud of me. He then followed with, "Karin, you need to remember that men hate fat women. They will have sex with you, but will never marry you, because they will be embarrassed." *Hmmm. What message did that send to her young brain?* I was 10 years old, and not entirely sure what all that meant, but it was not even close to the last time I would hear it. For many more years, those words would resonate with me, and affect me in incredibly dysfunctional ways.

Mom and Dad entertained many of his friends, and one couple I especially liked were the Hotine's. He was a Brigadier General my dad had met in England. During the time we lived in Wheaton, they came to visit on two occasions. The first time, I remember being so intrigued with their accent, and Mr. Hotine was especially nice to me. I recall him asking me if I had heard of the Beatles, and I excitedly replied, "I love them! I saw them on Ed Sullivan." He shared how they were all the rage in England. He also asked me about my school subjects, and I shared about my progressive school. He asked if I was taking any foreign languages, and this surprised me because the only school where I had been exposed to other languages was the private school in Norfolk. He said he felt I was a very smart girl, and I should learn another language.

Mr. Hotine was so loving to me, and the whole time he was there, he made me feel special. Complemented me on my looks, my drawings—which he asked to see—and he even wanted to see some of my schoolwork. This was all very foreign to me. And I ate it up. When they left after that first visit, I didn't know if I would see them again, and I was very sad to see them go. The kind of attention he gave me, I was starved to receive.

A few weeks later, I received a package from him, with three Beatles albums and a set of records that taught you how to speak French! I was ecstatic. I had a small portable record player that I usually played my 45's on, but now I had big records called 33's, and Dad had to show me how to change the speed on my player, so I could listen to them in my room. I felt so special.

A few months later, the Hotine's came to visit again, and he brought me more gifts! This time he brought me this super cool album of "monster" songs, like "Monster Mash" and a bunch of other songs. And he brought me another Beatles album that had not yet been released in the U.S. My friends would be jealous. I thanked him and gave him the biggest hug, and then went up to my room to listen to the albums. We had a wonderful evening with them, and when they got ready to leave, I hugged them both so tightly and thanked them. This time I cried when they left.

The next day, Mom told me that Mrs. Hotine had told her how very much her husband admired my talent in art and how well I expressed myself. She said he had talked about me a lot, and felt about me as he would a granddaughter. Mrs. Hotine even offered to allow me to come visit them in England, and they would foot the bill. I must admit, this gave me lots of warm fuzzies. I listened to the albums he gave me at every waking moment when I was home.

What happened within a few weeks of this special night is even now hard to write. I still can't remember what I did wrong, but I will never forget the punishment for it. I was in my room, playing my monster song album, when Mom stormed in and pulled the album off the record player, smashed it, and then proceeded to smash every album Mr. Hotine had given me. I was hysterical. I only remember her saying, "If Mr. Hotine knew what you were really like, he would never have given you anything." And then she was gone. I picked up the broken pieces off the floor, and tried to put some of them back together. It was useless. When I realized two of the French records had been spared, I hid them under my mattress. But I never played them again. I didn't play any records again until Aunt Ruby came back to stay with us. *My mom's words to me that day became part of a mantra within my self-talk that followed me well into my adult life. "If people knew who you really were—no one would like you."*

My School Experiences

When I started school that year as a fourth grader, I remained with fourth graders for social studies and music. I was in a fifth-grade language arts and gym class and sixth-grade math and art class. I loved art! We went on a lot of field trips. The National Gallery of Art, and the Philips Art Gallery, both in DC, were two of the places we visited. Other field trips we took were to see The Nutcracker, performed by the National Symphony, a movie about lions called, *Born Free*, and another African-based movie called *Hatari*. I loved this school!

I was picked for a part in the school Christmas play—a police officer. Even with my weight loss, I was still self-conscious about how I looked, but I didn't want to turn down the part, either. Of course, I hoped my parents would be there, but Dad was away, and to my surprise, Mom asked his friend to come instead. He and Dad worked together, and they were the same rank. He loaned me his officer's hat so I would have an official-looking uniform, and he and Mom came to the play to see me. It was a great night for me!

I can't remember Dad being home for Christmas that year. If he wasn't, we would have gone to Crisfield, and I would have remembered that. What does stick in my memory is sitting on the floor in our family room watching *Mr.*

Magoo's Christmas Carol, and *A Charlie Brown Christmas*—completely alone. No one sitting with me to share the fun. But even though I was alone, what I remember so clearly about that night was when Linus said to Charlie Brown, "Sure, Charlie Brown, I can tell you what Christmas is all about." And then Linus told the Christmas story. There was an excitement in me; something I had not felt before. I wanted to hear it again. I didn't tell anyone about that feeling. And it was a few years before I would feel it again.

I pretty much stayed a straight-A student all through fourth grade. I enjoyed this school a lot. In one of my classes, there was a boy, Alan, very small, with glasses, who carried a big briefcase for his books. He was quite smart, but acted differently than the other kids, and cried when they made fun of him. In those days, there were no back packs, just rubber "book belts" that strapped them all together for you to carry. So, Alan's briefcase made him different, and it became another source of laughter, so he got bullied. Kids made fun of his size and his glasses too. I knew how this felt; it happened to me on the playground a lot. "Fatso" and "tub-o-lard" were common to hear. And these were the same kids who teased Alan. The ringleader was a kid named Billy.

One day, when they surrounded Alan on the playground, making fun of him, I was watching. I felt so bad for him because Billy, who was the cruelest to me as well, was calling him "retard" and "four-eyes." Then he grabbed his glasses, and threw them on the ground. Alan started to cry, and they laughed harder. I felt something inside me explode, and remembered all the times Billy had made fun of me, so I ran to where they were and knocked him to the ground. I got on top of him and started slugging him as hard as I could. Two teachers came over, and one pulled me off him, but not before I heard her say to the other, "I wish she had knocked the snot out of him."

I didn't get in trouble for this, though a call was made to both our parents. I lucked out because Aunt Ruby had answered the phone. She never told mom or dad, but when I got home, with a huge smile, she said "good job." I don't know if what I did was right, because as an adult, I now know, that Billy was probably bullied at home. It seemed right at the time, to protect Alan, and it led to us being friends. And when I started doing carnivals at my house for Muscular Dystrophy (MD), Alan was glad to help me. The carnival was a big deal for us kids. Most of us were fans of the Labor Day Telethon that Jerry Lewis did. When you did a carnival, all the proceeds went to the telethon, and you knew you were helping Jerry reach the kids who had MD. We did two of them together, along with some other kids from the neighborhood, and raised a lot of money for the cause. I guess in our pain, we were kindred spirits.

At the beginning of fifth grade, I learned I could train to be a safety patrol. This was a privileged position in school where you were given a patrol belt to wear, and assigned a post on a street corner. Your job was to allow kids to cross the street when you felt it was safe. And they were required to wait for you to give them permission to do so. I started working with a sixth-grade boy whose post was at the end of our street. His name was Spiro, and I soon grew to like him. I think he liked me too, because we were in the same gym class, and he always picked me as his partner for square dancing. Now Spiro was a very small boy for his age, and as I shared, I was on the larger side—and tall for my age as well—so the two of us dancing together was probably humorous for the teachers. I clearly remember when we were supposed to "swing your partner" I would swing Spiro so hard, he left the floor!

Being a patrol was a big deal to me, because it meant I was trusted for the safety of other kids, I was looked up to by other classmates, but most of all because there was a big picnic, at an amusement park, at the end of the school year for all the patrols, and awards were given. If you were an "officer"—Captain, Lieutenant, or Sergeant—you got special recognition. I had been chosen at the end of my fifth-grade year to be the Lieutenant for our class. I was so excited for this honor, the coming award, and especially, the picnic! *More on that in a bit.* This would not be the last of my major life disappointments as Dad sacrificed the needs of his family to please others.

Some Good Memories with My Dad

When Dad was home, he started to take me for horseback riding lessons on Saturdays. I loved this! I had been attached to horses since the first time I could remember riding one at 5 years old. Dad said he had placed me on my first pony at 2 years old, but I don't remember that. However, I sure remembered every time after that. Even after I completed my riding lessons, Dad still took me to ride every Sunday morning, when he was home. Mom didn't ride so she did not come with us or take me when he was away. Consequently, I looked forward with great anticipation for Dad to be home.

After finishing up my lessons, I rode in my first Gymkhana. A Gymkhana is like a mini rodeo, based mostly in gaits, speed times and games. It was a blast, and I got a ribbon for coming in third place. As I got more practice with Dad on Sundays, my skills improved markedly. Unfortunately, because I loved it so much, this seemed to become leverage for my mom. The friend who came to see my play, Mr. Copeland, started coming with us to ride. He brought his two sons, Andrew and Tommy. I was excited because I had a crush on the older boy, and I looked so forward to riding with him.

One Sunday, I had spelling and math homework to finish and did not get it done before the reservation time. Mom said I couldn't go. Dad argued I could finish when I got home—we would only be gone for 90 minutes, but it fell on deaf ears. I cried all day. This happened on a few other occasions, and since I never knew when it would happen, I was frequently on edge. I didn't relax until I was actually in the car and on my way. My adrenalin was often on high alert. Anxiety can begin for many reasons, and trauma can be caused in many ways.

Another fun thing I did with my dad was slot-car racing. There was a place near us with three tracks, and Dad dived into this hobby—fully. He bought kits, and we built our own cars. We built the chassis, then painted the body, and then we raced them. Dad would notice which type won the most frequently, and then we would build that type. He bought each of us a case, like a fishing tackle box, where we carried our tools and cars. We did this on days it was raining, or when we couldn't ride. It was a blast!

The Rest of the Story

I have very few memories of my mom in Wheaton. Other than what I have shared. But I have a lot with Aunt Ruby. I have already described what an advocate she was for me. She seemed to temper my mother's moods, or maybe my mom just felt less stress and anxiety when Aunt Ruby was there to take care of me. Whatever the reason, she was my mother-figure now, and remained so for the rest of her life.

She had come to live with us at the end of my third-grade year. Mom said it was because Aunt Ruby had moved into her parent's old home, and she had only a small room heater to keep her warm. Living with us became a tradition—no matter where we lived. When we first moved to Wheaton, I had my own room, but when Aunt Ruby came, I moved into her room. We shared a bed, and every night we read till we got tired. Sleep came easy when I was with Aunt Ruby. It was safe. *It would be many years before I realized the probable reason I slept in her room. No one told, and no one implied, but I can bet it had a lot to do with keeping me safe.*

Aunt Ruby was an avid reader and passed her love of books onto me. Every Saturday, Mom or Dad took us to the library, and I would find all her books for her. She loved murder mysteries, and Agatha Christy was her all-time favorite. She also loved Ellery Queen, and a few others, so there was never a shortage of books for her. I loved books about horses. I discovered The Black Stallion series, by William Farley, and would get a new one each week. We cherished our times at the library, and reading together.

Another fun thing I did with her was go to the movies. We lived a few blocks from a local theater, and discovered we could take a shortcut through the back entrance of the People's drugstore, and save a lot of steps. Aunt Ruby was 65, but she never complained of anything. Because we used their backdoor, she thought we should eat lunch there, so we always got a burger on the way to the movies. I remember seeing mostly Elvis Presley movies, but she liked scary movies too, so we saw a few of those as well. On our way home, because we took the shortcut again, we stopped and got an ice cream sundae; she got pineapple, and I got cherry. Then we walked home. I looked forward to these times with her. I was experiencing something with her I am not sure I ever had with my mom or dad—attachment.

I had been a Brownie scout for a year in Aberdeen, so I asked if I could join a girl scout troop here in Wheaton. Brownies were the youngest of the Girl Scouts, and now I would be a Junior. I don't remember a lot about the meetings, except earning a lot of badges and selling a lot of cookies. Two of my new friends in school, Jill and Dawn, were also scouts, so we had that in common as well. We made a pact to see who could sell the most cookies, and I think we covered every neighborhood in Wheaton! In those days, parents didn't worry about their kids getting picked up by strangers. We were out till dark during both Girl Scout cookie seasons while I was at Bushey Drive, and we sold the most in our troop.

So, I was finishing up my fifth-grade year—I had nailed down the Lieutenant position as a safety patrol, maintained my grades, was taking mostly sixth grade level classes, continued to lose weight, had made lots of friends, was not bullied any longer, and was as happy as I could be. Then the bomb was dropped. I knew something was wrong because Mom and Dad were non-stop arguing. Aunt Ruby could not console her, and agreed "it wasn't fair." I kept asking what was wrong, and Aunt Ruby finally told me. The family we were renting from were coming back early. His tour had ended, and they wanted to move back into their home. We had a legal contract through the end of the following school year. We did not have to move. Mom's plan was to stay in this house until our lease was up, and fulfill our contractual obligation. Plus, she did not want to move any more than necessary. It would also be the end of my sixth-grade year, so all the things I had worked so hard to accomplish, I could still realize.

But Dad didn't want to upset this family and their plans to move back into their home. He didn't want them to have to rent a house for a year. He didn't want to "put THEM out." What? But somehow that was going to be okay for his own family? For his wife who hated moving—ever? For his daughter who had worked very hard to earn a goal she had set for herself?

I pleaded with him. Could they somehow keep me in the same school? Could we move into a house close enough that I could still walk to school? Could he just stick to the contract that we had? I cried, I begged, I bargained. Could I just finish my sixth-grade year at Bushey Drive?

Nope. He moved us. To Rockville. Five miles away from where we were living, but too far for me to go to the same school. And no one would drive me. I knew Aunt Ruby would have, but she had given up her license. I was crushed beyond words, but thought I would survive, because I could still be a patrol at the new school, though not the cherished position I had as Lieutenant, and I would still get to go to the picnic, and see my old friends there.

Ahh, the musings of one who thinks her hopes and dreams matter.

Alas, this was my first experience in discovering it was not safe to believe for, or hope for, anything. It was the first time I realized I didn't really matter to my parents. But far from the last. The things that were about to take place in Rockville, were worse than anything before. In fact, it was the beginning of some unhealthy and pervasive self-talk that would follow me well into my adult life—

I have no voice.

I have no one who cares.

I have no one who loves me.

I don't matter.

8

Summer in Crisfield

Dad found a house in Rockville that he was able to rent for one year. Aunt Ruby told me he expected to have his next assignment given in the next few months, so he was afraid to look for a longer contract. This assured me of my goal to get to the picnic at the end of the school year. He had already checked with my new school, and they guaranteed me a patrol position, but informed him the officers were already picked for their school. I had not really expected that honor anyway. I was just glad to get in.

My mother's fury (and that is not an exaggeration) about having to move unnecessarily, could not be quenched with any words or actions. She just told Aunt Ruby and me we were going to Crisfield for the summer. Her brother, Junie, was getting married, and that was her reason. As soon as the Mayflower truck was unpacked at the new house, we left. Dad was on his own. I had discovered there was a girl my age across the street, and a couple of boys a few houses down. It would be helpful to know some kids before I started this new school year. I was not looking forward to having to make new friends. I had only the experience I went through during my first year at Bushey Drive as an example, and that wasn't the best.

When we got to Crisfield, things seemed normal. Mom went to visit all her friends, and I stayed home with Aunt Ruby. I don't remember hearing anything about Uncle Junie's wedding. I don't know if Mom or Aunt Ruby went, or if they missed it. It's all a blank to me. I only knew they were married and living in my Granny's house. Things seemed good for the first few days we were there. However, it was not going to stay that way. In fact, there was going to be an explosion I don't think anyone was expecting.

I thought it was odd that my mom had not gone to see her brother, or vice versa, so I went to visit my uncle and his new wife, Teeny. She was the one who had been with him when he took me to see *King of Kings*, and I liked spending time with them. During one of our conversations that day, Teeny mentioned my mother had been married before—something I was totally unaware of, and it really upset me. It upset me because for some strange reason I immediately jumped to the conclusion that this meant I was adopted.

I went home and asked Mom about it and she completely blew a fuse. She went over to their house, and a screaming match ensued. Aunt Ruby just kept saying, "dear me, dear me" and pacing in the living room. Since I did not get any answers from Mom, I asked Aunt Ruby if my fears were true, and she hugged me and assured me my parents were my parents. She asked why I would think something like that, but I had no idea. *Maybe something to do with that story my dad liked to tell when he first saw me after I was born? Or maybe my mom telling me I wasn't her daughter when she was angry?*

The screaming match traveled down the lane to Aunt Ruby's house, and it was now in her front yard. Uncle Junie was involved, and Aunt Ruby went out to try to calm everyone down. It didn't happen. Mom was hysterical and Uncle Junie and Teeny finally went home. Mom came in the house and continued to rage about the "nerve of that woman."

As an adult, I can't really understand her reaction. Yes, it would have been better to hear it from my mom; however, a better choice would have been for her to allay my fears, and then tell Teeny she would have preferred to be the one to tell me. It caused me more anxiety to see her reaction. I think Uncle Junie and Teeny probably received some of what Mom never got to say to Dad before we left. As I got older, I was often the one on the receiving end of that one. *Another subject for a little later.*

So, for whatever reason, both Aunt Ruby and I were receiving the silent treatment for several days. Neither of us asked why. It was an unspoken understanding. Aunt Ruby and I played Rook (a great card game) almost every night, and watched TV together.

I used to think my mother's "silent treatments" were her way of punishing me when she was angry, or, well, for any reason she saw fit. I didn't realize until I was much older, it was also a tool of control. I had seen her do it to her younger brother, because he was marrying Teeny, someone she didn't like. She did it to my dad, and I had even seen her do it to my Aunt Ruby, when she defended me. It happened more than once during this summer trip.

One morning Aunt Ruby mentioned to me that the sister and brother-in-law of Miss Ruth, my babysitter in Wheaton, lived close by. Miss Ruth babysat for me when Aunt Ruby wasn't staying with us. I loved her! She was in her sixties and taught me how to play Canasta (another great card game.) My mom had heard about her from a neighbor and when she came the first time, I had mentioned Crisfield, and she said she was from there, too. I thought that was so cool. She told me her sister and brother-in-law, Miss Alma and Mr. Lewis, still lived there, and I should visit them. Aunt Ruby had found the address for me, so I could ride my bike over to meet them. I think she wanted to give me something to do, besides wondering why my mom still ignored us.

I went to visit Miss Alma and Mr. Lewis, and we really got along nicely. We played dominoes each time I went. Miss Alma always had either fresh baked biscuits or fresh baked cookies. So, it was not a chore to visit them, by any stretch. One of the things Mr. Lewis liked to do was carve ships out of wood. And they were amazing. I used to watch him as he worked on them, and his patience and talent amazed me. When he died, he left one of them to me in his will.

Riding my bike wasn't a problem until I started getting chased by a dog. He wasn't playing; he seriously tried to bite me. Aunt Ruby told me there was no other route for me to take, and offered her cane to chase him away if he got too close. I placed it over the handlebars as I made my way to their house, and it worked great the next few times I went. It was hard to steer because I was trying to hold onto the cane and the handlebars at the same time. But when I saw the dog, I would just pull the cane and shake it at the dog, and he would go back home.

One day, things didn't go so well. I decided to hang the cane on the handlebar which seemed like a great idea, because it freed up my hands to steer. I watched the cane as it swung back and forth, but my little inexperienced self, did not foresee the danger of this until the inevitable happened. I hit a bump in the road, it swung into the wheel spokes, and I promptly was flipped over the handlebar as the bike stopped abruptly. I lay in the road with extreme pain in my left thigh, and when I looked down at my leg, I saw the handbrake had punctured my thigh and had gone all the way in. I couldn't see any of the brake at all. The skin was sticking up as if an invisible pole had been implanted under it. I started crying, shaking all over, and scared to move. I also wondered if someone would run over me and my bike. Fortunately, I didn't lay there long before an old pickup truck came down the road. The truck

slowed, and then stopped. The driver jumped out, and looking at my leg, and cried, "Oh, honey, are you ok? That looks bad. I am a retired fireman. Let me help you."

He gently moved the bike into a position that relieved the pressure off the imbedded hand brake, and when in a good position, grabbed my hand and told me to hold on. He eased the brake out of my leg, wrapped it tight with a handkerchief he pulled from his pocket, and asked me where I lived. He gently put me in his truck and loaded the bike in the back. I was sobbing, and he told me I had been really brave, then held my hand as he drove the half mile to my house. He pulled into our yard, and jumped out, knocked on Aunt Ruby's door, then came around to help me out of the truck.

Aunt Ruby came out first, looked at my leg and put her arms around me. When mom came out, I wanted to go to her, but she had that look on her face that didn't seem to fit what I was expecting. She practically screamed, "What happened? What have you done?" Then she looked at the man and asked if he had hit me with his truck, and I said no, that I had fallen off my bike. The man began to tell her what had happened, and she burst into tears, then looking at me, cried, "How could you have done this? You are determined to ruin my whole vacation! What in the world am I going to do about this? You just can't let me relax for a minute!"

Aunt Ruby turned to her and told her to shut up and go back in the house, that she was acting like a word I had never heard Aunt Ruby use! The man had gotten back in his truck, and I am quite sure was eager to get out of there, but Aunt Ruby went to his window and asked him if he would take us to the doctor's office. He piled us in his truck and neither of them said anything.

It took five stitches to close the wound, and Aunt Ruby called my Uncle Junie to pick us up. When we got home, mom wasn't speaking to either of us, and packed her stuff and left me there with Aunt Ruby, until the following weekend. We never talked about it, and I had a great time with her—just the two of us! We played Rook every night and I always knew she would give big hugs and kisses before I went to sleep.

The following weekend, Mom came back, and everyone acted like nothing had happened. *Sound familiar?* No mention of my injury, except when she asked her brother to take me to get the stitches out. *Now if we stop here and look at this whole scene, what message is being sent to this kid? What did Mom hope to gain by her "silent treatments"?* Even at the age of 11, I saw how much fear she instilled in her brother and Aunt Ruby. The two examples I gave are the only two times I saw them argue with her, up to now. And both times were in the defense of someone else. But if the attack was personal, they just took it. I remember, on that day, hoping Aunt Ruby would always live with us, because I had begun to realize I was afraid of my mom, too. The next morning, Mom said we were going back to Rockville at the end of the week. Aunt Ruby was coming with us and that was a blessing. Because I was going to need her more than ever . . .

9

Rockville

When we arrived at the new home in Rockville, it seemed Mom and Dad had worked out some things. They were talking, and that was a good sign. The girl across the street came over with her mom and introduced themselves, brought some cookies, and invited me to play. They were from the South, and I loved their accent. Dianne and I became good friends, and we played together a lot. She introduced me to the two boys down the street, one was a year older than us and went to junior high and the other was a year younger than us, his name was Johnny. We played kickball in the street almost every day, and their mom became coffee buddies with my mom. It felt like things were going to be good here.

Sometime in August, Mom got an early morning phone call, and was crying when she hung up the phone. She told Aunt Ruby and I she had to go to Crisfield. It seemed like a big secret, and no one was talking to me about it. She called Dad and told him she was leaving and had asked Aunt Ruby to stay with the two of us. For some reason, Mom drove our VW instead of the Pontiac, which was considered her car. She took our dog, Brutus, with her and left the next day. That afternoon, Dad came home from work early and told Aunt Ruby and I we needed to come with him. Dad dropped me off at the Copeland's house (the friends we rode horses with) and Aunt Ruby went with Dad. I asked what was wrong but got no answer.

I stayed at their house for a few days, not getting any information about Mom, but I did hear a phone conversation that worried me. I heard Mrs. Copeland almost whisper, "Will she live?" What are her chances?" The next day, Dad and Aunt Ruby picked me up, and Brutus was in the car, but not Mom.

Dad drove us home and on the way, he told me Mom had been in a serious car accident, and she had not awakened yet. I thought of the phone call, and asked the same questions, but he didn't answer. Then Dad left, and Aunt Ruby told me a bit more of the details.

Apparently, there was heavy fog, and Mom had been at a stop light, behind an 18-wheeler. Another 18-wheeler approached Mom from behind, and because of the fog, did not see her car. He hit her hard, ramming the VW into, and partially shoving her under the truck in front of her. She was not wearing a seat belt, and was ejected from the car, on the passenger side, and apparently had been thrown into a ditch by the side of the road.

When the police arrived, the fog was still so thick they could not find her but heard Brutus whimpering. He had laid himself across her body and was whining. She was unconscious, and they took her to the hospital, where she was still in a coma. Aunt Ruby's next words were engraved in my memory, but I would not understand the impact of them for many years to come. She said, "The way your mom was thrown from the car was a miracle, honey. She was thrown out on the opposite side of the car from where she was sitting, even over the gear shift. Had she been thrown out on the driver's side of the car, another car could have run over her because the fog was so thick. And God used Brutus to keep her warm till she was found. She had angels protecting her, honey."

I had little knowledge of angels or God, other than what I had heard in Sunday school, many years earlier. But her words made me feel warm and safe. Mom had been protected. I asked when she would be home, and Aunt Ruby began to cry, and said it was unsure. For some reason, the answer was suddenly clear to me. If God protected her so much at the accident, He certainly was going to bring her home. It just made sense, so I said that to Aunt Ruby. She hugged me and told me she loved me. We went to bed with less heavy hearts.

Dad brought Mom home a week later. She looked rough. She had a lot of bruises, a black eye, and had lost some weight. It had been two weeks since I had seen her. Aunt Ruby made her a bed on the sofa, so she would not have to walk upstairs, and it was easier to get food to her since our family room was next to the kitchen. She didn't talk much but smiled whenever I would sit with her. She seemed different.

Mom recovered slowly, and things were getting mostly back to normal. She was trying to walk more and do more things for herself. She had not gotten to the place yet where she felt comfortable eating at the table, so Dad and I usually ate alone on Saturday and Sunday. One day, we had just sat down to have lunch, and I told him how cool it was how God had watched out for Mom, basically a review of my conversation with Aunt Ruby. His response surprised and hurt me. "If God was watching out for her, she wouldn't have had the accident in the first place!" And that was the last time I talked about it, for a very long time.

Dad was a tennis junkie. He had nagged me for a few years to learn how to play, so I finally gave in. I learned very quickly, and realized I had a knack for the sport, and I was soon ready for lessons to optimize my game. I played every day with Dad. I had a very strong forehand, be it topspin or slice, but I needed work on my backhand. Dad wanted me to learn the Chrissy Evert, two-handed back hand, but it didn't feel comfortable to me, so he asked if I wanted to take lessons. I agreed. In the meantime, Dad entered me in a 12 years-and-under girl's tournament. I only had to play three people to get to the finals, and I won! It was my first trophy, and I was proud of it.

I began my tennis lessons, working with an older man whom Dad had heard was a good instructor. He wasn't a pro, just someone with a lot of experience. I had lessons every Saturday, while Dad played on the adjoining courts. Dad reminded me I had missed a couple tennis lessons because of Mom's accident, and since he had a round-robin tournament the following Saturday morning, he asked me if he could set me up with my instructor. That was a resounding "yes" because I had missed playing and was excited to get back on the courts.

The following Saturday, I went with Dad for my tennis lesson. We were playing at the Montgomery College courts. There were twelve courts there, four sets of three courts each, and each set was separated with heavy netting, so you could not see into the next set of courts. Dad was playing on the set next to mine. My instructor was there, and I began volleying with him to warm up, and we practiced a bit on my serve and forehand. Then he began to focus on my back hand.

As he instructed me on my swing and follow-through, I noticed he had hiked his shorts up closer to his groin. This didn't surprise me because a lot of tennis players, when they perspire, have their shorts stick to their legs, and it's uncomfortable, so I didn't think much about it. Then after a few more practice swings, he hit a ball to me, and as I followed through and turned to face the net, I saw his penis had fallen out the left leg of his pants. My first thoughts were: Does he know? Should I tell him? I was almost 12 years old, but this was not in my knowledge bank. After all, I had said nothing to my own dad when I saw him naked.

At that moment, he called me up to the net. I went cautiously, afraid to look at anything except his face. He was smiling and told me we needed to practice my swing and he was going to show me how. He turned me around, back to him, and placed his hand over my right hand holding the racquet, and swung it a few times, replicating a top spin swing. I was so nervous, and became convinced, he had no idea he was exposed. I was just about to say something, when he closed his left hand over my left hand, and placed it on his penis, and with his hand controlling it, started to move it up and down. It did not feel like it had looked before. It was hard and stiff, and suddenly my whole arm, up to the elbow, was tingling and then went completely numb. I felt totally helpless, and then I saw my dad walk around the netted fence, and wave.

The instructor dropped my hand, adjusted his shorts, and waved back at my dad. I felt like I couldn't move or speak but forced myself to walk to the other side of the net and gather my racquets and bag. My left arm felt weird, and it took a few minutes for it to begin to feel normal again, but not fully. For some reason, I felt like I needed to hide everything that had just happened and say nothing. Dad asked me if I was ok, and the instructor answered for me, saying I had worked hard that day. I told Dad I was going to the car.

After what seemed a long time, Dad finally came. I had hoped he had been telling the guy off or something. When we got in the car, he asked me what was wrong, and I told him what happened. He didn't look shocked, or angry, or upset. He said these things happen sometimes and started telling me about his younger sister who had been walking home from school and a man approached her and revealed himself. Dad said they were called exhibitionists, and they were sick people. He did not address the other issue about how he made me touch him. He told me not to tell my mom because she was still recovering, and it would upset her. I asked Dad what he was going to do, and he said he had to think about it. I was silent the whole way home, and when we got there, Mom was sleeping. Dad took Aunt Ruby upstairs and they talked, then Dad made a phone call and left.

Aunt Ruby asked me how I was, and I told her everything. She said Dad was going to see the man and talk with him. I don't know what I expected, but when Dad got home, he said they had a beer together, and he found out the man was on the City Council, and a "big shot" around town. He had a nice family, and Dad didn't want to cause any waves. He said he talked with a police officer, who advised him not to press charges because they would "tear your daughter up in court." So, nothing was done. And it wasn't discussed further. No counsel. No doctor to see about what had happened to my arm. No answers as to why my arm went numb. Nothing.

So here we are again. What message did she receive from this event? How protected did she feel? Did her dad care what happened to her? What concerns did he have for her mental and emotional health? When she swallowed all of this, where did she hide it in her young heart and mind, and what were the consequences? More to come on that one.

It took a lot of time for Mom to fully recover, and she did seem different. Calmer, more patient. She and Dad did not seem to fight as much. And I started in my new school. I realized Bushey Drive had been paradise compared to what happened here. I had grown almost four inches over the summer. I was almost 12 years old, and 5'9". Much taller than anyone else in my class, plus I had suddenly needed to have my mom buy me a bra. It seemed like it all happened overnight, and I was feeling like a freak. I was the focus of everyone's jokes, and the things they said were much more hurtful than anything I had heard before.

Because we had not moved too far from our last home, I stayed in the same Girl Scout troop, and it was my last year as a junior. When I wore my uniform to school, I was called the "Jolly Green Giant." When I stood my patrol post at the end of my street, I was "beached whale, fatty, freak, etc." One kid even decided to sing "The Monster Mash" every time he and his friends waited for me to cross them on the street. I usually cried all the way to school and all the way home from my post because the teasing was brutal. I never let anyone see me cry, because when I had told Dad what was happening, he said, "Sticks and stones can break your bones, but names can never hurt you. So, ignore them and never let them see you cry!"

Well, that didn't do much for the pain I was feeling, or how much I missed my old school or all my friends. Plus, Dad's continued reminders to watch my weight because "men hate fat women" had been swallowed—hook, line, and sinker. So, the teasing was because I didn't have a boyish shape like most of the other girls in my class. Of course, this was a reality I didn't recognize until I became an adult. It didn't matter at the time, because Dad's mantra convinced me to believe I was fat, no matter what I weighed.

I made excuses not to go on the playground so I wouldn't be teased, trying to salvage some peace from the torment I knew I would receive there. But I was forced to, anyway. Of course, there was another "Billy" as at the old school, who was dedicated to finding me and reminding me how fat I was. The truth is, I wasn't "fat" anymore. I was at the weight I was supposed to be for my height, but not my age. And my new larger chest, and wider hips made me look heavier than the other girls because they were mostly flat chested. Remember, this was the mid-60's, and the models who were popular, were stick thin. In fact, the top model in that era was named "Twiggy." Every bone she had was clearly visible. Today she might be called anorexic. My body type could never look like that—I was too tall, big-boned, and an hour-glass shape. I probably would have fit in perfectly in today's culture, but not in the '60's. This was an issue that followed me throughout my teen years.

Though things were bad at school, life at home seemed to have improved. In November, Mom told me she was pregnant! This was great news because

I had always wanted a brother or sister. She started looking at baby clothes and baby toys in magazines, and sharing them with me and Dad, so I tried to keep my problems in school to myself. But I was struggling, especially in the subject I excelled in most—math. That's because "Billy" was in my class, and every chance he got, he made a comment. Also in that class, was the boy I had a crush on, Everett. So, I didn't like to go to the chalk board when called on, because I was petrified Billy-the-bully would make fun of me in front of Everett. It showed on my first report card. Straight A's except for math—I got a C.

As I shared before, this was my best subject, and it was my father's as well. I got a lump in my throat, so large, I could hardly swallow as I thought about taking this report card home. That morning it had started snowing, and we had about four inches on the ground by the time school let out. I loved snow, so this was the only positive thing I saw as I gathered my patrol slicker to wear to my post. The street was not too far, and as I walked, I struggled with what to say to Dad about my math grade. As I walked, I noticed there were people behind me, three boys, and for whatever reason, they had been let out too early. The patrols were supposed to have a fifteen-minute lead on everyone else.

"Hey, there's the beached whale!" The voice was way too familiar. It was "Billy" and he didn't even live near me. I heard the other boys laugh. And then the first snowball hit me. But it hurt really bad. And then more, until I was being pummeled with them. I started to run, but it was hard with my boots, and the snow made it slippery. I wondered what I would do when I got to my post, which was just ahead. How would I protect myself? I didn't turn around because I was afraid of getting hit in the face. The snowballs hurt so bad, which made no sense to me because I had plenty of snowball fights before, and they didn't hurt, not like this.

Suddenly, I heard, "Brian, get in this house!" The voice came from a house behind me on the left, and it sounded like a very angry mom. She was practically snarling at "Brian" and his friends (of which I guess "Billy" was one) until they disappeared in the house. I heard her offer an apology for them, but I didn't turn around. I had been crying and was embarrassed.

The time at my post seemed like it would never end. When I had crossed the last kid, out of curiosity, I walked back to where I saw some of the snowballs they had thrown. I picked one up, and the snow was packed tight around a very large rock. I began to cry again, wondering how they could be so cruel. No wonder they had hurt so bad. I walked the rest of the way home, my back still hurting from the pelting I had received.

I had not decided what to say to Dad, and when I turned the corner and saw his car in the driveway, my breath caught in my throat. My heart was pounding. He must have come home early because of the snow. I walked past my street and cut in front of the house next to ours, and then snuck back to the bushes in our front yard. I didn't even know what I was planning to do. I just knew I couldn't face Dad. I am not sure how long I stayed there, but when I heard Aunt Ruby calling me, I came out of my reverie, and stood up. I came around the corner, and she said, "Karin, where have you been? What are you doing in the bushes?" I followed her in and showed her my report card. She smiled and told me I had done a great job. I didn't smile back, or thank her, but instead told her what I was afraid would happen when Dad saw it. She assured me it would be fine.

It turned out she didn't know Dad very well at all. I was grounded until the next marking period, and that meant through the holidays. What else could go wrong? Well, in my family—that was a stupid question.

That night when I was putting on my pajamas, I heard Aunt Ruby gasp, and she asked me what happened to my back. Apparently, I had quite a few bruises where I had been hit. After I told her what happened, she didn't hide her anger, and shaking her head, she said we were going downstairs to tell Dad. I stopped her. He was angry enough, and I distinctly remember thinking, he wouldn't do anything anyway. I was still sharing a room with Aunt Ruby, and I just needed her compassion on this night. Nothing seemed to be going right since we had moved here. So, I focused on the one thing I could still hope for—going to the patrol picnic and seeing all my old friends. "I have to go to that picnic" was my last thought before I fell asleep.

The next morning Aunt Ruby announced she was going home. No reason was offered to me. Just before she left with Mom, she tearfully told me how much she loved me, and hugged me so tight. I didn't want to let go. I was devastated. I depended on her for so much.

A month passed, and a lot of activity began for Christmas at school, and I volunteered for everything I could. Even though I was grounded, Dad let me do things if it pertained to school or scouts. My language arts teacher found out I played guitar and asked if I would play "What Child Is This?" for our traveling school choir. That wasn't as exciting as it sounds. "Traveling" just meant going from classroom to classroom. I agreed and I played well. I enjoyed it, especially because Elliot was in the choir!

I also volunteered for all the Girl Scout Christmas events, and we did lots of crafts after school, almost every day, making things to take home to our parents for Christmas. This was my favorite time of the year! I felt like things may slowly be improving for me. Even the bully had laid off quite a bit, so my math grade was improving, too. I started feeling hopeful about the rest of the year.

We had a good Christmas season at home except Mom had started getting sick most every day. Aunt Ruby had returned for the holidays, and explained

Mom was older than a lot of women who get pregnant, and it would be harder on her. She was 42 years old, but I didn't know there was a good or bad age to get pregnant. In fact, I didn't know much of anything about the whole "sex" thing that I sometimes heard people talk about in school. I had broached the subject with Mom on only one occasion. Her facial expression, plus the curt, "We aren't talking about that yet" response, prevented me from going there again. I surely was not going to ask Dad. I had a lot of questions, especially since the tennis instructor.

In January, my mom's older brother, Alfred, and his wife and granddaughter came to visit. Cheryl's birthday and mine were both in January, and we were close in age, so they thought it would be fun to get us together. Dad had just come back from Switzerland. It was his first trip in a while, and he brought me a Tissot watch for my birthday. He said this was a very nice watch, and to take good care of it, so I was very careful. When my aunt and uncle arrived, I took Cheryl up to my room and we played with my Barbies for a bit, and then she wanted to look at my jewelry. I didn't have much, but I was proud of my new watch. She agreed it was nice.

We had a little birthday celebration over the weekend, and it was fun to play lots of games with my cousin. We had a good time, and I was sorry to see her go. The next morning, I was getting dressed for school and I went to put on my watch, but it was gone. I looked everywhere, and I felt that same terror I felt about my report card. But I had to tell my dad, and when I did, he exploded! First at me, then he went off about Cheryl, and Mom's family, and some things I won't print here. This started a war I had not seen since before Mom's accident. I was so sorry I had brought it up, because now it was my fault they were fighting again. And Mom helped remind me of that.

It was a while before things got back to any semblance of normalcy. Mom didn't talk to anyone for days, and Dad brought up the missing watch less and less. We had finally gotten to a place where all three of us were eating dinner together, and even though the eggshells were still on the floor, I felt a little more relaxed. But that was not to last. The following week, the atom bomb dropped.

Dad came home from work and announced, with much excitement, that he was going to be getting his master's degree in Geodetic Engineering at Ohio State! We were going to be moving to Columbus, Ohio! In two months! He was ecstatic.

None of us said anything. Mom finally said she was not moving while she was pregnant. That gave me courage to say I couldn't miss my picnic that I had waited two years to attend. Dad looked dumbfounded, shaking his head, as if in disbelief. He just looked at us and said, "I am sorry! It's not an option! I must be there in March to begin classes."

I started to cry. It felt like my heart had hit the floor. Mom told him to go by himself, and she would join him after the baby was born. He looked at her with the same look I got when he saw my "C". And through gritted teeth, he said, "You can't ever be happy about anything for me, can you!" I cried that night until I couldn't cry anymore.

After that, Mom stayed in her room most of the time, while Dad was busy getting the house ready to move. I was on my own. I can't remember Mom doing much to help him, or me. When Aunt Ruby was there, because I had such long hair, she would wash it for me during my bath. I can't tell you why I was not allowed to take a shower yet, but baths were the rule. So, when Aunt Ruby left, I had no one to wash my hair. My mom was isolating in her bedroom, speaking to no one, so I didn't feel I could ask her. My hair seemed to need washing more frequently nowadays. I had also noticed my skin was oilier too. Lots of changes going on.

On several mornings I had gone to school with oily hair. I kept it in a ponytail most of the time, but on this particular morning, I wore it down. As I said before, my "crush" was in my math class, and he sat directly behind me. Of all days, I felt him touch my hair, and the first thought in my mind was, "Why, today, when it's so dirty?" I immediately heard a chuckle, and when I turned around, Elliot and his best friend, who sat next to him, were both laughing. Elliot held his hand up as if he was trying to get something nasty off it. I felt sick—physically sick—and could not wait for class to end. After this happened, leaving Rockville didn't seem as bad, even if I was going to miss the picnic. I figured out how to wash my own hair and became meticulous about everything concerning my physical appearance.

However, my self-talk had become a mantra that began to play in my head—non-stop. I didn't have real words for it yet because I was too young to cognitively get what was happening to me. It was more like an understanding of what I believed to be the truth. Even years later, as an unhealthy adult, I didn't realize how these silent beliefs—this negative self-talk—were forming neuropathways in my brain that would affect almost every choice, every decision I made—then and in my future. I couldn't begin to understand the impact it had on my young, malleable brain, but I believe this was the point in my life where I began adding more skewed beliefs to my mantra. Unfortunately, I added even more in future years. And it would take decades for me to learn how to undo the damage they had caused.

I have no one who cares.

I can't trust anyone.

I have no one to protect me.

I am fat and that makes me ugly.

I am not enough.
No matter how hard I try, I am not enough.
I will never be enough.

10

Columbus

During the long drive to Columbus, I distinctly remember hoping I would still be able to watch my two favorite shows, "The Monkees", and "Where the Action Is." I wasn't aware of TV shows being "national" and I feared, along with losing everything else, I would also lose these. Some things had changed with me in the last couple months. I had started being more meticulous about my clothes, my hair, and how I looked in general. Maybe just the pre-adolescent years, but one thing was certain, the humiliation I had suffered with Elliot touching my hair, stayed with me.

The trip seemed long, and we had our whole menagerie of animals with us. Mom had her German Shepherd, Brutus, and I still had my three parakeets and hamster. Dad griped quite a bit about the noise in the car, but I don't think anyone cared. Even when he threatened to let them all loose, I felt certain he was just kidding. Dad had come out to Columbus by himself to find our house, because Mom told him she wanted nothing to do with the move. So, when we pulled into the driveway, she almost shouted, "This is ours?" A huge smile replaced the initial shocked look on her face. She was clearly pleased.

Our new house was huge, bigger than anything we had before. It had four bedrooms, three bathrooms, a large, finished basement, a beautiful sunroom, and a double garage. It sat on a corner lot and was a half-acre, according to Dad. Mom claimed the sunroom immediately as her sewing room, and I got to pick my own bedroom. With Mom liking the house, I had some hope things would be good here. My only point of dread was starting another new school, with only three months left in the school year. I had lost a bit more weight, probably from all the tennis I had been playing, but the first day of school would be a major stressor.

To my surprise, it went well, very well. The kids were friendly, and I made a lot of guy friends, because I played softball with them during recess. Two of them specifically, Myles, and Bill, were not only cute, but very nice to me. I played shortstop, and every time I got the ball, Myles would say, "Lookout guys, we don't have a chance now!" And I usually was successful when anyone tried to steal third, and I almost always caught the flies in my area. We had recess three times each day, which was new for me, though two of them were only twenty minutes long. Both Myles and Bill challenged me to tether ball almost every day, and my height became a big advantage. It took a bit longer to make friends with the girls, because they mostly played on the swings and talked.

I learned that one girl in my class, Paula, lived across the street from me, and she invited me over a couple of weeks after we moved in. She was so nice, and was as tall as me, and played basketball. She wanted me to play with her, but I could not get into basketball. Even my gym teachers nagged me through-out my school years to play. I guess if you're tall, it's an automatic assumption you will be a basketball player. Paula tried to teach me how to play; they had a nice basketball court in her backyard, but it just was not my thing. She and I played Barbies together and walked to school together most every day.

I had not met anyone yet who played tennis, but Dad told me he was going to join a club that had soft courts, or clay courts. He said the game would be a little slower, but it would help improve my game. There were also two pools that went with the membership, and one was close to my house. I finished my sixth-grade year with good grades and a lot of friends. I had discovered many of them were members of the pool close to me, so I planned on spending a lot of time there.

Since the local pool was part of the same club Dad joined for tennis, I could swim at the one close to me, or at the one next to the tennis courts. Dad and I played often, and he hired a pro to work with me. His name was Dick Frye. I was hesitant at first—considering my history with trainers. But Dick was awesome, He told me my forehand was a "killer" and really worked with me on my topspin. He also strengthened my weak spot—my backhand. He had me hitting my backhand an hour a day against the wall—topspin and slice. It improved but would never match my forehand. I learned a lot from him, and I gained confidence. During that first few weeks of June, Dad heard there was a 12-years-old and under tournament coming up in July and he wanted me to play in it. So, I worked with Dick twice a week until the tournament. And I won. He told me I had a lot of promise in the game. It was hard for me to be-lieve it. But it was hard for me to hear any compliment, and trust it to be true.

Mom was due in August, and she had slowed down a lot. Initially, she was very active, decorating the house, organizing her sewing stuff, and making maternity clothes. But she said the heat really got to her, and she always craved ice cream. I had started taking swim lessons and joined the swim team at the pool and was working toward being a junior lifeguard. I rode my bike there every morning, and after practice we would go just a few blocks to Baskin & Robbins and get ice cream. One night, Mom had an especially strong craving, so I offered to take my bike and go get some for her. The sun was just going down, but I had ridden at night before for evening practices, and night swims.

Everything went well, until I was on my way home. I had gone about a quarter mile when I noticed someone behind me, also on a bike. I didn't think much about it until I realized it was catching up to me, and quickly. I began to pedal faster and soon was peddling as hard as I could. I only had a little way to go, but I could hear the other person was right behind me. I looked to my right, and he was right there, a much older man. "Give me a feel of them!" He then reached out and grabbed my right breast and squeezed hard. At first, I thought he was trying to pull me off my bike, but he let go, laughed and turned down a side street.

By the time I got home, I was breathing so fast, it felt like I was going to pass out. I felt dizzy and sick to my stomach. Mom asked me what was wrong, but it was hard to talk, and after sitting down, I was finally able to breathe normally. I gave her the ice cream, and by then, Dad had come down from his office. I told them both what happened, and Dad ran out and took off in the car. He was gone for a while, and when he got back, he said he didn't find anyone. Mom asked about calling the police, but Dad said we didn't have enough information. Then Dad said, "If I had found him, I would have knocked him out!" Hearing my dad say that was amazing; in fact, seeing how concerned they both were, just felt wonderful! It made what happened to me seem—not so bad. But we never talked about it again, and the fear I felt was never addressed. So, maybe it wasn't that big a deal. Minimizing and swallowing traumatic events had become a habit for me. One I would see the fruit of in the years to come.

My summer was wonderful that year, despite having to get up and cut the half acre of grass, with a push mower, BEFORE I went to my eight o'clock swim class. My friendships grew, and no one teased me or made fun of me. One thing was happening that was embarrassing for me, and that was I was developing much faster, and my breasts were getting much larger than the other girls. I had to change bathing suit sizes three times that summer, and I recognized that boys were staring at me a lot. I didn't get to play much tennis that summer because Dad was taking his first class and he was constantly studying. It was almost three miles from our house, so I only went on weekends when he was available.

Mom was getting bigger and more uncomfortable. She wanted Aunt Ruby to come, but we couldn't just drive to get her anymore. And Aunt Ruby wouldn't fly. As things got closer to the birth, Mom started getting more and more worried about having help with the new baby. She cried a lot and she and Dad argued about how far he had taken her from Crisfield, and I started worrying about them bickering like they used to. I didn't miss that one bit. So, I started doing all the cooking and cleaning. I began to wonder what was going to happen after I went back to school. This was my first year in Junior High, and I was excited. Mom managed to take me to get a few new clothes, and Dad took me to get school supplies. I felt ready, as long as Dad could take care of Mom while I was in school.

The evening of August 21, we were watching TV and suddenly Mom grabbed her belly. Dad asked her what was wrong, and she said she was having a contraction. Dad was all a flutter. I had never seen him like this, and when the contractions got closer and mom said we should begin to time them, I offered to do it. Dad yelled, "No, you won't! I will do it!" I backed off and sat down. Mom told him not to be so rough on me, and he apologized but didn't let me near her. Mom said she was worried since the hospital was forty-five minutes away, and if the contractions got too close, they would need to leave immediately. I didn't feel I was going to be any help, so I ended up going to bed. Sometime in the middle of the night, they went to the hospital. Which was in downtown Columbus. A good distance from our house. While I was asleep. Alone in the house. After a man had tried to pull me off my bike just yards from my home. And I was 12-years old. *Hmmmmm. Guess it's a good thing I didn't wake up.*

The next morning, Dad woke me and told me I had a little brother, who had been named after him, so he was a junior! I was thrilled because I had wanted a brother. I asked about Mom, and he said she would be home in a few days. Things were very different back then. Mom was completely put to sleep, at her request. And you may remember Dad was not present at my birth, so he was all about making up for it with this one. I was never allowed to go to the hospital to see her, and when she came home with my brother, it took two days before Dad would let me hold him or let me do anything for Mom. But all that would change. And my excitement about junior high would dwindle with my new responsibilities.

I started school a few weeks later, wearing my new culottes and sweater Mom had bought me. I went by Paula's house, and we walked to school together. I had already gotten all my class assignments at orientation, so I reported to my home room. No sooner had I sat down, the teacher called me to the front of the room. She made me get on my knees and noted for me that my culottes were not touching the floor—but instead were two inches off the floor. She then told me I had to go home and change! I kid you not! These were the days before you could wear pants to school, so I had to walk back home and put on one of my new skirts. Dad drove me back to school, so I didn't miss too much time. Not the best way to start.

After a week of school, Dad was watching my math homework, and felt I was way past what they were teaching. I didn't want to move my class because one of the guys I played softball with was in there. I also had a couple of my swim buddies in that class. But Dad persisted, and I was placed in a geometry class the next week. I had a few friends in there too, so I acclimated. We were sitting in alphabetical order, and the boy who sat behind me was named Mark Taylor. He was exceptionally cute and nice, too. He sat behind me in a lot of classes, and in time, would become a "first" for me.

The first few weeks of school were good, and I liked all my classes. There was a lot of home-work, and Dad had set up a desk in my room. Mom cried a lot and wanted Aunt Ruby to come. She kept saying "she couldn't handle it" but I didn't know what "it" was. I soon found out. Remember those responsibilities I mentioned earlier? Well, they were here, and everything changed overnight.

Mom was unable to take care of my brother anymore, so Dad had to care for him during the day, and when I got home from school, I was appointed to care for him the rest of the night while Dad studied. This meant I had to do the nighttime feedings, so my brother slept with me. His crying woke me, and I would feed him, and then I had to feed him before I left for school. All the care I had been doing to look nice, went down the tubes because I was exhausted and never had time in the morning. After three mornings of being late, the school called Dad saying I was facing detention, and told him I was falling asleep in class.

Well, that phone call put things in gear, and before I knew it, I heard that Uncle Junie was bringing Aunt Ruby to come live with us. This was such a re-lief, because, though I loved my little brother, I didn't want my grades to suffer either. I had to maintain my grades because I didn't want to be grounded. My chores had increased to include all the cooking and housework, and I had little time for studying.

One more thing happened before Aunt Ruby came. It was very confusing for me, and I didn't know what to do with it, so I buried it—deep inside. One night I woke up to Mom shaking me. When I turned over to face her, I could immediately smell alcohol. I had smelled it on Dad, so knew what it was. She was kneeling by my bed and with a slur in her voice, said, "Karin, your dad did this to me. This is what he has driven me to."

I was stunned, I didn't know what to say or do, so I remained quiet. She leaned her head against my bed, with my brother sleeping beside me, then got up and stumbled into her room. I laid there a long time trying to understand what all that meant. Mom never drank, and Dad was almost always the brunt of her comments about people who drink. Why was she doing it now? Why was she waking me up just to tell me Dad drove her to this? Why was she telling me anything at all? Good questions for a 12-year-old to ask. Not so good that she needed to ask them. Aunt Ruby would be here in another week, and it couldn't come fast enough. I was one happy kid, and I counted down the days. I would soon realize how much I needed her there, because life was about to change drastically for all of us. In so many ways.

11

Columbus – My Awakening

The seventh-grade school year brought lots of different experiences, most of them new to me. At home, with the arrival of Aunt Ruby, Mom started to come out of the funk she had been in. Aunt Ruby took the room I had been sleeping in next to Mom and Dad's, and I moved into the room down the hall. My brother remained the focus of my parents' attention, and during a visit from some friends, one of them suggested he was a "chip off the old block" and recommended calling him that. Dad loved this idea! Up to this point, they had called him "Little Gene" and that was a mouthful, so this was the perfect solution. So, my brother became my dad's "little me" and I sank further into the background.

It seemed I suddenly had a lot more freedom, and not so many questions about what I was doing. When Halloween rolled around, I went out trick-or-treating with a bunch of friends in several different neighborhoods. That was the night I first got introduced to cigarettes. It was a chilly evening, so I pretended to inhale but actually just exhaled hot air, and in the dark, it looked like smoke. I didn't want to smoke, but I did want to be liked by them. These were the "cool kids" in my school, and I felt accepted. We stayed out till after 10 p.m. and one of their mom's drove us all home. It was the beginning . . .

On Friday nights, everyone went to the high school football games, and we would stand behind the bleachers and smoke, and some of the "cool" boys joined us. To my surprise, Myles was one of them and he had other friends, John and Fred who hung out with us also. My friend Shelly liked Fred, and his dad and my dad had played tennis together this past summer. Another friend, Jamie, went to a different school, but she and Shelly were best friends, so she always came with us to the games.

That was my first introduction to Teen Club. Someone's parents picked us up from the game and took us to another school that hosted it. All the kids there were junior high students, from different schools, and we all just hung out, listening to music, watching the bands play, and eating the snacks. I felt like I was really becoming part of the "in-crowd."

I usually had fun hanging out there, but it did include eighth and ninth graders as well. And it seemed I got a lot of unwanted attention from many of the guys. One uncomfortable thing that kept happening to me there was being inappropriately touched. I can't count how many times guys grabbed at my breasts. Once I was standing with Shelly along the wall, just watching the band, and a guy walked by and fully grabbed my breast and squeezed, like the guy on the bike. There was a feeling in my gut that this was wrong, but when I told Shelly, she blew it off and told me. "Don't make a big deal about it." I didn't tell anyone else about those times at teen club.

Other things happened in school like that. In art class, guys would make little balls out of clay and try to toss them down my shirt or sweater. Never told about those times either. *So, let's look at this. All this unsolicited, inappropriate touching, and I never felt I should tell anyone? Why would that be? Two traumatic events in my life prior to this, and both just dropped by the very people who were supposed to protect me. Not a word afterwards. What's the message? Hmmm. More on that soon.*

The first several months of my seventh-grade year went smoothly. None of my new friends were in any of my classes, except art class, and so I asked one of my teachers if I could change classes. She told me the classes I was assigned to were advanced learning classes, so unless my grades dipped, I was stuck. I knew better than let my grades slip, but I wanted to. My friends were about the only attention I got nowadays. At home, my mom was all about my brother, my dad was all about studying, and Aunt Ruby was helping Mom most of the time and had taken over the cooking and cleaning. Christmas came and went and then I asked if I could have a party for my thirteenth birthday.

The party was a bit of a discussion, but Aunt Ruby rallied for me, and she helped me plan it. We would have it in the basement so it wouldn't disturb Mom or my brother, and it would be a sleepover. I invited six girls, mostly the ones I knew from going to games and Teen Club. I invited Paula, my neighbor, but her mom wouldn't let her come. She had not been waiting for me anymore to walk to school and had not invited me over lately. And, truthfully, I had not really noticed or even tried to contact her. My need for attention from the "cool" crowd left my friendship with Paula by the wayside. Choices.

The night of my party, we went to Teen Club first, and then came to my house for food and cake. I had made some good snacks for us, and Mom and

Aunt Ruby made my favorite cherry cake with cherry icing. Apparently, at Teen Club my friends had informed some guys about the party, and it was going to be quite the surprise for me.

After we got home, we all went downstairs. I had taken my record player down there, and some of the girls brought their 45's to play (yes, I am that old!). I went up to get the food and when I came back down, there was a guy climbing through the basement window! I didn't even know who it was. Before I could say anything, Myles was climbing in, and then another guy. I started freaking out because I knew this was going to be bad news for me if Mom and Dad found out. My parents never came downstairs except to use the laundry room, but with my luck, tonight would be the first.

Shelly saw how upset I was, and told me to chill because no one would find out. They promised to be super quiet, so I relaxed a little. I must admit, it didn't seem like such a bad thing to have the "cool" guys at my party. However, I noticed there was some pairing up going on, and four of them ended up in the laundry room. When I went to check, they were playing a game called "spin the bottle" and I was not interested in what that meant. I told them they couldn't be back there, so they came out, and then all four of them climbed out the window. They went out to smoke, and I knew this wouldn't end well. The back and forth through the window continued until my dad heard something in the front yard, and when he went out to check, saw one of the guys climbing out. He exploded, Mom was hysterical, and the party ended with all my friends being invited to leave. During my weeks of being grounded, I would continually hear how my party had caused my mom terrible stress.

My forever advocate, Aunt Ruby, would invite me into her room during this time to watch TV with her, or sometimes to spend the night with her. She was the one person I could talk to about my feelings. One night she asked me if I would like to go to a class that a designer store was sponsoring for young girls to teach them how to do makeup, hair, and fashion. It was at a store called Lazarus, in downtown Columbus. I asked her how we would get there, since that was way out of Mom's comfort zone. She told me we would take a bus and she would go with me. The bus stopped right in front of our house, and it would take us there each week. I didn't hesitate to agree!

This turned out to be a wonderful time for me and Aunt Ruby. We caught the bus right after I got home from school, then I went to my two-hour class before we had dinner together, and then we caught the bus back home. The ladies teaching the classes were very nice and complimented me frequently. On the day we did make-up, the one who was putting eyeliner on me, said, "You are a very beautiful girl! Green eyes like yours are very rare." It felt like my heart would burst! I blushed profusely, not knowing what to say. She got the attention of the other lady, and said, "Look at this!" She nodded, smiled at me, and told me I had beautiful eyes, making me more uncomfortable. After that, I paid extra special attention to the way she did my makeup and loved how it made me look! I would have to get my parents to buy me some makeup!

The class lasted for eight weeks, and was to end with a big fashion show. Our parents were supposed to buy us a dress we would wear as we walked the runway. We were to have our makeup done by the instructors, and we would get to meet Miss Ohio, who was going to attend. Well, that didn't happen. I was told a new dress wasn't in the budget. Dad had a paper to finish for school, and Mom was not going to drive into the city. The buses did not run, on Saturdays. Aunt Ruby tried to explain how important this was to me, but to no avail. So, I didn't get to go. My heart was crushed.

I don't have many memories about the rest of the school year. But remember that inner mantra I had spinning in my head from Rockville? Well, add to that the events that had happened here, and the consequences of those feelings were soon about to rear their ugly head. A girl will do about anything to receive attention when none is coming from home . . . at least, none that is healthy. But I got a short reprieve. The best summer of my life was coming up.

12

Columbus – The Cup

Tennis had become a huge part of my life. The club Dad joined had six clay courts. Clay courts are great to play on for many reasons. It's a slower game, and when the ball hits the clay, the spot can be visualized easily, so no debate on the ball being in or out of play. The last few months of the school year, while Dad had a break in his classes, I went to the courts with him frequently and there was always someone there with which to volley. During some of these times, I heard about a tennis team called the Junior Wightman Cup. It was for young girls, under 16, who wanted to play competitively, and if they made the team, it was an inside track for them to eventually move up to the Wightman Cup. The ladies on this team almost always went pro and played the big games! Wimbledon. The US Open. The Australian Open. The French Open! These were for the elite players, and if you won all four, it's the Grand Slam! Few have accomplished that. Dad found out information about how to tryout, and I became determined to make the team.

There was a very sweet older couple, the Marvels, whom Dad and I played doubles with sometimes, and they complimented me frequently on my abilities. When Dad mentioned the Cup to them, they enthusiastically encouraged me to try out. Both seemed ecstatic that I was considering it and gave Dad some resources to contact. On the way home that day, Dad said they had both commented on how beautiful a girl I was. I blushed. I hadn't heard Dad say that before.

The courts were a little more than three miles from my parents' home, and for me to expect Mom or Dad to drive me there as frequently as I wanted to play, was a joke. So, Dad gave me permission to ride his 10-speed to and from the courts every day. That was a good thing since it helped build my quads which would improve my game. I usually got there right after school, about 3 p.m., and would just wait for someone to show up. I would stay till close to 7 p.m. every day, so I had enough time to get home before dark. With Aunt Ruby staying with us, my chores had diminished a lot. On weekends, the only thing I still had to do was cut the grass, and then I could leave to play by 9 a.m. Sometimes, Dad would have time to stop by, but it didn't matter to me. I played with anyone. I loved the game! And it was a thousand times better than being at home.

On one of those days, a girl and her mom came to play, and invited me to join them. The girl was a year older than me, and her name was Natalie. I discovered her dad and mine played together sometimes, so we began to meet whenever they did, or when her mom was free. Natalie and I became good friends, and I found out she was going to try out for the Cup also. She lived close to the club, and I would often spend the night with her, so I didn't have so far to ride. I asked her why she didn't ride her bike, since she lived so close, and she said her parents didn't feel it was safe for a young girl. *Hmmmm. Wonder how that message got internalized?*

Natalie's mom was kind of bold, and asked my dad one time, in front of me, if he didn't think it was taking a chance for a young girl like me to ride so far. His reply? "She's a big girl, she can take care of herself! I used to ride many more miles on my bike delivering newspapers, and I did ok!" Natalie's mom didn't say anything then, but Natalie told me later, her mom thought my dad was "ridiculous." *Guess he had long forgotten the summer before when I almost got pulled off my bike. Well, enough said . . .*

On one occasion, when I was at the courts alone, I saw the "cool" guys hanging outside the fence, and Myles gestured to me to come over. He said he had heard I played and wanted to watch me. John was there, and Bill, the one I had the crush on in sixth grade. But there were two new boys with them, Danny, and another Bill, who was a twin. They were really cute too. Though none of these guys had ever been anything but nice to me, my insecurities caused me to believe they were only there to laugh at or make fun of me. They hung around for a while, but no other players showed up. Myles said they had to get going, but before he left, made a comment to me about how he thought I looked "sexy" in my tennis shorts. I felt my face get heated, swallowed hard, turned on my heel, and went back and sat down. I was certain he was making fun of me, because Dad had convinced me I was fat, and "men hate fat women." I had even questioned Mr. Marvel's compliment. *The groundwork had been laid, and the negative thinking was on course.*

I heard the tryouts for the Cup were being held at our club the first weekend of June. Since school had let out, I was there all day, every day. Natalie and

I met at the courts almost daily to practice. We were both so excited, and even talked about what would happen if only one of us made the team. We hung out a lot together, even off the courts. We went to the pool and talked a lot about boys.

Well, the big weekend finally came, and Natalie's mom dropped she and I off an hour early to warm up. The Wightman Cup coach was there. He smiled and acknowledged us but wasn't overly friendly. He asked if we were there to try out and it made us both nervous to warm up in front of him. My hands were so sweaty, they made my raquet grip slippery, and my heart was pounding. Within a few minutes, several other girls showed up, and Natalie's mom came back with water for us. She spoke briefly to the coach, but he wasn't very friendly to her either.

Promptly at 9 a.m. he started the tryouts. He had us in alphabetical order, and he was all business. Natalie's last name started with a "B" so she was one of the first. Of course, I was next to last. The coach didn't make a lot of small talk, just ran us through all the paces—checking our forehand, backhand, net game and serve. He volleyed with each of us for about five minutes. Finally, it was my turn. His coolness made me even more nervous than I already was, and I knew I had not played the best I could. When he finished with everyone, he excused himself, and after five minutes, came back and called out four names. These were the ones he had chosen for the team. Then he called out two more who would be "seconds." Natalie and I didn't make either list.

I was crushed. It didn't seem to bother Natalie as much, but I had heard about all the travel they did to different states for competitions. I had dreamt about being away from home all summer, doing what I loved to do most. Now, that was shattered. Natalie's mom was very encouraging and said we could both try out next year. She asked where my parents were, and with much embarrassment, I made excuses for them not being there. She took us out to lunch and then drove me home. Dad was disappointed and mom was kind of oblivious. My brother had become her only focus these days. Which meant Dad and I spent much more time together.

The next day, Dad and I went to the courts to hit some balls, and the Marvels were there. They talked to Dad privately for a few minutes and then brought me into the conversation. Apparently, there was a big tournament coming up the following weekend. It was called the Columbus Invitational, for 16 and under girls. The Junior Wightman Cup team always played this tournament, and usually always won. It was almost like an opportunity for them to play each other competitively. I guess the Marvels had some clout and had been able to get an invitation for me. All I had to do was agree to go. Mr. Marvel put his hand on my shoulder and told me I needed to do this. He said

I had so much talent, and I needed to show it off. I was scared to play these girls, but he convinced me to try. And I had one week to get my confidence up.

Tournament weekend arrived and I could hardly take a deep breath. To add to that, neither of my parents were going with me. Mom was too tired, and Dad had a paper to complete, so he asked the Marvels to take me. I had the impression he didn't think I was going to fair well. The drive seemed forever, and when we got there, it didn't compare to the small tournaments I had played in the past. This was a big country club and over thirty-six girls were competing. Three rounds were to be played on Saturday and Sunday, with a one-hour layover between each. When you're young, I guess they think you have the stamina for that.

My first draw was a girl who had been on the Cup for a couple years, and she was the #2 seed. In tennis, "seeds" are how people are rated for their ability. So, a #1 seed is considered the best player, and so on. I didn't think I stood a chance. I was playing poorly; my nerves had the best of me. She got the first set 6-3. Between sets, Mr. Marvel gave me a pep talk, told me to relax and just imagine she was one of my friends—and to play like I did at home. It worked, and I won the second set 6-4. I was leading in the third set 5-0, when she said she was sick and dropped out. I advanced by default. I went on to win the next two matches, so I advanced to the Sunday finals.

I went home ecstatic! SO excited to tell Mom and Dad. I had no aspirations of winning, but I was at least competing against players on the Cup. Dad seemed very proud, and Mom congratulated me, but neither committed to come to the finals. Mom had tears in her eyes and hugged me. I went to bed that night pretty broken they wouldn't be there but kept my eye on the prize. The Marvels picked me up and took me again, and they didn't stop encouraging me. They told me I could win this tournament!

The #1 seed on the Cup was in the opposite bracket, and Mr. Marvel said that was good—it would be a showdown between us. I started to say, I would never make it that far, but he held up his hand to shut me up. He and his wife assured me I could do it. I won the next two matches who were the #4 and #8 seeds on the Cup. At 3 p.m., I was facing Judy Dillon, the #1 seed. I could not believe it! She was as tall as me, both about 5'10" but she was very slim and lanky. I had more muscle, but she was fast. I lost to her 6-3, 6-4. It didn't matter because I had held my own, and I was proud of myself.

After the trophies were handed out and the closing ceremony took place, the coach from the Cup, approached me. I was standing with the Marvels. He looked directly at me, and said, "I don't often have to do this, and I don't much like it, but I am eating some crow today, and I need to swallow it, and invite you to please join our Cup. I made a mistake, and I want to correct it. It would be my honor. I don't know how I overlooked your talent! You will be seeded #2 behind Judy!"

Well, I just about passed out. The Marvels immediately clapped and hugged me! I was so shocked I could hardly get out my very thrilled, "YES!!!" And then to add icing to my cake, I saw my mom! She had come. Alone. Without Dad. I could hardly believe my eyes. I hugged her and told her the news. She was so happy for me. On the way home she told me she understood my joy, that she had been in a place like that for basketball. It was the first I had ever heard her mention this. But when I questioned her, it was obvious she didn't want to talk about it. So, I let it drop with hopes of hearing more someday. Mom rarely opened up about anything in her past. I never felt like I really knew her. Maybe this new dimension of my life was an area we could share.

When we got home, Dad finally took a break from his studies and came down to tell me he was proud of me. It was the beginning of the best summer of my life. And one final thing happened that made it amazing! It was unfortunate for her, but Judy sprained her wrist, and that moved me into her spot. So, I joined the Junior Wightman Cup tennis team seeded #1! Wow. Just wow.

It was no easy feat being on the team. We practiced twelve-hour days, six days a week, from 7 a.m. to 7 p.m. The coach was not much different than when I first met him, all business. If he didn't think you were doing your best, he made no bones about telling you. We played tournaments in Kentucky, Tennessee, Michigan, Ohio, and Indiana. Traveling with the girls on the bus was a blast. We had so much fun! I became close to my doubles partner, Debbie. She was a lefty who also had a strong forehand. No one could get a ball past us! We went undefeated all summer.

My coach told me at the end of the season I had a lot of promise. He said if I stayed on the team, and kept improving, he would recommend me for consideration for the Wightman Cup when I was old enough. Judy was already 16 years old and was looking at that possibility next year. I had a few years to go.

It sounded like I was on the Cup for good now. No more tryouts were necessary!

A real chance to be a pro!

It was so exciting. Absolutely, the best summer of my life!

And a truly positive future for my life.

But this, after all, is MY life. And in my life, all good things must come to an end . . .

13

Columbus – The End

I named this chapter The End because, at that time, for me, it was the end—the end of all that could or would be good in my life. It was the beginning of a downward spiral that I didn't even realize was happening. Because it was all inside. Messages I had received, and those that had played in my head for years were now circling together—like buzzards who had visualized the roadkill. I didn't know what was coming, but the stage was set. A stage, I now know, was a formula to destroy the hopes and dreams of a young girl. A girl who wanted to be loved, accepted, and seen—just noticed—as someone with worth.

Toward the end of the summer, the award luncheon was held for the tennis team. To my shock and surprise, my mom offered to go with me. I guess

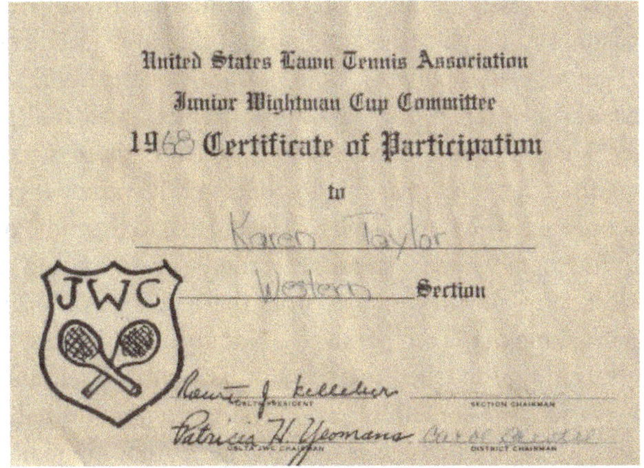

United States Lawn Tennis Association
Junior Wightman Cup Committee
1968 Certificate of Participation
to
Karen Taylor
Western Section

since Dad had been the driving force for me to play, I expected he would want to go, but he was studying.

Mom and I had a great time, and the shining moment of the day for me was receiving my trophy and my certificate of participation in the Junior Wightman Cup. It came from the US Lawn Tennis Association and that was a really big deal. I was so proud to be part of this team and already looked forward to the next season. Mom congratulated me as we drove home, and that felt really good.

When we got home, still in a celebratory frame of mind, Dad informed us he would graduate in January with his Master's in Geodetic Engineering. AND he would immediately be transferred out to Seattle to take over the survey ship, the Pathfinder. He would be the captain, and this was a big deal for him. It was apparently a great honor for anyone in his branch of service. It was the prerequisite to being made an Admiral. But, as usual, his family would be second on his priority list.

What it meant to me was no more Wightman Cup. No more fun. No more future I had dreamt of all summer. No more time with the friends I had made here. I had finally found a place where I felt respected and successful. A place where I could be something—somebody. Now all that was being stripped away. I was angry. I was sad. I was frustrated. I wanted to run away. Mom was furious, too. She said, in no uncertain terms, she was not moving, and she would stay put with me, my brother and Aunt Ruby until his eighteen-month tour was over. Well, that didn't fly, and the response was that would "never happen." Besides that, he informed us the lease on our house was up in January. I don't think Mom had been given that information before. War broke out again, and I retreated to my room . . . to a dark place, where I felt a door shut in my head. A door that was plainly marked—I AM DONE TRYING!

I was still putting my all into my tennis game—for the little time remaining in the season. But despair ruled me most of the time. It didn't occur to me things could get worse. *Apparently, I had not fully accepted the course my life seemed to always take.* Then one day, some friends asked me to meet them at the movies. I asked Dad to drive me, and we left early to meet my friends. He parked on the edge of the parking lot, and said it was a better view of the theater, so I could see when my friends arrived. He had the radio on, and I was watching out for them when he suddenly leaned toward me and asked me if I wanted to "neck." For all you youngsters out there, this was a term his generation used for "making out." I felt paralyzed. Not unlike the time with my tennis coach. Where Dad had touched my hand, it felt numb. I felt numb. I have a vague memory of saying something like "Oooh, gross" and tried to get out of the car. He laughed and said he was just joking. At that moment I saw Shelly arrive with her mom. Dad drove me down to the theater and dropped me off. It was never mentioned again . . . for many, many years.

The following week, things began to change for me. I took cigarettes from Aunt Ruby's room and started smoking in the attic, above my room. I had stairs in my closet, and I snuck up there every chance I got and practiced really smoking—inhaling and everything. I started spending more and more time with Natalie. We had drifted a bit because I was always practicing, and when the Cup ended for the summer in August, we were inseparable. I discovered she smoked too, and she lived so close to the local shopping center, we frequently went there to hang out. Her brother smoked, so we always had access to cigarettes, and it seemed the "cool" kids hung around us more when we stood around smoking.

Natalie and I often window-shopped as we walked around the center, and she showed me some makeup she thought would look nice on us—some Yardley stuff. As she was leaving, I decided to pocket it. Never done that before! And I got away with it! She was dumbfounded that I had done it, and we ran all the way home. I would like to say it was my last time shoplifting, but this book is all about truth. *Ahh, that adrenalin rush. Risky behavior beginning.*

During one of our outings, we ran into John and his friend Bill. Bill's twin brother was named Mike, and I had seen Bill with the guys at the tennis courts. Natalie and Bill were getting friendly, and the four of us ended up riding our bikes to Barrington, my old elementary school. Natalie and Bill ended up in the dugouts on one end of the field and John and I went to the other dugouts. I was so nervous, because he was one of the guys who always tried to throw stuff down my shirt and accusing me of stuffing my bra. Somehow, I felt like I needed to prove to him I didn't. He tried to kiss me, and I pulled away, so he asked me if I wanted to make out. I said no.

We sat there, awkwardly, for a few more minutes. He asked again about making out and then reached his hand up my shirt. I let him because I didn't know what else to do. No one had ever told me not to. No one had taught me what was right and wrong with sex. All through seventh grade, boys had been trying to grab at me, even the guy on the bike. I hadn't told anyone, because somehow, I felt all these things were my fault. After all, my parents had never done anything about any of my past encounters. And now I was feeling like I owed it to John to prove I didn't "stuff" my shirt. So, I let him, even under my bra. He tried twice to kiss me, and both times I turned my head away.

It felt like we were there forever, and then finally, Natalie and Bill got up and walked toward us. I was so relieved it was over. The boys rode off on their bikes and Natalie started bragging about what a great kisser Bill was. She asked me if I had kissed John and I said no but volunteered nothing else. She looked at me strangely, but asked no more questions, so we rode our bikes back to her house. *Hmmm. What was at work here? No kisses. Just proving her sexuality to a boy. As if she owed him something. A little strange.*

By the time school started, I had mastered the smoking and shoplifting thing. Took some things for some other friends as well as Natalie. Well, they were people I wanted to be friendlier with because they were so "cool." I guess I thought they would like me more by giving them gifts. *Gee, I wonder where I learned that one!* They seemed grateful. It almost felt like these new people were on a different level than even the "cool" kids I had already been hanging with. Some of the girls dated boys a lot older. Some had divorced parents, and instead of living in a house, they lived in an apartment. Their moms worked all the time, so they were on their own a lot. There was something that didn't feel quite right, but I couldn't put my finger on it. I was unsettled around them . . . cautious. It was strange.

The other strange thing that was happening was with Dad. I was now allowed to take showers, and he had started walking in the bathroom, almost every time I was in the shower. And it was a glass door, so he could see. He acted like he didn't know I was in there. They had their own bathroom, so none of it made sense to me. He also asked me if I was wearing a bra almost every time he saw me in my pajamas. I felt embarrassed when he asked because he would be looking at my chest. Mom was never around when these things happened, but Aunt Ruby noticed and told me to lock the door—something forbidden in my home. When I argued, she said to just do it, and she would handle it.

Then out of the blue, Mom said she wanted to start going to church. I could only remember going to church one other time since Crisfield. We had gone to a church in Rockville twice, for Easter and Christmas, and Dad had griped so much, we stopped. He griped this time too, but she was persistent, and when he had to study, she took me anyway. Aunt Ruby babysit for my brother, and the third time we went, a man approached my mom and asked how old I was. After she told him, he introduced himself as the youth pastor. He invited me to come to his youth group. I was a little hesitant, but ended up going, and I really liked it. We talked about family stuff, stuff in school, and just life in general. The kids were nice, but I didn't know any of them. They seemed different from who I had been hanging with. They seemed a lot like Paula had been.

After I had been going for a while, we were released early one night because the pastor had an appointment. I went out back behind a tree, and lit a cigarette, not really thinking about getting caught since I was in the back of the church. A couple of the other kids came back there and stood with me, then one of them asked me why I smoked. He had seen me play at the Invitational and told me it would affect my lungs and my game. I dropped the cigarette, and stepped on it, and apologized. He said it was no big deal, and we waited for our parents to come out.

The next time I went to group, the pastor pulled me aside and asked how things were at home. Since I had a clear, but unspoken understanding I was never to talk about family stuff, I lied and said it was good. He encouraged me to talk to him if I ever needed to. That night, I thought how nice it would be to talk to someone transparently, without having to hide anything. But the consequences of that felt worse than the freedom it might bring.

Mom was consistent in going to church, and so was I. It felt like we had grown closer just for sharing this experience. I talked with her about my concerns that I was putting some weight back on, since tennis had stopped, so Dad made an appointment for me with a doctor at Ohio State. I was about twenty-five pounds overweight, and the doctor asked me to keep a diary of everything I ate for two weeks. I did that and when Mom took me back, the doctor told her she was concerned I might have some thyroid issues and wanted me to come back for a "basal metabolism" test.

I had to lay on a table while it monitored my heartbeat, respirations, and other things. Afterwards, she said I definitely had to start on some thyroid medication. So, Mom got it, and within a few weeks, the weight started coming off. I felt so much better too. I had more energy and was grateful to have been diagnosed. The doctor said it was mandatory that after we move, Mom keep taking me to a doctor to get my meds on a consistent basis, because this was a lifelong issue. She gave Mom information on hypothyroidism, and Mom said she understood. *Famous last words.*

School was going well now, too. I had stopped the smoking and my other bad habit. I realized one day that Mark, the nice kid from last year, sat behind me in almost every class I had in eighth grade. We ended up talking a lot and he seemed to like me. When football season was half over, I ran into some of the kids from youth group and hung with them sometimes. I still joined friends behind the bleachers, and Mark was one of them, but something had changed. Something was going on inside me that felt completely new and different. I had no idea what it was, but I only felt it when I was in church or with the kids from there.

As it got closer to Thanksgiving, a few things were happening. Mark was finding me at the football games and hanging with me. He knew I was moving soon. Then one night, he asked me to "go with him." I knew this meant going steady, and it was my first time. We left the game, and went to the opposite side of the school, and I got my first kiss. We kissed a really long time and he never tried anything like John did. He told me he didn't have an ID bracelet to give me, but I didn't care. I was glowing.

At church, we started practicing for our Christmas show. We had a teen choir and I loved to sing! Singing Christmas songs with them felt different than anything I had ever experienced. Watching the Nativity play rehearsals continued to stir in me whatever it was that was awakening. Then we did this really awesome thing called a "progressive dinner!" It was a blast! We went to four different houses, having a different food course at each home. Everyone who hosted us was so friendly and nice—loving on us, hugging on us—and the feelings I was experiencing were very new. I clearly remember looking around in each home where we stopped, and thinking, "So this is how other families live." I had never witnessed so much love and care in a family. It was one of the best nights of my young life.

In school, the music director had asked for volunteers to sing for their Christmas show, and I was eager to join in. So now I was practicing for two Christmas shows, singing awesome Christmas songs, and feeling this wonderful feeling I could not name. It was distantly familiar, however. I had felt like this when I watched A Charlie Brown Christmas a few years earlier. And I was glad it was back!

At home I tried to get my parents to play Christmas music all the time. I believed this is what was making me feel the way I did, and I wanted it to rub off on them. They played the music, and though I had seen some good changes between my mom and me since starting church, little was good at home between mom and dad. The closer it got to moving time, the more depressed she got. And with every one of Dad's refusals to attend church with us, her anger grew. She did not want to move to Seattle and be "3000 miles away from my family." I felt the foundation was being laid for a major world war.

Both of my performances were attended by my mom. I sang my heart out, and I felt every word! I had grown to love coming to church and the friends I had there. With the loss of weight, I was feeling more confident, and getting more attention from boys. On my last day of school before the move, I was cleaning out my locker. Suddenly I noticed the twins, Mike and Bill, were standing on either side of me. They were identical and I had a hard time telling them apart. One of them asked if he gave me his address, would I send him a picture of me naked. I almost dropped my books and was unable to look him in the face. I said nothing, but the other brother said he was serious. I thought this was really weird since they were friends with Mark. Completely believing they were making fun of me, I closed my locker, said goodbye, and then walked away. I never told anyone, not even Mark. *I have thought about that over the years and wondered what was behind it. That almost 14-year-old, was very confused about her sexuality—and what she was supposed to be other than a sexual object. She had even wondered why Mark never tried more than kissing her. What had caused her to objectify herself?*

Christmas was coming and we spent it with Dad's parents in Massachusetts since we were moving so far away, he didn't know when he would see them again. This only caused another blow-up between Mom and Dad, because she didn't get to go see her family for the holidays. Aunt Ruby had taken a bus home after Thanksgiving, so Mom was facing this move alone. Dad had gone out to Seattle and bought a house for us. Our first. Mom wanted nothing to do with it, and all I could do is hope she liked it, as much as she had this one.

Over the holiday, we had to start packing. I spent a lot of nights with Natalie, so I could sneak out and meet Mark in their back yard. The last night we were together, he told me he would miss me. We exchanged addresses but neither of us ever wrote. My family left Columbus two weeks before my fourteenth birthday. No one was happy, especially Mom, because Aunt Ruby was gone. And she would be alone—often three months at a time, while Dad's ship was surveying. My thoughts went back to Aberdeen, and fear began to trickle in, as I remembered how that had been, but I hoped having my brother would make her happier this time. I felt little else besides dread . . . and rightfully so.

There is one more thing that has haunted me over the years. Though I really liked the church I was attending, I sure wish someone had told me about salvation. Nothing from the pastor. Nothing from the other kids. But it was still a warm, safe place. Safer than anything I had known since my days in Crisfield. The youth pastor had told us stories about Jesus, but not how to meet Him personally. I have often wondered how differently my next few years, heck, my next few decades, might have been, if I had known Jesus personally.

Because for all the good, warm, and safe feelings I was now experiencing . . . and for all the junk I wanted to leave behind . . . all the "really bad" that I thought had happened already?

Well, it was but a twinkle to what I was about to go through.

14

Seattle

After a lot of prayer, I felt it is best to write about these next eighteen months in small vignettes. There is too much to include everything that happened, and so I have only included those things that were the most traumatic for me—emotionally and/or physically. This time in Seattle began a complete shift in who I thought I was . . . who I had hoped to be . . . and who I became.

Every little girl just wants to know she is loved, protected, and most of all, adored by her parents. That doesn't change as they get older. In fact, during adolescence, it is even more important as the teen ventures out and experiments to discover who she will become. That "becoming" can be very twisted when there are no feelings of attachment to her parents . . . no feelings of belongingness . . . where she feels like an emotional orphan.

The First Three Weeks

Dad did the marathon drive in three days. We ate deviled ham and Vienna sausages out of a can, with crackers, for all our meals, and the hotels were not the best. We did get one steak dinner as we were passing through the Midwest. The fighting between Mom and Dad was constant. We had to stay someplace that allowed the dog and my bird. Yes, I still had Goldie. I had to give away the other parakeets, and the hamster, but Mom fought for Goldie. She was my forever friend, and had listened to sad stories, very late at night for nine long years.

Some friends of my parents, the Parkers, had invited us to stay with them for the six weeks we had to wait to finalize the sale of our new house. I liked the

Parkers a lot. They had three girls, two older than me, and one younger. Mom and Mrs. Parker had gone to the commissary together quite a bit when we lived in Wheaton, and I had become good friends with her second daughter, Lori. When we pulled into their driveway, all of us were relieved this marathon was over. I wondered if the "everything is wonderful" act that my parents were experts at, would start as soon as we rang their doorbell.

They had a beautiful house on the water, with a full basement, which they had offered to us during our stay. Bill Parker was coming off the ship that Dad was taking over. The act was on, and it was even believable—for a time. Soon however, Mom became moody, and things started to crumble. She didn't drink at all, and almost every night the rest of them had cocktails—nothing crazy— but had a lot of laughs. I noticed her going to bed earlier and earlier. I knew things were going south.

Pretty soon I became the focus of her anger, and it seemed everything I did was a problem. Dad had brought the bathroom scale with him and wanted me to weigh in every day because I was on the thyroid meds. I had lost all the weight I needed to and had hit my ideal weight while there. When I shared this with Mom, I thought she would be happy for me but instead it seemed she thought I had an ulterior motive—to get boys' attention. It made no sense since I saw no one else except my family and the Parkers. I couldn't start school yet because the Parkers lived in a different district than the one where I would be attending. I had nothing else to do until Lori came home from school, and then I hung with her a bit. So, my mother's fears were unfounded.

Mrs. Parker, Carly, was the first to notice the changes in Mom, and would ask me to go to the store with her, or anywhere she went, just to get me out of the house. She asked if everything was ok, and I kept to the family rule and said nothing. My brother was a year and half now, and still in diapers. He was the focus of mom's attention and the only one who got a friendly word.

Carly found out it was my birthday, and had a little family party for me, but it was not well received by Mom. That night, Dad went somewhere with Bill, and Mom started in on me. I asked her if we could just let me enjoy my birthday, which only aggravated her more. She then said, with dripping sarcasm, "I guess Carly is a better mom than me since she gave you the birthday party!" I knew this was going to get bad, and I tried to find a safe place away from her.

I went into the closet to get Goldie, and found her dead. I started crying and got no support from Mom. Carly heard me crying and came downstairs and helped me wrap up Goldie and bury her. Mom was incommunicado. I stayed with Carly for the rest of the evening—sharing with her how I had gotten Goldie from my Granny and how long she had been my buddy. I waited till

Dad came home to go back downstairs. There was complete silence between them, so I went to bed. I laid there that night blaming myself for Goldie's death. Mom and Dad had made me keep her in the closet so she wouldn't wake my brother in the morning when she sang with the sunrise. Maybe if I had taken her out and allowed her some fresh air, she would have lived. She was my last tangible memory of my Granny, and now she was gone too. It hurt my heart.

The next day started with an argument. I refused to get into it, so I got dressed and went upstairs for breakfast. I didn't see Carly, so I found some cereal, and sat down to eat. Mom came up and within minutes had started again. She was brutal with her words, and then Carly came out of her bedroom. I was crying, and Carly put her arms around me, then laid into Mom. I had never heard anyone defend me except Aunt Ruby, and especially someone who was one of Mom's friends. She told her she didn't know what her problem was, but the way she treated me was awful, and I didn't deserve it. Instead of feeling protected, this scared me, because I knew it wouldn't end well.

It didn't, and that night Mom had everything packed up by the time Dad got home, and we left to go to a motel. Somehow, this became my fault—in Dad's eyes as well as Mom's. On the way there, accusations of why I couldn't just keep my mouth shut and do what I was told, was all I heard, along with every other excuse they could come up with. One positive thing came out of it, Dad got a hotel close to my new school, so I got enrolled and didn't have to be with Mom and my brother all day. Her new thing had been hugging and kissing on him in front of me and telling him how perfect and sweet he was. Words I longed to hear. I thought how lucky Carly's daughters were to have a mom like her. I never saw any of the Parkers again.

The Next Three Weeks

The motel was a one-bedroom efficiency, and Mom, Dad, and my brother shared the bedroom. I slept on the pullout couch in the living room. My only memories of staying there were babysitting for him most of the time, while Mom and Dad settled things on the new house. Dad had promised Mom some new furniture, so they spent time looking for that as well.

One night they left me to babysit and went to Dad's welcome party. When they got home, my brother was sleeping, and I was in bed, almost asleep. I woke up when they came in, and Mom went straight to the bedroom and shut the door. I knew that was a bad sign. Dad sat by my bedside, and I could smell the alcohol. I pretended to be asleep, and he bent over and kissed me on the cheek. I turned my head slightly to say goodnight, and he kissed me on the mouth. Just then, Mom opened the door, and he got up to go into the bedroom. Mom made some nasty remark about how drunk he was, then went to the kitchen. I was grateful just to be able to go back to sleep. But I had turned a corner in understanding what was safe for me in my own family.

The New House in Bellevue

Fortunately, Mom loved the new house. And there was plenty to love. It was a large, two-level house, with living room, dining room, family room, half bath, and ranch kitchen on the first floor, and four bedrooms and two baths on the second floor. It also had a two-car garage, large patio off the ranch kitchen and a large fenced-in yard. Brutus loved the freedom here since he had to remain on a chain when outside our house in Columbus. Mom went through the house a dozen times and kept saying how much she loved it. This was the first home they had owned. And this made everyone happy.

Dad was to leave in three weeks, so when the Mayflower truck unloaded, the rush was on to get things set up in short order. Things went well for the first week, but when Dad pushed too hard, Mom pushed back, and the arguing began. Everything from how far he had taken her from her family. to him complaining how she was never happy no matter what he did for her. It was unbearable. I picked out my room from the three extras and concentrated on getting my stuff unpacked, especially my record player. My music could drown out the rest.

The closer it got to Dad leaving, the more the arguing and/or silent treatment continued, and the more afraid I became of having to stay alone with her again. Aberdeen had not drifted far from my memory bank, and I couldn't imagine having no one to talk to if she did the silent treatment thing again. I missed Aunt Ruby terribly.

Dad Leaves on the Ship

The time came too quickly, and I woke up crying the night before Dad was to leave. I was crying so hard, I went into their room and climbed in bed next to Dad. They were both asleep but as I scooted as close to the edge as I could, I felt him put his arm around me. I thought of nothing except how much I would miss him. Everyone woke at the same time, and I saw Mom glare at us, and I knew that look. Nothing was said, but I went to my room and got dressed. Dad got all his bags in the car, and he drove all of us down to the pier at Puget Sound. His ship was bigger than I had imagined. He had us come on board, and the cook had prepared a delicious meal for us in the captain's quarters. I ate as slow as I could, not wanting this time to end. The thought of going home with Mom was scaring me.

Finally, we all finished eating. Dad held my brother on his lap for the longest time, and I couldn't stop crying. We went back out to the dock as the guys made the ship ready to depart. Dad stood on the bridge as the ship backed out and I could hardly control my tears. Mom left quickly to go back to the car, but I watched until I could not see the ship anymore. When I got in the car, my brother was asleep, and mom said nothing. Halfway home she said, "All the tears in the world will not make any difference to him. You're wasting your time." I didn't understand that. It sounded as if I was acting? This was my heads up about what the next three months would be like. I felt like my heart hit the floor.

Point of interest: A person's perception can be very wrong based in what they expect, instead of reality. This is where "re-framing" their thinking—or their initial perception—can be life-changing for a person. More coming on that.

Another New School Adjustment

I had been in my new school for six weeks, and it was not bad. I had lost a lot of weight with the thyroid meds, so I wasn't dealing with that issue. But even though I had lost weight—I was not "skinny" and skinny was what was popular. I was curvy, and had big hips and thighs, and those were not viewed as attractive. They were great for tennis, but not for feeling accepted. To make matters worse, Mom had not taken me to get any new clothes, and that was embarrassing. The clothes I had were a bit large and definitely not the styles they wore on this side of the country. The other thing I dealt with was my accent. It was never mentioned in Ohio, but now it seemed I had a "southern" accent which was made known to me on a regular basis. Ironically, many of them had never heard of Maryland. Baltimore or DC, yes, they got that connection, but the East Coast geography was foreign to most of them.

I had made a friend who lived down the street from us, Pam, and we met at the bus stop each day. She was nice and came from a large family. She had two older brothers, an older sister, and two younger sisters as well. Her parents had an Italian accent, and I loved listening to them talk. I hung there a lot and ate meals with them. Whenever her mom would get frustrated, she would throw her arm up in the air, touch her fingers to her thumb and wave them back and forth, saying "Momma Mia!" I thought it was so funny, but Pam told me she did it when she was frustrated.

Pam and her family used to love to make cheddar cheese sandwiches with mayonnaise and mustard. I had never seen that before but found it tasty. The whole family loved to cook, and I enjoyed spending time there. Sometimes after we would finish eating, I would just sit back and watch the family interact. It was amazing to me that all these people could get along so well. I wondered if it would have made a difference if we had more kids in my family. But mostly I wondered if my parents didn't have me, if it would be better for them. Watching Mom with my brother made me sad because I don't remember her ever being that loving with me. I really couldn't remember any times at all.

School was going pretty well for me, except what should have been my favorite class and the easiest for me—art. We had a teacher named Mr. Ho, and he just did not seem to like me. Pam was in my class, and she noticed it as well. Everything I did, he had a problem with, and he would make me do my projects over and over again. I had always gotten A's in art, so when I got a half term grade of a C, my mom asked what was up. I told her what Pam said, so Mom decided she would go to the school and talk to the guidance counselor.

Well, we had a meeting with all four of us, and Mr. Ho said in the meeting, he didn't think I respected him. I had no idea what he meant, because I honestly felt no way at all about him, but my mother came out with this story that I could not even comprehend. She said it was probably due to my hatred of the Japanese because of what they did at Pearl Harbor and because my dad was an officer in the Navy. *WHAT?????* I wanted to say something, but knew that would be suicide, so I kept my mouth shut. The counselor looked at me, and explained Mr. Ho was Chinese, not Japanese, and I shouldn't hold any grudges. I was speechless. I had no feelings one way or the other. I didn't even fully understand what happened at Pearl Harbor, and certainly didn't hold a "grudge" against anyone. At the conclusion of the meeting, it was decided there would probably be no more issues now, and I ended up getting an A on my report card. When we got home that night, Mom seemed pleased with herself for making "headway" with the teacher. She said she didn't think he seemed very nice, but she straightened things out. I kept my mouth shut. But internalized the whole thing.

So, let's look at this. Here is my role-model making up a lie to fit what she feels will help the situation—bizarre as it sounded. So, if we have a difficult situation, we don't tell the truth, we just make up a story that will help us get out of it. Not the last time I observed Mom doing that. And, oh my, this was a lesson I learned well.

Mistaken Identity

It was getting close to Easter, and Dad would be coming home soon. Mom had not taken me to the doctor to get my medication, and the weight had started to creep on again. I had no form of exercise because it rained all the time, so no tennis. This was depressing to me, and I started watching more and more TV and learned to play Solitaire as well. I spent as much time as I could at Pam's which wasn't helping my weight much—but it was better than being at home. They were Catholic and had invited me to come to church with them, which I did. It was a little too weird for me, after what I had been used to. The whole service was in a different language that Pam told me was Latin.

At their church, I did meet a family who were looking for a babysitter. They, too, were Catholic and had twelve kids. When I went to interview for the job, they had concerns about me only being 14 years old, but I was excited to try it. I loved kids, and they ranged from 1 year to 12 years. They gave me a trial run while the mom and dad went to the grocery store. All went well, and they hired me. I only babysat for them about once a week, and never found it a challenge. Not even when I discovered the 1-year-old, after his nap, with poop all over his crib, and rubbed in his hair. The oldest girl helped me clean him up and it was quite the joke as I shared with the parents. I knew from my experience with them; I wanted a lot of my own kids. I loved taking care of my brother when I babysat for him, but having a bunch of my own was an awesome dream.

I counted down the days for Dad to come home, believing we could find an indoor court to play some tennis. Oh, I missed playing so much. I also hoped he would take me to the doctor for my pills. The day finally came, and when I saw him pull up in the driveway, I ran to the door! He had his bags in both hands, and when he got to the door, dropped them both, and grabbed me, kissing me right on the mouth. It was very awkward for me, and Mom was standing directly behind me. I ducked out and then he hugged and kissed Mom, but I could immediately tell something was wrong. She was as cool as a cucumber, and the whole welcome home thing was changed. My brother hid behind Mom, and Dad had to grab him for a hug. He cried and Mom scowled. "What do you expect? He never sees you!" Yeah, this was going to be a long night.

I got the silent treatment for days after that. Dad did too, but he took her out shopping a lot while I babysat, so eventually things calmed down between them, but not with me. I was afraid of taking time away from them, so I never asked dad to take me to a doctor. He was only home for a week—for Easter— and when it was time to leave, I stayed in the car at the dock and just waved.

That night, Mom hardly spoke a word to me. Or over the next several weeks. Those old feelings I had in Aberdeen were cropping up, because I couldn't figure out what was wrong with me that was so bad. My own mother ignored me. Did she hate me? I started coming home from school and making a batch of peanut butter fudge, two BLT's with the bacon still fatty and lots of mayo, and drinking two large glasses of whole milk. I did this EVERY day after school. And every day, the ingredients I needed had been replenished. This went on until I had gained sixty pounds in little less than two months. My teachers in school asked if anything was wrong at home, and I continued to deny it. (Please understand, at the time, I was unaware of my unconscious decision for this eating plan. This intentional weight gain was only something I recognized decades later with my counselor. And the lack of my thyroid medication, was another factor.) Even the guidance counselor had me in her office, asking questions. I denied any problems. Then Aunt Ruby came.

Rescued

It felt so good to have Aunt Ruby here. Just to have someone else to talk to was wonderful. She noticed my weight gain right away, and I told her I believed it was from not having my pills. She talked to Mom, but there were always excuses. Dad was gone again for three months, so he would be home in July. I did everything I could to help Aunt Ruby acclimate to her new surroundings. She felt like I felt about the constant rain, and she even believed it was what was affecting Mom. As it got closer to summer, I noticed some of the rain had subsided, and I was amazed at how beautiful the sky was—some of the bluest skies I think I had ever seen.

As the school year was ending, I found out I would not be attending the same junior high next year. A new school had opened, and it was more of a progressive school, like Bushey Drive had been. Dad was all about that. I would be allowed to take as many classes as I could handle, and I could earn high school credit. I was kind of excited about that. Sadly, Pam, was not going to go there. I had felt her pulling away a little. Since she was my only confidant, I think I had shared too much about my family with her. I was getting fewer and fewer invites from her mom, and by the end of the school year, I didn't even see her at the bus stop. With Aunt Ruby here, it didn't seem to be as hard to take another rejection.

When Dad came home in July, he had just missed the first lunar landing. It was something Mom and I shared with enthusiasm. She put away her deck of cards and watched it every day with me. We even missed out on watching our favorite TV show, *Dark Shadows*, so we could watch the men on the moon. I was excited to talk to Dad about it since much of his work dealt with astronomy. But when he got home, he was clearly not happy with my weight gain. The "men hate fat women" litany began again. However, it was noteworthy there was no kiss on the mouth this time for Mom to get angry about. He almost acted angry with me, and so there were no tennis outings with him, either.

Eventually, he warmed up again, and he found a ranch where we could go horseback riding together. I really enjoyed these times with Dad. This was our one area where we still connected. Tennis sure didn't seem to be an option anymore. He was home for the whole summer but would have to go back the end of August. He had met another officer who had shared with Dad how much he and his family enjoyed camping. So, Dad thought this would be a great exercise for our family. He rented a small camper, and it was small enough that we were able to pull it with our Pontiac. My brother and I loved it! We thought it was so cute and cozy. Mom and Dad had a full-size bed and we had bunks. There was a full kitchen and a small bathroom. Aunt Ruby stayed at home since the camper only slept four. It was hard to get a read on Mom. She didn't seem terribly thrilled. Dad made reservations at a national park near Mt. Rainier, and we were camped right on a lake. It was beautiful!

But this was not Mom's thing. She griped and complained about everything from it being too cold, to the beds being uncomfortable, to having to deal with a tiny kitchen. No one was having fun. On a couple days, Dad took my brother and I on hikes, and we found gorgeous waterfalls and trails. But Mom wouldn't come, and when we got back, we all got the silent treatment. They started arguing, and so I took my brother out for a walk just to get away from it. Finally, Dad packed us up and we went home a day early. This unsuccessful family trip had made things rough for Dad's last month at home. I am sure he was eager to get back to the ship.

But Aunt Ruby was here for good. And that was a very good thing.

15

Seattle – Bad Company

Another New School

I started 9th grade in my new school, and I really liked it. I was taking many more classes, and meeting lots of people. One girl I was friendly with, Jewel, seemed to be in the "cool" group—something that seemed unimportant at the last school. Pam hadn't been in any group at all, and I wasn't either. Jewel wore a lot of make-up, and she was very pretty. I started hanging out with her and going to her house quite a bit. It didn't take long to discover she was a smoker, and with only a little resistance, I started smoking again. Her older brother had dropped out of high school and was home most of the time. He smoked and often supplied our cigarettes. Many of the people we hung with were her brother's friends. So, this became my new hangout. No parents, lots of rock music, older and experienced kids, language I had not heard much before, and it felt like a better place to be than home.

Mom didn't seem to care where I was, as long as I wasn't in "her hair." Aunt Ruby continued trying to communicate with me when she could, but I even started shutting her out. I pretty much played music whenever I was home and had adopted music styles of my new friends. Before it had been Gary Puckett, Jay and the Americans, Otis Redding, etc. Stuff Mom even listened to as well.

Now it was the Stones, Beatles, Iron Butterfly, and Hendrix. Some new groups came on the scene too, like Crow, The Who and other psychedelic bands. To my complete shock, Mom actually liked Iron Butterfly and played my In-A-Gadda-Da-Vida album frequently. Neither of us understood what it was about but liked the beat. Aunt Ruby used to laugh at us because she didn't even understand the lyrics. I wasn't sure we were supposed to.

Dad was due home again in November, in time for Thanksgiving, and would be there through the holidays. I really didn't care much anymore if he came or not. Nothing ever changed when he got home. We couldn't ride horses in the rainy season—which was all winter. He had stayed clear of me since I had gained weight, and that was ok with me. I had started to feel like being at home was like a black hole. One from which I couldn't escape. I existed there, with no connection.

Bad Company

Jewel and I had started going with her brother to the local hang out, Lake Hills, which was a roller-skating rink. It was kind of like the teen club in Columbus, but they had big bands there sometimes. I heard Heart played there once, but they weren't called Heart at the time. Someone said even Hendrix had played there before he got famous. A lot of the kids from my new school hung out there.

One night Jewel was talking to two guys, Morgan and Chris. They both had long hair and were really cute. They asked if we wanted to go outside to smoke, and that led to us crossing the street and going into the woods. Chris had the cigarettes, and we all sat together for a while, but Chris kept putting his arm around Jewel, and soon they walked off to be alone. I was super nervous since I didn't know Morgan. I had seen him at school, and he was always nice, but I just didn't know him. He moved closer to me and put his arm around me. I turned my face to tell him I was nervous, and he kissed me. It was the first person I had kissed since Mark, but he seemed a lot more experienced. I was feeling things I never felt with Mark, and the more he kissed me, the more he pushed toward me until we were laying down. I had such conflicted feelings; I didn't know what to do with them. It was awesome and scary at the same time. I had no point of reference as to if this was good or bad. Mom never brought up anything about boys or relationships. And of course, we never discussed it. He didn't try to go under my bra, but there was a lot of rubbing, and I was feeling even more confused.

Just then, Jewel and Chris came back, I must admit I was grateful, and we all headed back to the rink. Jewel's mom came to get us, and after we went to bed that night, it's all we talked about. I didn't know if this meant I was his girlfriend. I didn't know if I should not talk to him because he might be embarrassed. I didn't know what to think. Jewel seemed pretty confidant she would see Chris again. I wasn't confidant of anything.

The following Monday in school, I saw Morgan in the hallway, and ducked inside a classroom so he wouldn't see me. Later after lunch, I saw him as I was leaving the cafeteria, and he waved, but I hid again. Every time I saw him, my heart felt like a triphammer in my chest. On the way home on the bus, Jewel said he had talked to her about it, and had seen me both times trying to hide. She asked me what I was doing, didn't I like him? I honestly didn't know. She and Chris were going for pizza before going to the rink on Friday, but I couldn't bring myself to do that if Morgan was coming. I hid from him on two more occasions, and he ended up telling Jewel he thought I was crazy. It wasn't long before I saw him with someone else. *Here we go. The symptoms are beginning to show. And they are becoming more ingrained in her self-worth and how she defines herself.*

I had gotten a job at K-Mart, to meet Dad's requirement for me to pay $50/month for rent. On a few occasions, I saw Morgan come into the store, and I did the same thing I did in school—I hid from him. I tolerated the comments thrown my way from different people over how I had treated Morgan. I knew I deserved it, after all, being "crazy" wasn't a foreign term in my house. If it wasn't Mom, it was me. With the way Dad threw the word around, it became second nature. I maintained my grades because I was desperate to be able to graduate early. I thought if I could just get into college, it would get me out of the house, and I couldn't wait for that chance.

Another friend I had met, Karen, had a boyfriend who was a lot older than us—in his 20's—and the few times I went to her house, he was there. He always winked at me and smiled in a way that made me uncomfortable. One night he called me, telling me Karen had given him my number. I thought it was weird, but he was very friendly, and soon I felt relaxed. He started talking about things he and Karen did together, and how he would like to do those things with me. It was strange how he did it. It felt sneaky, because before I knew it, he was saying things that made me feel the way I had felt when Morgan kissed me. It didn't make sense because I was on the phone, so it couldn't be wrong. Could it? When I hung up, I realized my body had reacted in ways I was very unfamiliar with, and I didn't know who to talk to about it. Certainly no one here at home. And I couldn't tell Karen, but I never went to her house again, or took any more of his calls. So, I stuffed it. Deep. *But not deep enough for it to do no damage. All of this was laying a foundation built on sand and this young girl was about to crash.*

Desperate and Deadly Choices

Time passed and Dad was going to be home in a few weeks. Jewel told me the band Crow was coming to the roller rink the first weekend in December. That was exciting, so we made plans to go. I waited till Dad got home to ask permission, and he said it was fine. Besides, they were going to a wedding. A very important wedding. The Admiral's daughter's wedding! It was a very big deal, and it was being held in downtown Seattle. Well, that was great news for me because it meant my curfew was wide open. I knew Aunt Ruby would be ok with me spending the night at Jewel's, and her parents were always gone, so no one would know when we got home. Seeing Crow would be so cool! I loved their song, "Evil Woman."

The week before the concert, Jewel suggested we take some alcohol with us. Her brother had snuck some to her on occasion, and she liked the way it made her feel. I had not experimented there yet but was willing to try. She said she could steal about a half bottle from her father's bar. I told her I didn't know how I could get any, and she reminded me about my dad's very well stocked bar. He had even added more to it for the holiday season since they had some parties coming up. So, one night while Mom and Dad were out, and Aunt Ruby was upstairs with my brother, I found an empty fifth bottle Dad had tossed, and filled it up with a little bit of everything he had in his bar. Gin, rum, bourbon, scotch, vodka, creme de cacao, creme de menthe, tequila, brandy, and whatever else was in there. I filled it to the top and hid it in my room.

Both of us were so excited about going to the concert. Jewel's parents were going to drop her off at my house since I lived within walking distance, and we would drink what we had as we walked to the concert. I kissed Aunt Ruby goodbye and told her not to worry about us. We began walking, and after reaching the end of my street, we pulled out the bottles. Jewel's bottle was about one-third full, and when I showed her mine, she thought it was a lot. I had little experience here and didn't know what to expect. So, as we walked, we both started drinking what we had. It was tough going down at first, but as I felt a bit numb in my fingers and toes, it went down easier. By the time we actually finished walking through my neighborhood and onto the main road, both of our bottles were empty. I recall trying to light a cigarette and telling Jewel I was afraid when I lit the match, I would blow fire like a dragon because of all the booze. She thought that was funny. I don't remember crossing the street to take the short cut through the shopping center, but I do have a vague memory of walking through one of the stores and weaving badly.

Everything else I am going to share, came from other people. I have no other memories except a couple of fleeting ones.

So, apparently, I passed out in the field between the roller rink and a 7-11. Someone saw me there and tried to wake me up. When they were unsuccessful, they called the police. While they waited, they tried to revive me by pouring a Slurpee in my mouth. This initiated the gag reflex, and I apparently spewed out my guts like a fountain. When the cops got there, I had no pulse or heartbeat, and rescue was called. They did CPR till the ambulance got there, and after loading me in, they shocked me and revived me. I woke up once at that point, as they were putting an IV in my arm. I tried to say something but had an oxygen mask over my face. The girl working on my IV just said, "Shhhh." And I was out again.

When they got me to the hospital, I was diagnosed with alcohol poisoning. The alcohol level was so high, they gave me a blood transfusion. I remember waking once in the ER and the nurse had such a look of disgust on her face, I said nothing. I was evidently covered with vomit. I have no other memories until waking up the next morning in my bed at home. Mom and Dad had to be called out of the wedding, and I think that was a bigger deal for them than what happened to me.

Orphaned

I woke up in my room at home, and the smell was nauseating. Aunt Ruby was with me, and she took me into the bathroom three times to wash my hair, which was very long at the time. It was a mess. She was so gentle and kept saying, "What were you thinking, Karin?" I was still very sick and at that time, had no idea what I had been through. After Aunt Ruby changed the sheets, she sat by the bedside and tried to warn me what was coming, but she didn't have enough time.

Mom came to the bedroom door. She just stood there. Her expression of disgust was similar to the nurse in the ER. Through pursed lips she said, "You are not my daughter. I disown you. You are disgusting. Don't refer to me as your mother—ever again." Aunt Ruby looked at her in shock, and said, "Don't say things like that." But she was told to stay out of it. And Aunt Ruby knew better than argue. Mom left, and then Dad came in, and told me to get up and get dressed. He informed me we were going to the police station. I was clueless. Aunt Ruby didn't have enough information to fill me in. My head felt like a brick was banging both sides at the same time—and it was nonstop. My stomach was working in reverse more than it felt normal. But I got up and went with Dad.

There was no conversation on the way to the station. The officer there was apparently the one on duty the night before. He was very compassionate and seemed to really care. It was this officer who filled in all the missing pieces for me. He told me in graphic detail that I was dead when he found me, and he was actually shocked that they were able to revive me. Someone in the hospital informed him the saving graces for me were my size and the person who poured the Slurpee in my mouth causing me to throw up. At one point, they had even considered doing dialysis. They felt by the amount of vomit on me, I had pretty much emptied my stomach of most of the alcohol. Otherwise, it would have been hopeless. There were no charges, but the cop asked me to promise not to drink again until I was an adult. I told him with the way I felt, I would never drink again. *We all have famous last words.*

The ride back home was silent. The only thing said is how I had ruined his night at the wedding, thoroughly humiliated he and Mom, and I better stay clear of her for the next several weeks. That was going to be a problem since I was "grounded for life." When I got home, I could tell Aunt Ruby and Mom had gotten into it, and it looked like both had been crying. My hair still smelled like puke, so I went up and took a full shower. There are no words to describe how I felt—physically or emotionally. But there was a nagging voice inside me that kept saying it would have been better if no one had found me in the field. And I found myself agreeing with it.

Ruined Holidays

Christmas was two weeks away, and I have no memories of it being celebrated. I have plenty of memories of being told I had ruined the season for them. Not enough to cancel any of their parties, however. It always amazed me how completely friendly and sweet they could be when their friends showed up, regardless of what had been happening before the doorbell rang.

My fifteenth birthday was three weeks after Christmas, and I have no memories of that either. Did we celebrate either of them? Did they have Christmas, and I wasn't included? Did they just skip my birthday? I can't answer those questions, and I have no one to ask. I remember Dad went back out on the Pathfinder near the end of January. It would be the next to the last time he had to go out for his tour. He was gone for three months and would be home for Easter.

Mom had few words for me once Dad left. Aunt Ruby was always there for me, but it seemed she wanted to wait to talk until Mom went to bed. There was almost a fear in her to show me any attention if Mom was around. This was new for her. And it only added to all the junk already going on inside me. I focused on school and getting as many courses done as possible. And I kept up my grades. I was determined to get out of here as soon as possible. I also met someone who went to the ranch where I used to ride with Dad, and her mom offered to take me with them to riding lessons. I couldn't afford the lessons, so I mucked stalls each week, and they let me ride for free. It made the time pass, and the horses seemed like the only friends I had.

By the way, Jewel was not allowed to hang with me anymore. I was "bad news."

Promises, Promises

When Dad got back home, he took me horseback riding at the ranch where I worked, two or three times a week. This was unusual because last year, it had only been on weekends. I always rode a quarter horse paint named Shiloh, and Dad rode a bay. We would get deep into the woods where we had found a clearing, and then we would race—full-tilt-boogie. I could hardly breathe! I remembered to bury my fingers in his mane and just gave him his head. There are no words to describe the feeling you get riding a horse at a full gallop. You can feel his muscles gathering and releasing beneath your legs, and its powerful.

Sometimes the horses didn't want to stop at the opposite edge of the trees, and we would still be at a full gallop as we entered the woods again. You learned quickly to keep your head low and be prepared to jump anything the horses chose to leap over. These were good times with Dad. It was almost like my substitute for tennis with him. During this time, I realized I had given up horses when I moved to Columbus and substituted tennis. Now I had to give up tennis, and I was back to horses. These were the two things I loved the most.

On one of our visits to the ranch, the owner, who raised Appaloosas, showed me a picture of a mare and her foal. They were beautiful! She told me the foal was about three months old now, and she wanted to sell them together. She knew how much I loved horses, and asked if I would like to buy them, I was speechless! Was she kidding? Dad was right there, and I showed him the picture, with little hope that we could afford it. When she said both for $350, I almost cried. I told Dad I would keep my job and earn the money. He told the lady we would buy them. But not until he finished the last sail of his tour.

When we got home, I ran in the house and told Mom. Aunt Ruby was thrilled for me. Mom just had that look—the one that said she didn't approve. I didn't care. This was a life-changing moment for me. I was so excited; I could hardly sleep that night. I decided I would spend every waking minute on the ranch when school was out.

I promised Dad to keep my grades up and started saving all the money I could from Kmart. Dad would be back home in July, and I would be able to get the horses then. I finished up school on the honor roll. I had earned enough credits to graduate in my junior year in high school, and I was going to own two horses of my own. What could possibly be better than this? *Oh, child. Have you learned nothing yet?*

Dad came home in July. There was a big party for him for completing his service on the ship, and a party for the new Captain. The aspiration for everyone coming off the ships was to make Admiral, and Dad was no different. We had assumed he would take over the Pacific Marine Center and be promoted accordingly. But that wasn't going to happen. They wanted him back in Rockville to take over as Director there. This would be his steppingstone to Admiral.

Mom was livid. She hated living this far from Crisfield but having Aunt Ruby had helped that a bit. However, this was her first home that they had ever owned, and she didn't want to leave it after only eighteen months. She and Dad argued well into the night, and it was bad. I had not correlated what this meant for me yet. I just expected his promise would be kept—somehow.

The next day, I asked Dad how we would get the horses back to Maryland. I was even willing to give up one of them to make it easier. Dad's face told it all. Nope, there would be no place to keep them. It would be too hard to travel 3,000 miles towing a horse. We had enough to worry about selling this house quickly and buying a new one. I immediately got a lump in my throat, and I was unable to swallow it. I could not speak. I could barely breathe. How could this be happening—AGAIN! For my whole life, every time I got my hopes up for something, it blew up in my face. I begged Dad not to do this. I had saved money. I had waited since he left. This could not be happening. But it did.

We sold the house, packed up everything and headed back to Maryland.

No tennis future.

No horse future.

No future. Period.

I went to a dark place. A place where there is no room for hope. Or dreams. Where the only safe place is the one where you take care of yourself, because no one else will.

I was now in "who cares" mode, and that led me to places no one should ever go.

Ever.

No. Never.

16

Seattle – The Rest of the Story

To save space and time, I have listed some other memories along with the rest of the traumatic events in Seattle. In short, less-detailed form, no chronological order—and as bullets. No pun intended.

- I hate this place. It does nothing but rain. Fog and rain every day. It definitely affects Mom and her moods, worse than ever before.

- Brutus ends up biting my brother. Dad suddenly decides we must get rid of him. I asked why, since I knew how much the dog has meant to Mom. After all, he had bitten me twice and it was never a consideration to get rid of him. The response? "You probably did something to provoke him to bite you. We can't take the chance of him hurting your brother again." Both times I had been doing one of my daily chores, which was brushing him. *Can you say, "Do ya feel like chopped liver?"*

- Mom discovered Solitaire. She played constantly while my brother took his naps. No conversations with me, however.

- One day I was in my room doing homework. Mom walked in and handed me a book. She said flatly, "This is all you need to know about sex, so you don't have to ask me any questions. Just know you need to remain a virgin until you're married." The book was about human reproduction. I found out the definition of virgin elsewhere.

- Another day I was in my room studying, and the hanging lamp over my bed started swinging back and forth. Then I heard the toilet sloshing. Mom screamed from downstairs for me to come down there right away. Then it's over. We have apparently experienced an earthquake—probably an aftershock from a Mt. St. Helen's eruption. Mom freaked out, and called Aunt Ruby, telling her she can't live here alone anymore, and begged her to please come.

- In the whole eighteen months we lived there, Mom didn't take me clothes shopping or to get my hair cut. Not once. She seemed oblivious to my changing sizes. I was always embarrassed that I had clothes that were the wrong size, out of style, and too short.

- Mom made me take ski lessons. I went every Saturday on a bus with other kids from my school. I didn't have ski clothing or my own equipment. They did. I wore jeans and my CPO jacket. I rented my equipment. On the fifth Saturday, I ended up hitting a patch of ice, then I hit a tree, and my bindings didn't release. I ended up in two removable casts on my legs to help heal the torn ligaments. I was on crutches for six weeks.

- Mom and I picked a bunch of blueberries, and she asked me if I would make some blueberry wine. I found a recipe and we worked on it together. The fermentation process took some time, and when it was finally done, she tested the wine on her bi-monthly bridge group. They all got buzzed. It was a good time and a good memory.

- Dad kept R-rated joke books in the guest bathroom for people to read. I was one of those people. I got some pretty skewed ideas on a lot of different things from those books.

- The first summer we were there, Dad took me to see *Easy Rider*. Mom refused to go. There were many things in the movie I didn't understand, and many things I should not have seen or been exposed to. Over the years, he took me to a few movies which were totally inappropriate for a young girl to see. And especially not with her father. By the way, some of those feelings I mentioned earlier, the ones that had been awakened, were piqued with this movie. And I was way too young to be feeling them.

***

Another thing that was becoming blatantly clear to me was my parents' inability to recognize my need for them to pay attention to my health issues. The medical care that had begun in Columbus, needed to be followed up on by a physician here in Seattle. This was a major dropped ball.

My thyroid medicine prescription was never refilled. I ended up putting on sixty pounds in eighteen months. It was embarrassing and I didn't feel I could ask to see a doctor to get my meds. In school, I had met a girl who told me how she controlled her weight—she made herself throw up after eating a meal. She said it wasn't that hard, and proceeded to educate me on the process. So, I began to practice this. And it seemed to work. I started to drop a few pounds. The one thing I needed to stay on top of was keeping the bathroom trash can clean after each purge. But it wasn't good enough for Mom. I guess she smelled it a few times, and sarcastically addressed it, "If you are going to throw up, you better clean the trashcan with bleach! I don't want to smell that again."

When Dad came home on leave, she told him about it, and he added, "Why the heck are you wasting food like that? Are you an idiot? Just don't eat it!"

Okay, well she had her priorities established for her. If she is going to be a bulimic, she won't be taken to the doctor to see why she is doing this, or to see if something is physically wrong with her, but she will keep the bathroom trashcan bleached, and try not to waste too much of their food. Got it.

Never did see a doctor for the bulimia, and I controlled my weight like this for seventeen years.

Here are some other times a doctor's visit may have been in order:

- I was invited to a birthday party. It was summer and I wanted to add a little color to my face, so I took Dad's tanning lamp and laid under it. I fell asleep. When I woke up, my skin felt tight. I went into the bathroom and touched my face, and water sprayed out. Dad's sister was visiting, who was an RN. When I told Mom what I did, my aunt said I should go to the hospital because I probably have 2nd degree burns—"and after all, this is her face." Mom said I would be fine and gave me some Noxzema. I applied it constantly but after four days, my face looked like leather. It was hard and tight. When it peeled, it came off in large pieces that felt like leather. Never saw a doctor. *I guess this was like a natural chemical peel. Maybe I should have been grateful for it?*

- Dad had purchased an electric lawnmower, and it had continued to be my job to cut the grass. Aunt Ruby was outside with me, and after I had finished, she pointed out a place I missed. In a hurry, I ran back over the spot—and the electric cord—at the same time. She had just finished watering the plants on the patio, and I was standing in some of the water when I picked up both ends of the cord and tried to put them back together. Don't ask why. The next thing I knew, I was against the fence about twenty feet away. Aunt Ruby ran in and got Dad, and when he came out and saw me breathing, he said I would be fine—"just a little shock." *Yep! Pretty shocking!*

- On another occasion, Mom and I got into an argument because I didn't want to take the ski lessons. She told me it wasn't an option, and I raised my arm in the air in frustration and said, "Mamma Mia!" This, of course, was mimicking what I had seen Patty's mother do numerous times. Dad misread my intention, and thought I was flicking her the "bird" and kicked me as hard as he could on my outer thigh—with his heavy work boot. I immediately went down on the floor, and my leg felt like it was on fire. Even after denying that I was not flicking the middle finger, he didn't believe me. That night I took a shower, and the leg was completely black and blue from knee to hip. I was too afraid to show my parents or say anything.

- The next day, in gym class, I was asked what happened and I told them I fell down the steps. I was sent to the office, and a social worker was there to talk with me. I told her the same story. She didn't believe me and asked if I had seen a doctor. I told her no, and she explained she was fearful a major vein or artery had been ruptured. I shrugged and told her I would be fine. She gave me her card and asked me to call her if I ever had another "bad fall." I was never taken to a doctor. *Note my response: "I will be fine." Sound familiar? I learned that line by rote—well into my adult years.*

- Two days after that incident, Mom started in about the ski lessons again. She told me she needed me out of the house on Saturdays so she could have some time to herself. I had begun to put on weight and was embarrassed to try and ski with all my friends who were already experienced with skiing. The next day in school—my leg still black from the bruising—my gym teacher approached me and told me no one believed I fell down the steps. She was pleasant but persistent, and I worried what would happen if Social Services got involved.

- By the time I got home that night, I had decided there was just no way out of the life I lived, so I decided not to deal with it anymore. I looked through my mom's closet and I found a new bottle of aspirin. And I swallowed the whole bottle. Nothing happened to me except I got very sick to my stomach. I also got very sleepy and slept for almost ten hours. When I woke up, the ringing in my ears was so loud, I couldn't hear anything else. I was very worried this might be a permanent thing, so I told Dad what I had done, and he told me I was crazy. "You're some kind of a nut." And, again, no visit to the doctor, and no further discussion of the incident. He returned to his ship a week later, and I still had to go for ski lessons. My hearing did return after several days. *What I learned as an adult, is I could have destroyed my stomach—caused an ulcer, a GI bleed, any number of* serious medical conditions. But there were no lasting symptoms, not even as an adult. One of many mysteries.

- After my alcohol poisoning incident, I was never taken to a doctor or a counselor. Both had been recommended by the policeman at the station. During the next three years of my high school life there were many times I should have seen a doctor, but it didn't always happen. Sometimes not until someone else brought it to my parents' attention.

So, the messages haven't changed much for this young girl. The messages she has internalized for quite a few years now. And now she has added a few more. These are the messages she didn't speak in words, but the sheer negligence, lack of care and compassion, and abuse must have screamed them in her head constantly . . .

You have no one who cares.
You have no worth.
You have no one who loves you.
You can't trust anyone.
You have no safe place.
You have no one to protect you.
You are not attractive.
You have no voice.
You don't matter.
You are not enough.
You will never be enough.

Part Two:

Some Family History

17

Digging Deeper

I am going to leave my story there for now. There will be more trauma in my young life. Much more. Oh. So. Much. More. But up to this point, all the things that happened to me were beyond my control—well, with a couple of exceptions. But even those exceptions were preempted by things beyond my control. No one made me take that alcohol and drink. However, what a lot of people don't realize is that the brain develops in stages. A part of the brain known as the amygdala overseas immediate emotions and reactions and develops much earlier than the frontal cortex, which controls reasoning and logic. In this later developed part of the brain, a person can identify and consider long-term consequences as they make decisions. Consequently, much adolescent decision-making is driven by the amygdala because the frontal cortex doesn't finish developing fully until adulthood.

So, when I left Seattle, my brain had still not reached maturity, and to add insult to injury, the traumatic events I had experienced had caused emotional stunting as well, so I was not operating with as much as I might have, but I did move into an older brain development. Although I was still not fully able to recognize all the consequences of my behaviors, I was now, at least, able to make choices for myself—most of the time—regardless of how reckless they were. No, they were not healthy, and they were still driven by great pain, but my choices could have taken a different direction, had there been someone in my life to guide me.

So, it's here I need to take you to a different place. A place where I can offer some partial understanding of how one could have parents like mine. To try and comprehend what they experienced that caused them to react and respond the way they did to me. As a person walking through the healing process, I had to come to a place of realizing my parents didn't wake up each morning wondering what they could do to mess up my life that day. The things they did, the reactions they had, the behaviors they exhibited were all learned—just like mine were. I had to accept that my parents were not evil people with a goal to make me miserable. I had to understand something had happened to them to cause them to be like they were.

This realization eventually helped me to learn to forgive. To have compassion. To look at them with Jesus' eyes, and not the eyes of a victim. There is a part of the healing process when you must look at your parents with cold, hard truth. To admit what they did to you. To scream out all the injustices. To recognize you were a victim of their dysfunction. But you can't stay there. You can't live there. Because if you do, you will never truly heal. You will stay a victim, with a grudge in your heart and an axe to grind away at them every time you get a chance.

I was there. I wanted justice. I wanted them to feel the pain I had felt, and still felt. I wanted them to hurt like I had. I wanted them to sit in front of me so I could tell them about every horrible and sick thing they had done, and watch them squirm in their seats. Only then would I receive my reward from them— the apology and repentant attitude that said it was all a mistake, that they didn't mean it, and that they would spend the rest of their lives making it up to me.

Well . . . I would settle for at least the apology.

Then there is reality. The truth is—my parents HAD been there. They had both experienced relentless pain in their lives. They had suffered, and they had hurt. The difference between us was I had met the One who could help me—and could have helped them, had they known or been willing. I had been led to Christian counselors to help me work through all my junk. I had been told what was unfair about the things I had experienced and what I could do to NOT carry them into the rest of my life. I learned I needed to forgive, because holding onto all that was only hurting me. I had learned all the places where I needed to also seek forgiveness because now, I knew there were things I needed to repent of as well, especially with my own children.

For someone to repent, they must know they have done something wrong. Without knowing you made a mistake . . . how do you repent of it? Without being educated to what is and isn't healthy, how do you discern which direction to take? This isn't learned through osmosis. It's to be learned by watching your role-models—usually your parents—and only when they are healthy themselves and able to do that modeling for you. If you weren't blessed to receive that kind of healthy upbringing, you must learn it somewhere else, and I was blessed with that opportunity, but my parents were not.

Without that knowledge, there can be no restoration of who you were meant to be before all the abuse happened. There needs to be a transition from victim, to survivor, to thriver. And the only way to get there is to walk through the fire—your own fire. And to understand your family of origin, and the fire they walked through. And unfortunately, sometimes, the fire your children walked through before you stopped being a victim.

Please let me state again—if you're reading this and are relating it to similar things in your own life, it's mandatory to recognize you were once a victim of abuse. It does no good to deny what happened and continue to pretend your parents were great people. This is the hardest thing about counseling with those who have issues and behaviors you know are due to childhood trauma. They often refuse to admit their parents were anything but "great parents." This is usually due to a fear of disrespecting them, or not honoring them. Truth is truth, and the sooner we look at the cold, hard facts, the sooner we can heal. It's not disrespectful to be honest about what happened to you; its disrespect when you aren't. It's dishonoring to the young parts of you who suffered. The little boy or girl inside who is still crying out for justice . . . the little person who can only temporarily be quieted or placated with all the adult defense mechanisms we learn to employ.

This is how generational trauma continues. People deny. People hide. People run. People keep secrets. They protect the abuser and disregard the victim. Even when they are the victim.

And with all that, they lie to themselves. "Things weren't that bad. It could have been a lot worse. Let the past be the past and leave it there. What good does it do to dig it up?"

They minimize. They believe they must protect the family reputation . . . the family name. When, what they are really doing is allowing the abuse to continue from one generation to the next.

For me, the buck needs to stop here. I wanted to do that years earlier when I realized how badly things had truly been. When I realized other families didn't necessarily live like mine. When I realized everything I had blamed myself for over the years was beyond my control. When I heard my counselor say to me, "None of what happened to you was your fault."

But my healing crossed a couple decades of work. Hard work. Painful work. Because there was a lot from which to heal. And unfortunately, that meant my kids were affected by my lingering dysfunction. The things that had happened to me, the things even I was unable to admit, were too humiliating to confess to anyone. Even God. Though I knew God had forgiven me, forgiving myself was a whole different ballgame. And so, I dragged my feet. I can only pray that this book will be the piece that can change the direction for the next generation. That it will help them see there is work to be done in their lives. That they will know how very much I wish I had been the person then that I am now, and if I had been, I would have done so many things differently.

My kids are gold to me, and I will live with the regret of passing down to them any part of this sickness, until the day I take my last breath. But I pray the words in this book will save them a lot of time and research. Save them years of wearing a victim hat they don't need to don, because now they can heal. They can grasp the truth so the buck can stop here for them as well.

My search for answers took a lot of work, digging into my parents' past, and then their parents' past, to discover how I got here. I have included that research in the coming chapters. Those answers allowed me to understand them. To forgive them. And to love them with all the love a daughter can have—as if they had been the perfect parents I always wanted. Because now I can see them through Jesus' eyes.

And love them as He loved me . . . in all my mess.

And that is a very peaceful place to live.

18

The Unspoken

Most of what I will share about my mom and dad, didn't come from them. It came from family members, friends, and newspaper articles. Dad shared some things about his young years, but very little came from Mom. The things I learned when I set out to discover who they really were, who they had been, and how they grew up, were both shocking and sad. It helped me understand how they became the parents they were, and why they had so few tools in their tool belts in which to know how to love me the way I deserved. There were no great parenting books back in those days, and even if there were, you wouldn't look for one unless you knew you needed to. So, they both did what they knew, regardless of the how damaging it might be.

This is Dad's story.

My dad was born on September 15, 1926. My grampie was 21 years old and a butcher. His wife Medora was 19, and an officer in the Salvation Army. She was also the leader of the local Women's Christian Temperance Union (WCTU.) With some research, I learned this group was a major force in pursuing and accomplishing the passing of the 18th and 19th Amendments to the Constitution. The 18th Amendment prohibited the manufacturing, transportation, and sale of alcohol within the United States, and the 19th Amendment gave women the right to vote. (This helped me understand a little bit about the genetics that drive me—to stand up for justice, defend what is right, and give a voice to the voiceless.)

My grandparents had been married almost two years when Dad was born. When I graduated from Bible college, I learned about Medora being in the Salvation Army. Dad came to my graduation and talked with a lot of my friends there. Many of my fellow students were in the Army, and for the first time I heard him talk about his mom in regard to her faith. It was a conversation filled with emotion. His love for her, and his loss of her at such a young age was palpable.

On the morning of October 9, 1929, one month after Dad's third birthday, he and his mom were at home. His dad had gone to work at the butcher shop next door. It was a chilly morning and Medora was stoking the fire to make the house warmer. She was eight months pregnant and was standing close to the stove to get warm, when her apron

caught on fire. Within seconds, her dress was in flames, and she was screaming. Dad was with her in the kitchen and ran to her, but she pushed him away, protectively, and told him to run and get Grampie. A neighbor in the building heard her screams and called for a doctor. He came and dressed her wounds and proceeded to take her to the hospital. When Dad returned with Grampie, the neighbor explained all that had happened and drove them to the hospital. When they got there, Grampie learned she had burns over fifty percent of her body. Her life, and the life of Marjorie, the baby girl inside her, were of great concern.

Medora was admitted to the hospital so she could get ongoing treatment for pain and seemed to make slow progress toward healing. Marjorie, however, was stillborn on October 15. Though this was a tremendous blow, everyone held onto the hope that Medora would improve and Grampie had even started planning to celebrate her birthday, while in the hospital. Grampie had sent Dad to stay with Medora's mother, right after Medora was admitted and Dad wasn't allowed to come to the hospital to see her during this time. They did celebrate Medora's birthday, a few days early, possibly to offset the loss of their baby. Medora had been improving, but after this celebration, went downhill very quickly, and succumbed to the burns on the morning of October 18. She would have been 22 years old the next day.

Having to plan a funeral for Marjorie, and then immediately having to decide on arrangements for his wife, Grampie found himself incapacitated by grief. He realized he was unable to care for Dad, or keep him in the same house, so he left him with Medora's mother. Grampie buried himself in his work to try and cope, and saw Dad on occasion, but did not bring him back to live with him for several years. Not until he remarried.

Dad must have felt orphaned. Remember my original definition: "a child deprived—by death—of one, or usually both parents" and a second definition of "one deprived of some protection or advantage." Dad had experienced the first definition in the death of his mom, and now he was deprived of the advantage of having his dad care for and protect him. So, he could still feel he belonged. To feel attached. Loved. I am not saying he did not receive those things from his grandmother. I wonder, knowing his dad was alive but staying away from him, except for brief visits, what damage was done to his heart . . . and to his young developing brain?

So, Dad never got to see his mom again, and the last memory he had of her was seeing her in flames. Grampie never discussed the death of Medora or Marjorie with Dad. But in 1972, when Dad was 46 years old, he finally shared with his dad his vivid memories of what happened, including the color of the dress she was wearing, and her screams for help, while she tried using a throw rug to douse the flames. After Dad shared this memory, with heavy sobs, Grampie told Dad his feelings about what happened. "It was important we celebrated her birthday because she was improving so much. Then  we had the party and suddenly she started going downhill. And it happened so fast. I just knew it was my fault. I could not give Medora a reason to live."

On June 24, 1935, Grampie re-married, and after their honeymoon, they brought Dad to live with them. He was 9 years old. They bought a farmhouse in Fitchburg, MA, and in the winter of Dad's tenth year, Grammie and Grampie went to a concert in Boston. It was a very cold night, not unusual in Massachusetts, and without the modern-day ability of knowing the weather forecast, they were not concerned about leaving Dad alone for a few hours.

The next events are still puzzling as to the sequence but what was reported in the paper is that a huge snowstorm hit with blistery winds. A temperature change of thirty-eight degrees took place in a very short time, dumping a lot of snow—known today as a bomb cyclone. A fire had mysteriously broken out in the chicken shed, and then proceeded to the barn. Some workers who were spreading sand on the road, saw the flames and using a special phone, called the fire station. By the time the fire truck arrived, the wind had brought the sparks to the main house, which was soon ablaze. A couple neighbors had come over and successfully removed the horses and cows from the barn. No one had checked the house yet, believing it was empty since the car was gone.

When the fire truck arrived, they found the pond they wanted to use for their water supply solidly frozen, so there was no source of water with which to hook into. With pickaxes they worked for over an hour trying to get through the thick ice. When they finally broke through, they discovered the pump on the truck failed, and they had to begin a bucket brigade. The shed and barn were a complete loss, so they focused on the house, but were beginning to lose the battle, as the wind was relentless. The firemen had done a sweep of the house and determined that no one was in it. But one fireman felt he needed to check the house once more, and against the advice of the others, went back in. He went up the stairs, and while searching each room, discovered Dad. He was asleep, and unaware of the crisis. By this time, the fire was raging, and the fireman wrapped Dad in a blanket and carried him downstairs and outside.

Some neighbors who lived about a quarter mile away, took Dad back to their house. The fireman was taken to the hospital for smoke inhalation. Many attempts were made to reach Grampie and Grammie, but were unsuccessful. When they were finally able to get home, they found their house mostly burnt to the ground. The firemen who remained at the scene told them Dad was safe, and where he was taken. Grampie and Grammie picked him up and spent the night with family in Fitchburg.

In 2014, when I found this article about the fire, I called Dad to ask him about it. He had no memory of this incident happening. Even after I read it to him, it didn't trigger any memories. Against my better judgment, I chose to share with him how much God loved him evidenced by the fireman risking his life and going back into the house to discover and rescue him. This was the first time, in all my attempts to share God's love and care for him, that I didn't hear a guffaw, and a sarcastic comment. There was silence. And when he did speak, it was obvious he was crying. He thanked me for sharing the article, asked me to forward a copy to him, and said goodbye. This was the beginning of some miraculous changes Dad was about to make in his life. And, more importantly, in his spiritual life.

Some other situations had laid the groundwork for those changes. Dad came with me to my graduation from Bible college in 2012. We stayed in an Airbnb, and did a lot of sightseeing before my graduation. One morning, I woke relatively early and heard Dad speaking with someone in the kitchen. I waited till Dad hung up, and then went out to join him. He was sitting at the dining room table and was quietly crying. He said he had been talking to his cousin's wife. His cousin, Jimmy, was related to him on Medora's side of the family, and had passed some time ago.

His wife had called Dad to give him a message Jimmy had wanted to share with Dad. The message? God is real. Jimmy's relationship with Jesus had changed his life and he wanted Dad to experience the same freedom. When he shared this with me, I told him I also knew this was true. Though I had seen counselors and therapists, over the years, it wasn't until I met Jesus that things changed for me. I also told him the promise of eternal life is getting to see again all who went before us. It was his chance to see his mom and dad again. The conversation ended abruptly when he straightened himself, got control of his emotions and began his usual description of science, astronomy and all the reasons God could not be real.

Though our conversation ended, the tears I had seen were real. Something was moving in Dad, and I felt sure it was the Holy Spirit. I knew time would be the only way to discover how much he was listening to the still, small voice. I prayed it would be sooner than later.

Years earlier, when I was a teenager, Mr. Miller, one of the other officers Dad worked with, became a close friend. He and his wife were very open about their relationship with Jesus, and often when having dinner at our home, talked about their faith. Dad listened and never argued or made the kinds of remarks he would make to my uncle or myself. Anytime Dad brought up anything good that had happened, this gentleman gave the glory to God. Dad would just be quiet. Interestingly, I knew Dad respected both Mr. Miller and his wife, and I never heard any negative comments about them, even after they left our home. Uncharacteristic for him when he had conversed with other Christians. Another seed was being planted.

As I continued to collect information about Dad's history, many events arose that involved fire. I had to wonder how that little 3-year-old boy—who was never permitted to deal with the trauma of his mother's death—acted out some of those feelings or may have been triggered by events in his future. He clearly had disassociated from the house fire. What other things may have driven his future behaviors? Here are some of the events I discovered, plus situations I recalled myself, that may have been related:

- In the research I did about Dad's family, I learned Grampie's grandmother was a nurse. She ran into a house that was on fire, trying to save a baby who had been left inside. She didn't make it out and died in the fire.
- Dad had a bad scar on the index finger of his right hand. I asked him one time how it happened. He said his dad had caught him playing with matches and held a candle to his finger to teach him not to play with fire. The scar clearly replicated a third-degree burn, and I remember thinking how horrible it was to do something like that to a little child.

- There was an incident in Wheaton involving an aluminum tree Dad had bought for us for Christmas. These trees came with a rotating wheel that changed the hue of the tree as it cycled through the four colors. We had family visiting and we were eating dinner. I am not sure how it happened, but the wheel caught on fire, and Dad completely freaked out. In all the years I lived with him, before and since, I had never seen this kind of triggered reaction in him. He was screaming for everyone to get away, grabbed a broom, picked up the wheel, and threw it out the front door into the snow. It took some time before he calmed down, but he was successful in shutting down the emotions, as he often did, and everyone returned to the table for dinner.

- We had a fireplace in four of the houses we lived in. I rarely if ever, saw Dad start a fire, with two exceptions—Christmas morning or when we had company and they requested one. I never thought about this possibly being connected to his past issues with fire, and I can't say now that it did. But it's an interesting consideration.

- We went camping on a couple of occasions, and Dad did build a fire in the evening, but we were not allowed to get close to it. Not even to toast marshmallows. However, he toasted marshmallows for us.

There were other things I learned about my dad's exposure to traumatic events. One of the things he talked about with obvious disdain were his experiences in school. Being a Protestant in a mostly Catholic population was hard on him. His size was another issue in school that only added to his feelings of rejection. Dad was small for his age. These are some of his memories and articles I found.

He shared once how hard it was to be a Protestant in the schools in the Boston area. Most of the kids he went to school with were Catholic, and the "class" separation in those denominations was tangible. The boys made fun of his faith, and his size, calling him "mouse" and having "mouse-sized faith." It was extremely hard on him, especially in gym where he got teased even more relentlessly in the shower room. Dad also said how he hated having to eat fish every Friday.

I found an article about Dad getting five teeth knocked out and a badly cut lip during a Boy Scout outing where Grampie was the scout leader. It didn't say how the accident happened, but Dad had told me over the years about someone throwing a rock at him and knocking his teeth out. I had not heard about it being in Boy Scouts. I called Dad and read the article to him, and he told me that was when it happened. Many of the boys in the Scout troop were from his school and were Catholic. The one who picked on him the most in school was the one who had thrown the rock. Grampie was up ahead of them and didn't see it happen. Nothing happened to the boy because Grampie didn't want to ruin the reputation of the scout troop. I can't imagine the pain Dad experienced both physically and emotionally. Bullied. Betrayed. Neglected.

My grandparents had their first son together on February 28, 1939, when Dad was 12. They then had a daughter on June 9, 1942, when Dad was 15. Things were very different for Dad after this, as in most blended families. But it also seemed to intensify the feelings of insecurity he had with his stepmother, as evidenced by the things he shared with me. There was a life-long belief that his stepmother did not love or respect him. This caused him to constantly try to prove himself. There were quite a few events in his young life that drove those feelings.

- Dad told me about a time when Grammie had come into his room without knocking and had caught him masturbating. She told him he was going to go to hell and threatened to put a clothespin on his penis. She put him in the closet in his room and made him stay there. Dad didn't know how long, but it was very dark, and he said he was scared.

- I also learned Grammie and Grampie did not sleep in the same room when their kids were young. Grampie and their son slept in one room, and Grammie and their daughter slept in the other room. After they had grown up and married, I remember visiting Grammie and Grampie one time. I was still a young girl and noticed they had twin beds in their room instead of one large to share, like my mom and dad. I asked Grammie why they had two separate beds in their room, instead of sharing a bed. I didn't get an answer to that one.

- Dad told me he never felt his stepmother loved him. When he was 14 years old, she told him he should not have any aspirations of going to college and that he should find a trade he liked and plan to go to a trade school. "You will never amount to anything. You are not smart enough. Find something you can do with your hands." Dad said he buried that deep in his heart, and it became the driving force to succeed in whatever career he chose. There was nothing in his life more compelling than his desire to prove her wrong. And he did.

- Dad told me once, he felt so unwanted at home, he decided to get out as soon as he could. At the age of 16, he lied about his age, and joined the Navy.

He was assigned to work evenings on airplanes at the navy base and finished earning his high school diploma during the day. He used his GI Bill to get his degree in Civil Engineering at Amherst College in Massachusetts.

- After Dad went into the service, and later when he was attending college, he told me Grampie would sneak him money whenever he came home for a visit. He would hide it inside Dad's suitcase, and then tell him not to tell Grammie. He would always get teary when he shared stories about his dad. He loved him very much.

- Another story he told me about Grammie, was her partiality to his half-brother. She made it clear in her words and actions how much she favored him. Dad told me while in the Navy, he had saved money to buy her a purse she wanted for Christmas. He came home on leave and gave it to her. When she opened the present, she thanked him and seemed to appreciate it. But when the rest of the family came for Christmas dinner, she told them her son had given it to her. When Dad shared this with me, he became very emotional, but shut it down very quickly. He would not answer any questions about his feelings.

Some of the rivalry Dad felt with his half-brother carried into the years that made up the rest of his life. I have pretty much determined it was only one-sided. As I have had an opportunity to grow my relationship with my uncle in my later years, I have come to know him as a very humble and caring man—one who was extremely proud of his brother, and deeply desired for him to have a personal relationship with Jesus. Unfortunately, it would be many, many years before Dad viewed him with the same love and affection. Dad just carried too much baggage. Too many times he felt abandoned. Neglected. Unloved. Second best. He had to do what he knew to prove himself. And his brother was one tool he used to satisfy that need.

- Over the years I heard—and witnessed—the ongoing tennis competition between them. At every opportunity, Dad would challenge, and usually win these tennis games. This went on until they were too old to play anymore. Dad bragged about his wins to Mom and me. Even as a young person, I remember thinking how very important it was to him that he was the victor in these games. I didn't understand what drove this rivalry because I didn't know about their history. I did overhear conversations between Mom and Dad about a camaraderie Dad and their younger sister shared. Kind of an "us against him" partnership. For lack of a better term, I guess it was sibling rivalry.

- On June 15, 1963, my uncle got married. I was only 8 years old but remember thinking how cool it was that my new aunt and my mom shared the same maiden name. This wedding was HUGE! It was the most beautiful thing I had ever seen. I think both Mom and Dad felt some things they didn't know how to express appropriately. I recall what WAS said—by both my parents—were words that conveyed undercurrents of jealousy. Their wedding had only been attended by four people—the best man, maid of honor, and my mom's parents. Grampie and Grammie did not attend. It seemed it only added to the negative perceptions Dad already had about his being the "redheaded stepchild."

- I don't remember many visits from my aunt and uncle, but when they did come, I could feel the tension in the air. Dad bragged quite a bit about all his accomplishments, his big home and all the work he had done on it. I didn't hear these things when we had other people visit—well, except when Grammie and Grampie came. It was as if he was compelled to prove to them, he was successful.

- The tension between he and his brother continued, especially because my uncle would gently try to share with him the love Jesus had for Dad. He had dedicated his life to sharing the gospel. He was an ordained pastor and had also been an administrator in Christian schools and he recognized the lack of peace Dad exhibited. He saw Dad's search for anything that would bring him feelings of affirmation, never feeling he was enough.

Dad was adamantly opposed to any talk of God, and seemingly enjoyed bringing up Scriptures that he felt were contradictory—his "proof" the Bible was "fake." I recall him sharing with me, his belief that the Bible was written by William Shakespeare. His "proof" was from something he read about Shakespeare's name being found in code throughout the Bible. These types of discussions were something I experienced myself after becoming a Christian. When they were unsuccessful with me, there was a 3-year period where he pretty much disowned me because I had chosen to follow Christ. He wanted nothing to do with anyone who knew God or who wanted to discuss anything Christian.

I often wondered in those early years of my own walk, what caused this hatred toward anything Christian. It wasn't that way with other religions. Our family home was full of things he had brought back with him from around the world. Statues of Buddha, pictures of Indian gods, he even had a picture of a ship at sea during a storm, with a prayer to the "gods" of the ocean to bring it home safely. He brought home several "dolls" that he had gotten on one of his travels and told me they were voodoo dolls. They came with long pins stuck in them, and he told me he could use the pins to hurt whoever the dolls represented. I sometimes wondered who he thought they represented.

What would cause that kind of disrespect—no, hatred—for God? As an older person who had experienced my own struggles in this area, I realized I needed to find out what had driven this man I called, "Dad." As I have shared here, there were many areas where Dad may have felt his self-worth squashed. Let's examine some of those.

When a child loses a parent, his concept of death is not fully formed—he has no frame of reference—and so all he feels is abandoned. This is especially true with the loss of a mother. Dad experienced this at the tender age of 3, with his mother who was eight months pregnant with his little sister. He saw her in flames, in an intensely traumatic way. And this trauma led to her death. Add to that, he was never allowed to see her in the hospital, attempting to recover. So, his last memory of her was seeing her dress on fire, screaming in pain, and protectively pushing him away. Then he was sent away to live with his grandparent for years—essentially losing his father, too. This was a huge blow to this little child's need for attachment formation and belongingness.

Erik Erikson, a developmental psychologist, identified eight stages of psychosocial development and called the second stage of life, autonomy vs. shame and doubt. During this time, a child acquires trust in his caregivers, and is supposed to begin to branch out. That rug was pulled from under Dad, and he was suddenly without either of the caregivers he had grown to trust. He was essentially orphaned of the things he knew. An emotional stunting took place in Dad's life at the age of 3. And without help in understanding how this had affected him, it could influence his relationships for the rest of his life. And it did. I don't doubt his self-talk sounded like, "What is wrong with me? My mother left me. My dad didn't want me and got rid of (abandoned) me. What is wrong with me?" Of course, none of this is based in fact, or at least all the facts, but a little child blames himself—and feels responsible—for almost everything around him.

I have a memory of going to Fitchburg, MA with Mom and Dad to see family there. Dad had stopped at the graveyard where his mother and little sister were buried. I was going to get out of the car with him, but he told me not to. It was the first-time I had ever seen Dad cry like that. Not just tears, but sobbing uncontrollably. I wanted so desperately to do something, but before I could even think of an excuse to get out of the car, he had gained back complete composure and stepped back into the car. I asked him if he was okay. He blew his nose and said, "Why wouldn't I be?" Dad was well practiced at stuffing his feelings.

The experiences he had with his stepmother were also bordering on mental and emotional abuse. Punishments and threats that were cruel and unfair.

Statements of discouragement about his ability to learn, and his hopes for the future. Dismissing his efforts to please her and "earn" her love and affection. And worse, crediting those efforts to someone else. Realizing his father had to sneak money to him because she obviously didn't want him to give Dad any monetary support. And as an adult, seeing his sibling's children favored over his own. The messages Dad received, though probably filtered through incorrect perceptions, only contributed to the already bruised and bleeding ego, attempting to form. And he had no one to correct it.

There were even things that happened with his dad that probably fed some of this. The time his dad held a candle flame to his finger to teach him not to play with matches. And held it there long enough that it caused a third-degree burn. This may have been the first time Dad felt the same pain, he had seen his mother experience. He was only 5 years old. What damage might that have left in his young developing brain? Or the time he got his teeth knocked out and nothing was done about it, because Grampie wanted to protect the reputation of the scout troop. This is hauntingly familiar to the incident that happened to me when my tennis coach molested me, and Dad wanted to protect his reputation. Learned behaviors being passed to the next generation. Not intentionally. But because it's all he knew.

Dad's feelings of low self-worth and low self-esteem played out in his life-long obsession to succeed. He strived in every way a man could. His house had to be perfect. His yard had to be perfect. His family had to look and act perfect. This was evidenced in many ways. Dad would frequently correct Mom's speech, how she ate, how she talked, and her lack of a college education. Mom had to be perfect. And when she wasn't, it led to multiple infidelities. It was much worse for me because perfection was demanded. I don't know how it was for my brother, because I was not around much after I turned 18. But with the ongoing dysfunction in our family, I would bet he had similar experiences.

Dad's work had to be perfect also. He was rarely home as he traveled the globe as the satellite triangulation Chief of Geodesy. His work in that area led him to receive the Gold Medal of Accomplishment from the Department of Commerce. To keep the upward momentum, the job required we move constantly, and his family's pleadings fell on deaf ears. He was determined to climb the commissioned officer's ladder. And he did. He made it all the way to Rear Admiral. The first phone call he made was to his parents. He wanted Grammie to know he made it.

His next striving led him to Virginia Tech, where he told me he was going to become a professor. He would be teaching astronomy, with hopes to be tenured so my brother could attend the school at no cost. And he did. My brother graduated from there with his degree in architecture. Dad just didn't know how to retire. He didn't know how to stop striving. I never saw him at peace. And he didn't let anyone else in his family have it either. It makes me intensely sad when I think about how many years were wasted by him trying to be something that he didn't need to be. At that point, he had no concept of God's unconditional love for him. No concept that he was enough—right where he stood. No understanding of a life without condemnation.

He was 89 years old when he finally experienced it. It was close to two years since I had shared the story of the fireman who saved his life. Shared how much God loved him to have sent that man back into the fire to find him. My uncle never gave up on him, and during a trip he made to Florida to visit Dad, he again addressed the issue of salvation. And this time Dad said yes. He received Christ into his heart. It was a joyous time indeed!

For the first time in my life, I had phone conversations with my dad that ended with, "I love you, Karin. I am praying for you!" Those words were gold to this woman's heart! We had wonderful talks after that. I was even able to hear him ask forgiveness for how he felt he had failed me as a father. How he wished he had let me stay in Columbus and pursue the Wightman Cup. How he wished he had bought those horses for me and trailered them back to Maryland. We reminisced about our tennis games, our horseback riding races through the woods, and our games of Memory. He laughed and said he was never able to beat me in that game. That was the last conversation I had with him that I was certain he remembered our times together.

God had allowed Dad's mind to stay lucid until his salvation and the redemption of our relationship were both accomplished. There are no doubts about the authenticity of it. No doubts about it being genuine. And then, he started to decline. His ability to remember things started dwindling. And I lost him in December 2019. He chose to be buried with his father and mother. Not with his wife of fifty years. That spoke volumes to me.

There are no regrets. Because there are now no doubts about his love for me. He loved me in the best way he could. There are no more feelings of anger at the way things were when I was young. But there were many tears realizing how much he suffered growing up. I know now he did the best he could with what little he had to work with from his own toolbox. The only sadness I feel is about all the years lost because of the dysfunction. All the time we could have had together. All the memories we could have made.

And that is the purpose of this book.

***

An epilogue to my dad's story.

As I shared earlier, Dad had some deeply buried emotions that would show themselves at unexpected times—when he saw anything patriotic, when he talked about his mom or dad, when he watched a competition where the underdog was winning, and when he talked about how hard he had to work in college to be successful. His feelings of abandonment and rejection as a young child, could not be bridled when he witnessed things that triggered those feelings.

When I was a teenager, Dad took me to an air show, a Blue Angels exhibition. I saw him tearful and asked what was wrong. This is what he said, "Those pilots represent the best of the best. They have worked hard to accomplish what they have succeeded in doing. Nobody gave them a nod or a wink. Nobody gave them an easy ride. Nobody gave them anything. They just dug in and did what they had to do to be something in this life."

It took many years for me to realize what Dad was really saying . . . he was describing himself.

19

Family Secrets

This is Mom's story.

My mom was born to Frank and Pearl Ward on May 13, 1923. She was the middle child of three with an older and younger brother. My mom didn't talk much about her young life. Happy or sad times. Over the years, I learned most of what I will share from Aunt Ruby, and some from my Uncle Junie.

Mom was considered a very attractive young girl. Her dad was the deputy sheriff of Somerset County for twenty-five years, and she towed the line to make him proud of her. She loved her mom, but Aunt Ruby said Granny never treated her kids with a lot of affection. I found this interesting because she was very loving with me.

Mom strove hard at school and maintained good grades, and when she reached high school, which in those days was after sixth grade, Mom discovered she loved playing basketball—and she was very good at it. She was tall and slim, unusually tall for a woman in those days—at 5'8"—and very fast. She was so good in fact that in her third year on the team, she learned she was being considered for a scholarship to play in college. Mom had many dreams and aspirations to go to college, but her family was not well-to-do, and so this was an awesome opportunity for her.

Just before her fifteenth birthday, Mom had stayed late for a practice and was walking home. It was a bit of a hike, but it was not uncommon in those days, to walk that far to school. It was the edge of dark when she left the school, as reported by her coach. When it got past the time when she should have been home, my grandfather went out to look for her. He drove the whole route she would have walked and saw nothing. Because of the high-water level in Crisfield, almost every road has a drainage ditch on both sides. Tracing her route back home, he finally saw something in the ditch on the side of the road. It was Mom. She was unconscious, and it seemed she had been laying in the water for a while.

Grandpop drove her to the hospital, and after examining her, the doctor was unable to determine if there had been a sexual assault because of how long she had been in the water. Her underwear, however, had not been found. Mom stayed at the hospital four days. Though she woke the next day, she was unresponsive to anything. She just stared into space, almost like someone in a catatonic state. She would eat when someone fed her, go to the bathroom when someone took her, but made no attempt to do these things on her own. After she came home, she remained that way another four days.

When Mom finally came out of the psychological state she was in, she had no memory of anything that had happened to her—not even her basketball practice, or any part of walking home. But though she seemed improved, she was not the same, according to Aunt Ruby. She never played basketball again, and where she had been an outgoing young girl, doing things with friends whenever possible, she was now a recluse, and rarely left the house. No matter how hard they tried to encourage her, she was unable to venture out. Aunt Ruby said it was a few years before she seemed more like herself.

It was never discovered what happened to Mom that night. No suspects. No evidence. No justice. And she never received any counseling or therapy for any of it. Why? Because in those days counseling was not even considered an option.

Some other stories I got from both my aunt and uncle were about what it was like growing up in the home of a sheriff. My grandpop was a very fair man, and had no racial bias, even in a town that did. There were black and white schools, and neighborhoods that were also completely segregated. This was the 1930's-1950's and not much change had transitioned into Crisfield.

My grandpop was the person in charge of taking prisoners to trial. The courthouse was in Princess Anne which was about a half-hour drive from Crisfield. His practice was to bring them to his house and give them a good meal and a comfortable place to sleep on what might be their last night before a conviction. In their home, they had a back kitchen where Grandpop housed them, with a single bed, but he still shackled them to the stove overnight. There was a chamber pot available so they could relieve themselves.

Mom shared some of these memories, and denied ever feeling scared. She said most of the men were so grateful, they just kept thanking my granny and grandpop. Mom said her mother always made them a full dinner, including homemade yeast biscuits, and the next morning she made them breakfast before Grandpop took them to Princess Anne.

A story both Mom and Aunt Ruby shared with me was about a young black boy who had been arrested for the assault of a white girl. The truth was that he and the girl were good friends and had fallen in love. The father of the girl caught them on the porch swing and accused them of being sexual. The girl tried to convince her dad that nothing had happened, but he made the accusation, and in those days, there was no way to get physical proof. Her father was a person of means and so because of the accusation, the boy was arrested. The girl stood firmly on her word, and promised to go to court and claim his innocence.

The night before he was to go to Princess Anne, Grandpop had him at their house, and a group of men with what looked like potato sacks on their heads, came there. They all had weapons, and one of them fired his gun to bring my grandpop outside. Aunt Ruby was there that night, and said the gunshot had scared all of them. My grandpop had a Colt 45 that was his work pistol, and he always kept it in its holster. He yelled out to them that he would be right out, and took the gun from the holster and went to the kitchen door. Aunt Ruby said Mom and Granny were both crying, begging him not to go outside. At that point Granny took Mom upstairs. Uncle Junie was hiding behind the kitchen door so he wouldn't miss anything, but his dad made him go upstairs with his mom and sister. Grandpop asked them what they wanted, and they told him to just turn the boy over, and they would leave.

Aunt Ruby, who was watching from the sitting room window, said Grandpop aimed his gun right at the man speaking and pulled the trigger. The bullet intentionally missed everyone, but they all jumped back. He called them each by name, and told them the next shot wouldn't miss. He told them if they didn't

get off his land right away, he would round each of them up the next day, and charge them with whatever he wanted to, and then lock them up. Aunt Ruby said they believed him, and they all got in their car or wagon and drove away. She said Grandpop didn't sleep all night, but guarded the door until morning, and then drove the boy to his trial. He was found not guilty. Both those kids were only 15 years old.

According to Aunt Ruby, anytime there was some action around town that Grandpop had to be involved in, my mom worried about him, and she worried about him a lot. Just another place where stress and anxiety were present in my mom's life. The sad end to my grandpop's story is that during one of those trips to take a prisoner, a truck crossed the center line and hit him head on. Mom told me his chest had been crushed against the steering wheel and he was having a hard time breathing. Instead of running, the prisoner pulled him from the car and got him on the ground to help him breathe better, and stayed with him until help came. That was on his birthday, and he died the next day. Mom was pregnant with me when it happened.

Uncle Junie told me the church was so packed at his funeral that they had to prop open the front doors because so many people were standing outside. He was well loved, and many people wanted to pay their respects. He said there were as many black folks as there were white, and for him—and me—that was the greatest compliment to the kind of man my grandfather had been, especially in those days when racial tension was so high. I never got to meet him, but I sure wish I had.

Another story Aunt Ruby told me was about Mom's first husband. On Labor Day weekend, Crisfield puts on a Hard Crab Derby. It's a three-day weekend of festivities consisting of a beauty pageant, the Derby, (which is where people race their crabs), a dance, and a boat docking contest. Mom had been chosen to be in the Miss Crustacean beauty contest. She was 19 years old, and it was an honor for Mom, and though she didn't win, she came in as first runner up. After the contest, Mom was asked out by a few local boys, but it was a very charismatic older man who won her attention. He was close to twelve years older than she, and completely swept her off her feet. They married after only a short time, and it didn't take long to discover he had quite the drinking problem. And a lot of anger issues.

Soon after their marriage, he was apparently going out quite a bit by himself, and Mom suspected he was not alone. She worked at the local pharmacy, Peyton's, and people had come in to tell her they had seen him with other women. Mom started driving around town looking for him, and sometimes she would ask Aunt Ruby to ride with her to try and find him. And they often did—with another woman.

At first Mom didn't do anything, but soon, she confronted him, and that's when the real trouble started. He slapped Mom around the first few times, but then it became more violent. Somehow Mom was able to hide the bruises while she worked, but Aunt Ruby said people were suspicious.

Mom only confided in Aunt Ruby because she knew what her dad would do, and she was trying to protect her husband. But Aunt Ruby had been through this with her ex-husband, and knew nothing about boundaries or self-protection for herself. She had no resources to teach my mother how to be safe. So instead of telling Mom to leave and get help, she confided to me that she repeatedly warned Mom not to do anything to upset him.

Aunt Ruby said someone told my grandpop what had been going on (I have a very sneaking suspicion it was her) and so he paid a visit to Mom's husband while she was at work. The outcome of the visit remains a mystery, but my grandpop shared with Aunt Ruby that he had made it abundantly clear to this man that his home sat on a lot of acres, and if he ever touched Mom again, his body would never be found. Soon after that, her husband left town, and he and Mom were divorced. She never knew about the visit from her dad, or the reason her husband left. She just assumed it was with another woman. And I never knew about this marriage until Uncle Junie's wife let it slip. I shared that big argument in a previous chapter. I didn't hear anything else about it from Mom. Not once. And Mom never got any counsel or therapy for any of this either.

Uncle Junie told me a story about a man she had fallen "head-over-heels" in love with a few years after her divorce. He was a very kind person, well liked in Crisfield, and seemed to be very much in love with Mom. They dated for quite some time before he was shipped out after joining the service. He was gone for over a year, and, though she never gave me a lot of details, Mom did share with me some of the cards and letters he had sent her. They were very sweet, and he professed his love to her in each one. She believed they would be married when he finished his tour of duty. I asked her what happened, and she said they just grew apart. But Aunt Ruby had a different story.

Apparently, when he got home, and told his mother he was going to marry my mom, his mother had quite the fit. She didn't want her "one-and-only" son marrying a divorced woman, especially one with such a "torrid history with which the whole town was familiar." There was quite a bit of discussion between he and his mom, and since his father was dead, he felt a great deal of loyalty toward her. He felt terribly torn. His mother won the tug of war, and Aunt Ruby said Mom's heart was shattered. The night he came to tell Mom, she completely fell apart, and begged him not to leave her. My granny got in the middle of it and told Mom, in front of him, "not to ever lower yourself to the place to beg a man for anything."

Both Aunt Ruby and Uncle Junie told me Mom was a recluse again, just like when she was a kid, and she buried herself in her work, now determined to become a pharmacist. Her work with Dr. Peyton gave her some of her confidence back though it's obvious Mom never got over this soldier, since she saved the cards and letters—even after being married to my dad for many years. I possess them now. My dad gave them to me among other memorabilia belonging to her before he died. I have no idea if he read any of it before giving it to me. It was never discussed. But the cards from this man were beautiful, and heartfelt. Mom must have been crushed. An interesting note: in her things were no cards or letters from my dad.

Her pain in this situation must have been devastating for her. She was never afforded the opportunity to talk it out, to recognize this was not her fault, and to see how the judgment she felt from the mother was terribly unfair. So, I am assuming she internalized it all. Add to that the trauma from her childhood, plus the loss of her scholarship—and her dream for college. And then having been beaten down physically and emotionally by a man—her husband—whom she thought she loved and who loved her. Well, by the time she met my dad, there was a lot of junk in her suitcase, and she would carry that baggage into their relationship.

Assault. Abuse. Rejection. Abandonment. Betrayal. Condemnation.

Yep, that's a load to carry around. And Dad was going to bring his own trunk of pain and unhealed wounds. Not a prescription for a happy marriage. Not a prescription for a happy ending. Not a prescription for bringing up healthy children.

So, they met by chance. Mom was working in the pharmacy when Dad's ship docked in Crisfield. Just for one night, on the way to Norfolk. He had come into the drugstore to purchase some personal items and mom was doubling as cashier that day. From what I have heard, Dad swept her off her feet and five months later they were married in Mom's small church with only four people present—her parents, her best friend, and his buddy off the ship. The storm was about to begin.

The rest of what I am going to share are things that I saw myself. More traumatic events for her. They are not in any chronological order. Many of the things I didn't even realize were strange—at least not at first. After all, doesn't every family have issues like this?

- Mom tolerated my dad "reading" *Playboy* every night when they went to bed. I often came in the room to say goodnight, and Dad would be looking at it, with Mom laying right next to him. I didn't comprehend what this must have done to her psyche, her self-esteem, until I was much older and sought counseling for myself.
- Mom was in a serious car accident in 1966. I was 11 years old. She had gotten a phone call from Uncle Junie telling her he and his wife were having serious problems. Mom had taken our VW bug to make the trip from Rockville to Crisfield. I shared about this in one of my earlier chapters, but wanted to reiterate, since she was in a coma for several days, and experienced another loss of memory, this was quite traumatic for her. It also left her with chronic back issues.
- Mom told me Dad gave her an allowance of $50/month. This was what she could use from the budget to spend on herself. That changed drastically after Mom learned about the "other women." Her allowance was then increased to $350.
- There were many incidents over the years, where Mom found condoms in Dad's things. I can't tell you why she was looking, other than being suspicious because of her first husband's infidelities. Since they didn't use them personally, it was obvious what Dad was doing. And this triggered that unhealed issue from her past. There were a few incidents in Rockville, but more when they transferred to Seattle, and more when they lived in Blacksburg, VA.
- Her discoveries of infidelity became major wars—not the old type—where it was just yelling, screaming, and throwing. Now it was with weapons. I remember one in particular. I heard her screaming, and ran upstairs to their bedroom. Mom had a knife, and Dad was trying to calm her down. I had never seen her this bad. Her face was red and contorted with hatred, and her eyes were slits of rage. I got in the middle of them and grabbed the hand holding the knife, and tried to calm her down. Her eyes looked right through me. She kept saying over and over, "He did it again, he did it again." I knew what she was talking about, but Dad just kept telling her she was crazy, along with his other gaslighting comment, his favorite, "You're some kind of a nut." *We will look at gaslighting a little later. I got my share as well.*
- After that incident, Mom learned to "cope" with Valium and Xantac. Because that wasn't the last time. It wasn't even close to the last time. When

she and Dad got into it, there would be a lot of ugly screaming, and then she locked herself in their room for three days and didn't come out. Dad slept on the couch in his office. When she did come out, she acted as if nothing had happened.

- As I got older, I had really had enough and would beg her to let us pack our bags and get out. Take my brother and go to Crisfield—anywhere—just get away. She would look at me with almost a confused expression and say, "Why would I do that? Nothing's wrong. Why are you trying to start something?" This happened a handful of times, and I walked away from each scene wondering if I was the crazy one. I couldn't wait to turn 18 and get out.

- When they moved to Seattle the second time, I got frequent calls from Mom about how depressed she was. She was unable to acclimate to the constant rain, exacerbating her depression, and her back had become very painful, causing her to be hospitalized several times. She wanted me to move there, but being in nursing school, it was an impossibility. Aunt Ruby ended up going out there, and this seemed to offer some relief for her. But she then discovered more evidence of infidelity, causing her to sink deeper into depression.

You may wonder how I knew about a lot of this very private information, that should only be between a husband and a wife. I knew these things because I was their confidant. Didn't want to be. Didn't ask to be. Tried not to be. But that was my role. If I tried not to engage them, I "didn't love them." Or I was "taking sides." Or I loved one more than the other. It was a no win. So, I listened. Mostly Mom at first, but when Dad discovered I was being told about the infidelities, he also began telling me "his side of the story" which basically consisted of my mom starving him sexually, and he had to find relief wherever he could. Both were committing emotional incest, or treating me as a surrogate spouse. And a child—no matter how old—should never be exposed to this abuse. Parents' business is parents' business.

As she got older, I often saw Mom looking into space, even when she would be talking to people. They would have to redirect her to the conversation. I realized she had stopped doing the things she enjoyed, like crafts, sewing, calling and visiting friends, working in the garden, and caring for her appearance. I didn't recognize these things for what they were—a deepening depression—but I did notice when I tried to talk with her, she would have a smile on her face, but she was somewhere else. It was a vacant look. A dissociative look. One I would recognize in the mirror in my own future.

I talked to Dad several times about my concerns, but he refused to take her to a counselor because "Psychiatrists are all a bunch of nuts!" I tried to explain to him, therapists and psychiatrists were two different animals—she just needed someone with which to vent. Even when her family doctor prescribed anti-depressants, he wouldn't let her take them. Family secrets stay secret because people don't tell. Or they are not allowed to tell. Because if someone finds out the truth, things may have to change. And we couldn't have that happen. Not in my family.

As I did with Dad, I want to look at some of the things that happened to Mom. Try to unpack the trauma she experienced and how it impacted the rest of her life. And why she tolerated the rest of the traumatic events that continued to affect her psyche.

I know nothing of Mom's young life other than the events I have shared. It seems she lived a normal life except for being the daughter of a sheriff who brought prisoners home to show them kindness. This compassion was a trait I saw in her and experienced as a teenager. Any friends of mine who were having problems at home were welcome at my house. She opened her home to all of them. A trait she passed onto me.

But when she was 15, there was the event after school. It's the first trauma she experienced of which I am aware. And I don't even know what truly happened. We can assume it was an assault, knowing she did not have on underwear when she was found. How far it went is unknown. Trained as a forensic nurse examiner, I learned many of her symptoms were not unique following a traumatic assault. I don't know how sexual assault physical exams were done back then, but now we know it is very important the victim feels she has some sense of control during the exam. For example, in the book we use in training, *The Atlas of Sexual Violence*, it states, "It is important to understand the actions, attitude, and approach to the patient by the examiner, and it may impact the patient's ability to make a healthy adaptation after the assault" (Henry, 2013, p.6). We don't know how her exam was performed, or how she was treated during the exam. But her inability to work through it, or receive any counsel or therapy, caused her to "swallow" it, and this led to many of her long-term symptoms of being isolated and housebound.

Stage five of Erikson's developmental theory is identity versus identity confusion. "If adolescents explore roles in a healthy manner and arrive at a positive path to follow in life, then they achieve a positive identity; if not, then identity confusion reigns." Erikson's theory in describing this explosive life stage is considered a hallmark in understanding it. He described the time between "childhood security and adult autonomy" in a term known as "psychosocial moratorium." In a healthy situation, the adolescent experiments with roles, careers, clothes, and personalities and eventually discards those that are undesirable. However, the teen who doesn't resolve this crisis of identity ends up lost and choosing one of two courses: isolation or loss of self in others. I would venture to believe, the years of isolation following Mom's assault were suggestive of the first course.

Her attraction, and eventual marriage to her first husband, are indicative of the other course—of being lost in others—otherwise known as codependency. Her lack of boundaries, and an understanding in her inability to control another's behavior, are classic symptoms of codependency. In her marriage she also experienced what is known as sexual betrayal. In Sheri Keffer's brilliant book, *Intimate Deception* she reveals the trauma a woman feels during relationship betrayal. And when it continues, the trauma is replicated over and over, and the symptoms worsen.

Sheri described three responses to continued betrayal trauma:

1. Hypersexual – moving toward the person betraying you by taking responsibility for the betrayal, blaming yourself, fear of losing the person. All fueled by false shame and the deep desire to be loved (Keffer, 2018).
2. Hyposexual – moving away from the person to avoid further pain and shame by shutting down—it is self-protection. This is recognizable in becoming depressed, shutting down all self-care, and listlessness (Keffer, 2018).
3. Sexually reactive – This is moving against the person by seeking outside "relief" to the feelings of not being wanted. We seek retaliation by being aggressive in seeking illicit relationships to feel desired (Keffer, 2018.

From the things Aunt Ruby shared, Mom was in the hypersexual mode, taking on all the responsibility for her first husband's betrayal. She wanted to fix it. In fact, the person who helped her during this time, Aunt Ruby, had also suffered from these issues, and her advice to Mom had been "not to start anything." Consequently, I would bet Mom held onto some false guilt and shame for the outcome of that marriage. Add to that, domestic violence, and you have a recipe for serious PTSD consequences.

And there is another issue that could have added more damage to her already fragile ego. I don't know specifically if she experienced this in her first marriage, but gaslighting is also a common practice in domestic violence situations. Gaslighting is defined as an insidious form of manipulation and control. False information is systematically and deliberately fed to the victim, to intentionally cause them to question their own sanity—their own reality. Again, Mom did not receive any counseling to help her know the truth and resolve these false shames. Again, part of the problem lies in the fact, counseling was not offered in these situations during that time. A woman was to submit to her husband and if that included name-calling, shoving, pushing and punches, so be it.

Her relationship with the young soldier, though not peppered with abuse and infidelity, was a full slap of rejection and the abandonment of her hopes and dreams of a good and healthy relationship. Understanding his mother saw her as a "used" woman only exaggerated her already desperate feelings. She had been dismissed as a candidate—not good enough in his mom's eyes.

Mom's fragile and damaged ego was fertile ground for this soldier and his mother's rejection to take flight. She knew nothing else to do except shut down, and isolate. I could imagine her believing she was the focus of gossip all over their small town. It was easier to stay home and focus on becoming a pharmacist. She could possibly gain back her lost respect in this pursuit. Of course, none of this was probably true. But due to her repeated traumatic experiences, it was her perspective of the truth. And, again, she didn't have the blessing of a counselor to re-frame her thinking.

The relationship betrayal continued when she married my dad. In the pornography. In the infidelities. In the gaslighting. In the constant berating of her not being enough. My dad's narcissistic symptoms, due to his own feelings of inadequacy, were exactly what Mom DIDN'T need.

And there was one more incident I believe impacted Mom greatly. I alluded to it in Hawaii. The time she was throwing dishes at my dad as he was running out the front door. What led up to that was her walking in on Dad playing his tickle game with me. In this game, I didn't wear any clothes. Dad was fully dressed, and this was actually a game I found to be fun. I laid on my bed while Dad tickled me. There was no inappropriate touching, just tickling me which caused me to spread my legs. And if it didn't, Dad asked me to spread my legs. This explains the behavior I exhibited with my cousin when I was 5 years old, and in the bathtub in Norfolk. And it explained how that aberrant behavior followed me through the years, until it was healed in therapy.

Mom came home from shopping and caught us playing our game. And she lost it. She was furious. But as she often did, she swallowed it. She buried it. And she didn't leave. She stayed with him. And what I have come to understand over the years is that I became the "other woman" in her eyes. Because of that incident, much of the attention Dad showed me caused Mom to be jealous. And when I became older, his inappropriate behaviors with me were triggers for her. I "belonged" to him, and she was left on the outside. I didn't stand a chance at a healthy mother/daughter relationship. And I had done nothing to cause it.

For her, the relationship with Dad was the fuse in a gigantic explosive that had not been ignited yet—but it was coming. Her shutdown was coming, and it was going to end in a full-blown depression that became so severe, her neurologist, after performing an EEG, called it pseudodementia. It would eventually lead to a complete neurological flatline.

My mom never had the opportunity to heal that I had. She never had the blessing of a personal relationship with Jesus—a place where she may have finally found some peace. She never knew what it felt like to be truly loved by a man, unconditionally. And she never knew the joy of knowing she was protected and secure. Writing about my mom has been a very sad experience. What I understand now allows me to realize how very much she needed these things. The first three were necessary before the last could be possible.

Trying to love someone the way they deserve to be loved, and allowing them to love you the way you deserve to be loved, is an impossibility until you have learned to love yourself. Jesus said it, "Love your neighbor as you love yourself." When we have been hammered our whole life with guilt and shame, our thought life becomes twisted with negative self-talk. And our thoughts affect our feelings, and our feelings affect our behaviors. We do everything we can to find an escape, a way to numb the pain. We bury ourselves in someone else, codependently, and believe we can change and control them to be everything we need them to be. Or who we think they want to be. When all along, we are the ones who need to change. We are the ones who need to learn boundaries. We are the ones who need to find peace in who we are—no matter how painful that journey may be—even if it means subsequently being alone. Because there are many things worse than being alone.

When I learned Mom could possibly improve if given the right meds, I took her to a psychiatrist who admitted her for two weeks into a psychiatric unit. She improved markedly in that short time. Being away from Dad, and on the proper meds, made a big difference in her behavior. When she was discharged, the psychiatrist suggested having her stay with me, where she could continue on her meds, and where I could perform a mini-mental test on her daily. This test just checks the cognitive impairment and identifies changes. And she was improving.

One day, during the short time Mom came to live with me, we decided to go shopping. As we were going out the front door, she stopped me. She had tears in her eyes, and I asked her what was wrong. She took my hand and said the strangest thing, "I so wish all these years you had been mine and your brother had been your dad's."

I was perplexed and told her I had always been hers, too. She shook her head, and said, "No, you were always your dad's. I was left out."

My heart just leaped. I hugged her and felt the tears come. These were tears that had been stored away. Bottled tears. Long since abandoned—by me—as wasted tears. The tears representing the desires in the heart of a little girl who just wanted to belong and feel loved. A little girl who cried herself to sleep on so many nights, wondering what was wrong with her, why she wasn't lovable. These were those bottled-up tears. The ones God Himself had collected, keeping track of my sorrows, and recording them in His book. (Psalm 56:8 NLT). These were my redeemed tears. They were being turned from sad bitterness to sweet understanding. My mom loved me.

Those were words I never thought I would ever hear from my mom. I had spent my whole life believing she didn't want me. That my brother was the favored one, the loved one. It was never a consideration that she might feel I didn't want her in my life. After sharing these things with her, and as I began to release her from the hug, she said, "Karin, I love you." I honestly believe that was the first time I could remember her ever saying those words to me. If she did, I didn't internalize them. Or maybe didn't believe them. But now, they were gold.

Mom went back home soon after that. Dad had put the pressure on hard and she gave in. And things went very bad after that. So, this was one of the last lucid conversations I had with her. I know now, God provided that special moment, at the front door of my house, to hear my mom say words to me that healed decades of pain, hurt and rejection. God gave me, for just a brief time, the relationship I had always wanted with her. And I was changed. Unfortunately, I would never have the chance to experience this again.

A lot happened in the next few months. Dad ignored the diagnosis of pseudodementia. Would not let her take her anti-depressants. Would not let her go to counseling. Then I got a call from one of the nurses I worked with who asked me if I was aware my mom was in the hospital. I went right away and found out she had "fallen down the steps" at their home and now she was unable to speak, or walk. She appeared to be someone who had a stroke. Her request for me to make final decisions for her was overwritten by a new power of attorney—my dad. I knew Mom had not signed it. My attempts to get guardianship failed because the cost was more than I could handle, and Dad was successful in getting her into a nursing home.

God gave me one last blessing with her. My aunt and uncle came to visit, and Dad allowed them to stay in his house. He was traveling with his girlfriend. They shared that they would like to see Mom and I was able to pick her up and bring her to the house to visit with them. She was aphasic but was still able to show us what she was trying to say.

While there, Mom asked me to take her to her room, and she found a hidden jewelry box with all her "special" jewelry. She handed it to me, gesturing she wanted me to take it. I asked her what she wanted me to do with it, and she made it clear she wanted me to keep it. These were things she had had her whole life. A baby bracelet of mine, her wedding rings from her first marriage, things belonging to her mother, and things I had given her. Mom owned another large jewelry box, but this small one had all her special memories—not the expensive things, but the important things—and she wanted me to have it. A special gift from my mom. Another gift from God.

Soon after that, Dad and his girlfriend sold their homes, and moved to Florida, taking my mom with them. I knew nothing about this until I went to visit her at the nursing home with my daughter and was told she had been taken. No goodbyes. No last hugs. No nothing.

Dad put her in a nursing home near his home in Florida. She was only there a few weeks before she was gone. She died on Good Friday, 2001. Dad didn't tell me. I learned about her death from my uncle. On Easter Sunday.

I tried to find out what happened, but Dad had closed every door very tightly. I was not privy to any of her information. I only knew the tale he wove of her dying of starvation couldn't be true because she had been carrying at least twenty-five extra pounds the last time I saw her. I knew she had been eating well before she was taken to Florida. And if she had stopped eating, a feeding tube would have been ordered, and I learned they had never given her one at the new facility. Something wasn't right, but my hands were tied. Too many things were hidden, and too many doors were closed to me. I had to be content with the gifts God had given me.

***

An epilogue for my mom.

When my mom showed up on the day of my tennis finals, during the Columbus Invitational, it was such an odd thing for her to do. She was just never invested in what I did. But I was so happy she was there. On the way home that day, she shared with me, for the first time, her dreams of being a basketball player. She told me about the scholarship, and how much she loved the sport. "I can see that same thing in you, Karin. Don't stop playing if you love it that much, and don't let anything get in the way of your dreams."

I asked her what happened with the scholarship, and she just got one of her faraway looks, and said nothing. I know now, what happened, and how her dreams had been dashed. And now I realize she tried to keep me in Columbus so I could continue on the Wightman Cup. But she was not mentally or emotionally strong enough to believe she could take care of us while Dad was in Seattle. And she wasn't strong enough to stand up to him.

My mom loved me in the best way she knew how. The person whom God created her to be was forever changed by her multiple traumatic experiences. I saw glimpses of that person in how she loved animals. How she fed the racoons and deer on her property and how she had always allowed me to have so many pets. I saw her love of crafts, and how she excelled in all of them. I saw it in how she let me have my friends stay at our house when they were having troubles at home. I saw it in our all-night Rook or Pinochle games she participated in with my friends.

I saw glimpses.

I saw her.

The real her.

And I know I will see THAT person again. And we will finally have the relationship I have always desired—for eternity.

20

Return to Rockville – The High School Years

"Dear younger me, I cannot decide,
Do I give some speech about how to get the most out of your life,
Or do I go deep, and try to change,
The choices that you'll make, because they're choices that made me.
Dear younger me."
Mercy Me

Now, back to my story. As I left Seattle, feeling angry, betrayed, and ignored, it was hard to anticipate anything positive happening on my return to Rockville. The first time I lived there had been a nightmare, and I didn't expect a miraculous transformation to take place this time. Especially after the way things had been in my life since then. Little did I know, returning to Rockville was going to be how I acted out all the trauma that had happened to me up to this point. And in my ignorance to what I really needed in my life, and in my parents' inability to understand the professional help I required, I was about to add so . . . much . . . more . . . trauma to my already full plate.

I will be transparent here, I had very large gaps in my memory when attempting to recall specifics of these next few years. Maybe everyone does, when having to go back half a century. I believe some things that happened in my three years of high school, were so traumatic, there may have been some dissociative times as well. The only events that seemed fully available were the bad ones. And those were crystal clear. I know for sure, that any feelings of being "orphaned" earlier in my life, were absolutely intensified during my high school years. I became invisible.

I was 15 years old, and my parents never asked where I was going, what I was doing or with whom I was doing it. If I asked to spend the night with a friend, no one checked up to see who the person was. Or if I was going into a safe environment. Or what the parents might be like. Or even who the parents were. This led to an ease of going wherever I wanted, whenever I wanted, with whomever I wanted, for as long as I wanted. The only rule was I needed to be home to go to school. I had an open door to find all kinds of ways to numb my pain. And I did. Alcohol, pot, Quaaludes, over-the-counter cough syrup, black beauties, etc. I walked through that open door. Boldly.

I had one guidance counselor who I felt tried to help me on two separate occasions. Both times he had called in my parents and recommended professional treatment for me. The first time was in my sophomore year, and he referred my parents to a psychiatrist. I went willingly, believing I would have someone with whom I could ask questions about things I didn't feel I could ask my parents. I saw him three times and at the end of the third session, he told me he was requesting to see my parents. Well, Dad was not happy, and Mom was non-committal. But they went together and when they came home, Dad said the guy was "some kind of a nut" and I wasn't going back. That made me sad, but I wasn't making the final decision or paying the bill.

The second time the guidance counselor called them in was during my junior year, and this time he referred me to a therapist. I met with her a few times, and she, too, wanted to meet with my parents. They met. She was "some kind of a nut." I never went back. I realize now, the subject of family counseling probably came up, and that was NEVER going to happen. Or they may have suggested some other form of counseling, requiring their participation, and which could have revealed too much truth about our family. Whichever the case, Dad wasn't having any of it.

✳✳✳

The purpose in sharing my time in high school is to reveal the damage that had been done. How all that had happened in my formative years was now affecting my ability to think, feel and behave. The symptoms I had started to display, and my inability to make good choices for myself were a direct response to the lack of being parented properly. Years of being ignored, experiencing silent treatments, feeling betrayed, hungering for acceptance, enduring physical and emotional abuse—were culminating in the traumatic responses I would now display.

As I have prayed about how to share my high school years—the twisted and entangled mess that it was—I realized the best way to present it was through the people who played a major role during that time. I felt it best, for the length of this book, to break it down to very specific events that were life-changing for me—good and bad—through the interactions with those people. Those who inspired me. And those who played a role in my downward spiral.

These are the ones I think about, even today, and wonder if they found healing and truth in their lives. The Truth we all need. The Truth that sets us free.

Part Three:

The Players

21

Ivy

Leading Role

When we moved into our home in Rockville, directly next to us lived Ivy, her husband JD, and her three little girls. Almost immediately after moving in, Ivy came over and introduced herself. She was very friendly and after she met me, asked if I did any babysitting. This opened the door to a regular Saturday night job for me, as she and JD went to the horse races at Pimlico every weekend. After just one night, I knew I wanted to keep this job because JD paid very well.

After only a few months, Ivy started asking me to hang out with her after JD went to bed. He was much older than her, and she liked to "unwind" after they got home which was defined by her making a pitcher of martinis and consuming it. After a few of these nights, she started making drinks for me, too, even though I had promised myself not to drink again. The Seattle incident had been a nightmare, but having an adult offer—and knowing I wouldn't get caught because my parents were always in bed when I went home—well, it was too much temptation to resist. So, this became a regular thing.

Months passed and we spent more and more time together. While JD was at work, she started asking me to bring my friends along, male and female, on some of our outings, and she would turn them onto drinks too. We all had to skip school to do this so it wasn't that often, but we enjoyed it when we could. Those times transitioned to her taking us to bars where they didn't card us (drinking age was 18) and buying us our drinks. She even bought pot for some of them. She started writing notes for me to be excused early from school, and would pick me up, and then wait for my friends to get out, then take us anywhere we wanted to go.

"

It is hard for me to remember what excuses she gave to JD, but she would have her girls spend the weekend with friends and rent a hotel room for all of us, and provide all the alcohol . . . and whatever else we wanted. Sometimes she even bought tickets to see concerts—we saw Sly and the Family Stone with her. Every outing was a party with Ivy. To clarify, she was 40 years old. We were all 15-17. She was the "mom" figure every teenager *thinks* they want at that age. And this orphaned girl had found a new mother. She had no problem calling parents to assure them we would be having "a well-chaperoned time together, and not to worry!" And she was a very good liar.

It wasn't long before some of the party weekends turned south. She would make excuses to JD as to why she couldn't go with him to Pimlico, and would rent a motel room. There was a lot of drinking going on. Her inhibitions started getting very loosey-goosey and soon she started renting an additional room for herself, and taking some of my male friends with her. This only happened a few times, because it was a turning point for a lot of them. I think it was a novelty at first, but grew old quick—no pun intended. My girlfriends started feeling she was weird and weren't comfortable around her anymore. The parties dwindled, and soon it was only a couple of my girlfriends who hung out after that. Interestingly, it didn't feel weird to me. It was something to do—attention—and I was lapping it up like a thirsty animal.

All the above happened in the first six months of my sophomore year. As you can see, my ability to make good choices was in the dirt, and during the next few years it was going to get worse.

Ivy had taken me to her family farm a few times and I had gotten to meet her cousins, and some of their kids. One of her cousins had committed suicide a few years earlier, and her youngest son, Brandon, had found her in the kitchen. She had shot herself. He and his older brother Garret still lived in one of the houses on the farm. When we went to visit, we spent most of our time with them. I really liked Brandon, and we would go for walks and talk a lot.

In July of my sophomore year, Ivy said they were going to have a big party for Brandon's birthday. She invited me to go and offered to pay me to help babysit for the girls so we could stay a couple days. I was thrilled to go, and the girls were too. We arrived on Friday night, and I got to spend quite a bit of time with Brandon while she visited her other family. Saturday was spent decorating, and the party started at 3 p.m. It was mostly family there, with a few of Brandon's friends as well. A couple of Garret's friends showed up later. Alcohol was flowing freely, and everyone got lit. The party was pretty much over by 8 p.m. and most everyone had gone home.

Ivy's girls had no desire to sleep yet. They had fun at the party and had eaten lots of cake, so were on a major sugar rush. Ivy was determined to get them to bed because she was ready to keep partying. I encouraged all of them to come upstairs with me. The younger two were less resistant to bedtime, and I got them dressed for bed and helped them get tucked in. But the oldest was angry, and stomped downstairs to let her mom know. I came down too, and found Ivy in the kitchen mixing up three glasses of chocolate milk. She was emptying the contents of small red capsules into each glass. I asked her what she was doing, and she said she was going to help the girls sleep. I asked her what it was, and she told me Seconal. I knew that was a sleeping pill because my mom had taken them. I didn't like that she was drugging her girls and I told her so, but she was determined. She and her daughter went upstairs with all three glasses.

When she came down, she said that would take care of them for the rest of the night, and now we could party. She turned up the stereo, and started dancing with a few of Garret's friends who were still there. Brandon and I started playing a board game, and it seemed like it was going to be a fun night. The attention he gave me and the way he looked at me made me like him even more. But Ivy had been drinking all day, and she was not slowing down. Pretty soon she was dancing seductively and coming on to one of Garret's friends. She was really acting like an idiot; I was embarrassed for her. The guy was clearly uncomfortable, and left. Then the other guys left too, and Garret looked disgusted and said he was going to bed. That left the three of us.

Ivy was too drunk to join us in the game, so she went into the kitchen and within a few minutes called Brandon. He asked her what she wanted, and she just repeated for him to come to her. He rolled his eyes and went into the kitchen. I didn't know what to do, so I just waited. And waited. And waited. Finally, after about twenty minutes, I went to look for them. They were not in the kitchen. The house was huge, and I tried looking in all the rooms. I finally found them in the "servant's quarters" where there were a few pieces of furniture, including a bed. And they were in it. And they weren't sleeping. Brandon had just turned 16.

The betrayal I felt was heavy. I went upstairs and went to sleep. The next morning was awkward for everyone. The oldest girl was still angry with her mom, and I was right behind her. But I swallowed it, as I did everything else.

***

Ivy had plans to indoctrinate me into her "shopping" days. Soon after all the partying stopped, she started calling the school—pretending to be my mother—and would get me released early. Then we would go shopping. What I didn't know was that she was a professional shoplifter. Not the petty little things I had done, but major stuff. She could go into the jewelry store and get the salesperson so confused; they didn't know what she had looked at and what she had not. I have often thought she may be one of the reasons, when looking at fine jewelry, they only take out one piece at a time.

She was well equipped for her "shopping" days. She had transformed a pillowcase—sewn a zipper on the open side, cut two holes in the back, and threaded a belt through the two holes. She then belted it onto her waist. She also had an inflatable pillow she blew up and placed inside the pillowcase. She wore a poncho over this and . . . Voila! She looked like a pregnant lady!

When she went into clothing stores, she took as many articles of clothing as possible in with her to the changing room and then had me bring her more. So, no one could really keep track on how many she had. She then deflated the pillow and filled it with the clothes she wanted, returning the rest. She was a pro, and she taught me everything she knew. This went on for a couple years until we got caught. The charges were dropped for lack of evidence, but it was the end of my ride with "shopping." My parents never knew any of it.

I didn't have her boldness, but I still had much to ask forgiveness for when I met Jesus. I actually returned to some of the stores that were still open and spoke to the managers, asked forgiveness and offered restitution. All of them, without exception, just thanked me for my honesty, and asked what had brought about the confession. That blew me away. It was always awesome to share how Jesus had changed my life.

One night, after JD went to bed, we both got really sloshed, and Ivy asked if she could dance for me. Okay, a little strange. I had witnessed this on the farm, but I was too drunk to argue, and so she started dancing, and then she started to take her clothes off. I felt terribly awkward and pretended I was sleeping. Then I felt her touch me. I asked her to stop, but she persisted. I got off the couch and firmly asked her to leave me alone, and got into the bed I used when I spent the night. She didn't follow me, and it was never discussed again. But my desire to pull away from her was at its strongest.

One friend I hung out with, Willow, also a player in my story, and whom you will meet in more detail, was more brazen than me about asking for things. Willow had accompanied me on a family trip to NH, in June of that year, and while there, met a guy whom she really liked. So, she asked Ivy to take us back. And she did. She called both sets of parents saying we were going to a NJ beach. We took off for five days. It was a wild time, since the guy Willow had met was a horse trainer and all his friends found Ivy to be a lot of fun. We stayed in a motel, and it was just one big party. Almost everyone except Willow and I were of age to drink, so I guess Ivy wasn't worried about getting caught.

My days of drinking increased exponentially with Ivy. I had gotten through my sophomore year, but not with the grades I had been accustomed to getting.

In August, I had started hanging with a girl who was a year older than me. Her name was Darla, and I hung out with her at her house a lot. She had a brother, Marty, a year younger than me, and we started liking each other. He is another player I will introduce to you later. Suffice it to say, Ivy had a large role in undermining my goal to remain a virgin until marriage.

My junior year started off strong, and I had enough credits to graduate, but the vice-principal wouldn't let me. This made me angry since I had worked so hard in Seattle to be able to graduate early. I was pretty sure she was on to my antics from the previous year. Though I had taken alcohol to school in my sophomore year, I had not gotten caught, but she still might have been suspicious. So, when I got the bad news about not graduating early, I just kept up the practice in my junior year. That, plus the relationship with Mike consuming me, caused my grades to suffer so badly, it became fruitless to continue. And alcohol wasn't all I was doing now. I will share more on that as we get into other players.

Again, how I didn't get caught, and no phone calls made to my parents, was a "mystery." One of many I will share.

When I told my dad I was dropping out, he was furious, and told me I was going to start paying rent and I better get a job. The money I still made babysitting for Ivy wasn't going to cut it, and I ended up getting a job at the local Grant's store, the same chain where I had gotten Goldie. I did short-order cooking during the day. At night, I also worked with my friend Camellia (another player you will meet) at Computer Learning Centers. I was making $2/hour and thought I was rich! Dad took $50/month and I have no memories of my mom's response to any of this. Ivy and I still hung out, but now it was mostly weekends. It was during this time she told me about her murder charge.

During one of our long Friday nights, Ivy had gotten particularly sloshed. I had started spending the night in their basement on the heavy drinking nights because I didn't want to walk home lit. On this occasion, she asked me if she had ever told me about who JD really was. It turns out he was the stepfather of her dead husband. I knew the girls' father was dead but had never asked how he died, so I asked her, and she told me she had shot him. I assumed it was an accident, but she corrected me and said, "No, I intended to shoot him." This had apparently been a domestic violence situation, and she was tired of the beatings, waited for him to come out of the bathroom one night, and shot him. She had told the police it was an accident, that he had been cleaning his gun. I was a bit in shock, but then she went on to share—since this seemed to be the night for True Confessions—that her middle daughter was not her husband's but an affair she had with the "love of her life." This was believable since that girl looked nothing like the other two. I was speechless, and pretty wasted, and I didn't think I could handle anything else, so I told her I was going to bed.

When I woke the next morning, I hoped she would not remember our conversation. I really had not believed the story, and didn't want to know if it was true. While I was contemplating all that had been said, she came downstairs and brought me breakfast. She asked if I remembered what we talked about from the night before. She then made it clear I needed to keep my mouth shut, so nothing happened to me like happened to her husband. Then she winked at me. This exponentially increased my desire to pull away, but she had instilled quite a bit of fear as well. Remember, I was only 17 years old. I increased my hours at my night job, and the only time we got together was on babysitting nights. I hung with the other players in my life during this time. But unfortunately, my time with Ivy had not ended.

My relationship with Marty was over in June of that year. I was completely devastated, so started doing even more stupid stuff that summer. My friends and I hitchhiked even more to meet people and to find parties. I will go into more detail as I share the other players, but as I mentioned earlier, my risk-taking behavior was on the rise. And it showed up in a lot of different ways that summer. Ivy was always available to hang out. She even planned her family trip to the beach the same time my parents planned ours, two years in a row. When my friend Camellia and I went with my parents on those vacations, Ivy covered for us so we could go to plenty of all-night parties with people we had just met at the beach. Yeah, living risky was becoming commonplace. And it's yet another "mystery" how I got through the summer relatively unscathed.

I knew I wanted to graduate, so decided to sign up for my senior year. I enrolled, and while picking my classes, the vice-principal told me she would be watching me. I still suspected she was privy to my drinking, but she had not been able to prove it, so I cautiously responded that I would not be a problem this year. I only needed five classes, and I had decided I was going to make it work. Because I had to quit both jobs, I started working for Ivy again on a full-time basis. That was a huge mistake.

Just a few weeks into my senior year, she made one of her calls to the school and I was brought to the office and told my mom was waiting for me. Of course, it was her, and she said we were going on a shopping trip. I told her I didn't want to do that anymore, and she said it was a legit shopping day. We went out of state, and she took me to the town where she had lived before moving to Rockville. Where she had lived with her dead husband. We drove to the library, and she pulled a bunch of archived articles for me to see. Articles about her husband's death. Articles proving to me, she had been a suspect but passed a lie detector with flying colors. Articles showing suspicions of foul play but with no proof, had been ruled a "gun accident." Today, I can still remember the catch in my throat and the thought that she knew too much about me and

I knew too much about her. It was a moment where I felt completely victimized, and completely terrified. But I swallowed it. We spent the rest of the day shopping, and things seemed good. Until we got home.

As soon as Ivy drove up in her driveway, I saw Dad walking over to her house. Strange for him. He ordered me out of the car. Then JD came out of the house and ordered Ivy out of the car. Both were yelling at us. I was hearing about skipping school and Ivy was hearing about calling me out of school. It seemed the vice-principal was onto more than we realized, and had called my mom to verify the phone call to excuse me. Mom then called Dad and he came home from work and stopped by the school, then went to talk to JD. He had been given all the notes from the past two years that Ivy had written. And there were a lot of them. Dad told me to go home and when I got to our driveway, Mom was standing there, furious, announcing for the umpteenth time in my life, she had disowned me. JD had gone into their house and Ivy had followed Dad and me.

When Mom saw her, she lost it and the two of them faced-off for quite some time. I recall feeling a lot of fear that Ivy was going to tell everything, but she didn't. And when Mom ordered her off our property, Ivy said, "Someone had to take care of her!" And just like that, Ivy was out of my life.

For a while.

22

Camellia

Leading Role

Camellia was my very first friend after moving to Rockville again. She was in my geometry and English classes, and because we were in alphabetical order, she and I sat next to each other. When we started hanging out together, there was always a hesitancy about me coming to her house. She finally shared, that because I wasn't Jewish, her mom didn't like her spending time with me. Usually, what Camellia did for fun was to go to the Jewish Community Center where they had activities for teens. So, she started inviting me to go with her—which *was* approved by her parents.

When Ivy had asked for me to invite people to her parties, Camellia was one of the first to come. She was not a huge drinker, but she loved to do Quaaludes (714's, Sopers, etc.). This was the drug of that era that has since been outlawed because of its severe addictive qualities. After Camellia turned me onto them, I can vouch for the truth of that assessment. The feeling you got was one of pure relaxation and euphoria. They were expensive, so we didn't get them often, but Ivy helped with that when needed.

I don't know how it started—who first thought of it—but Camellia was my first partner in crime with hitchhiking. I can't recall the first time or why we even did it, but because we met some nice guys who took us to a party and then brought us home, we thought this was a pretty good way to meet people. And it became a regular thing. With most of my friends. Camellia's parents were very invested in her two older brothers, but not in Camellia. So, we were the perfect prescription for risk-taking behaviors.

Camellia had been sexually active for a while before I met her. She had a boyfriend who went to a different school, and he was a year older than us. I only met him a few times, and he seemed okay, but I didn't feel like he treated her very nicely. But she said she loved him. Camellia is the one who taught me about birth control. She is also the one who taught me about abortion. *More on that soon.*

Camellia and I had many escapades on our hitchhiking excursions. Once, we got picked up by some old hippies in one of those classic VW vans. They turned us on to some weed that was so strong, Camellia and I could not stop laughing—for hours. I didn't like to smoke because I usually just went to sleep, or got paranoid, but Camellia didn't want to smoke alone and with a petulant glare, convinced me to try it. We laughed so hard, they finally said they had to dump us off.

So somewhere on Connecticut Avenue, we found ourselves with ferocious munchies, and went into a Gino's restaurant, still laughing. The guy tried to take our order and we were unable to even tell him what we wanted. He shook his head and started laughing too. It was just before closing time, and no one else was in there, thank goodness. The guy kept chuckling and suggested he would read the menu to us and when he got to the items we wanted, we would raise our hands. That was incredibly hilarious to us, but it worked. I think we got enough food for four people, and he looked at both of us when we were paying, and said, "Munchies, huh?" That sent us into another tirade of laughter. We sat outside and ate our food, and decided to wait till we straightened up a bit before we stuck out our thumbs again.

Toward the end of our sophomore year, our school had a Community Day. Different groups in the community did presentations in our school to teach us about businesses, recreational opportunities, health clubs, etc. One of the presenters was going to be from Planned Parenthood. I knew nothing about them other than this is where Camellia got her birth control pills.

On the day of the event, we discovered our principal had cancelled Planned Parenthood. What started as a small group of incensed students, turned into a full-blown protest. Because so many students used their services, this was a major insult. Camellia talked me into joining in the protest. Over a hundred of us walked out of the school with handmade posterboard signs, hailing the glory of Planned Parenthood. We marched four miles to the Montgomery County Board of Education. Yes, having good judgment was in short supply on that day.

Ironically, just a few weeks later, Camellia found out she was pregnant. Her boyfriend wasn't interested in being a father, so she was left with deciding for abortion. She said her parents would kill her if they knew, and at that time, abortions weren't legal. She found out she could go to Baltimore and have the abortion, at a major hospital up there. I don't remember which one, but I learned many of the students used that facility for termination. When she told me about her decision, it felt wrong. I asked her about adoption, and she reiterated how her parents would react. I didn't know what to say, so I said nothing. I just felt sad for her.

When she got it scheduled in late July, she asked me to go with her. She had her own car now, but it was the same weekend I was going with Ivy to her cousin's birthday party, and I was supposed to babysit. I asked her why her boyfriend wasn't taking her, and she said they had broken up. That was a blow for Camellia. I could hear in her voice the pain of losing him. So, when I told her I was not available, she ended up going alone. That was tough for me to hear. And when she came back home, she was changed. I would experience changes like that in my future, also. And they weren't changes for the better.

Toward the end of that summer, she went with me and my family to Ocean City, MD. She was quiet and pensive unless we snuck some wine from my dad's stock. We always vacationed with another family, and there was much drinking going on, so no one missed a few snorts of their liquor or a few glasses of their wine. I was more than willing to acquire alcohol for her just to see her smile. Ivy vacationed in Ocean City at the same time, and we spent a lot of time at her condo, and at parties with people we had met there. Of course, these were all times for getting smashed, and Camellia was now drinking much more than before. Ivy always covered for us with my parents.

We started going out with Ivy a lot. She had discovered some bars in Prince George's County that didn't card as strictly as Montgomery County, so we spent a lot of weekends partying at these places. Ivy always picked up the tab. Sometimes, we took the whole gang with us, and stayed till closing time. Those were some wild days, and how none of us ever got caught, picked up for a DWI, or killed ourselves driving drunk, was a "mystery." Ahh, so many "mysteries."

During my sophomore year, I had experienced some scary times hitchhiking with my other friends, but I didn't share them with Camellia. Why? I didn't want to stop hitchhiking. I didn't want to miss the "fun." But the reality was, I didn't want to miss the adrenaline rush I got every time I stuck out my thumb. The same adrenaline rush you get when you live in a home full of people who are unpredictable. Where you must learn to read their signs and signals, so you can avoid the backhand slap, the kick in the leg, the silent treatments for days on end. My adrenal glands were always in high gear as a child, and that became an addiction. I got used to the feeling—it was comfortable—because it was all I knew. And that caused the idea of relaxation to feel awkward—*un*comfortable—so I would create ways to get that feeling. Voila! Risk-taking behaviors. Maybe that's why Camellia did it also. Ever wonder why an "adrenalin junkie" does what he does? That could very well be the reason.

While hitchhiking during our junior and senior years, we both met guys we ended up having long-term relationships with, and they turned out to be men who were abusive. During those times, our friendship dwindled a bit because the guys were so possessive, and our codependent behaviors were escalating, so we allowed ourselves to become isolated. Camellia got out of hers first, but afterwards, it seemed she jumped from one guy to the next. I asked her if she was staying on top of her birth control pills, so there was no chance of another "accident" and she assured me she was. I wondered if the changes I had seen in her would get worse if she had another abortion. I had already seen what abortion had done to my other friend, Heather, another player you will meet soon. Too bad I didn't internalize some of those observations, and apply them to my own life.

For the purposes of this book, I am only including the high school days. But Camellia and I remained friends for forty years. We had a lot of ups and downs, especially after I got some healing in my life. I longed for her to experience the same. There was a period when we separated company. We came back together when I learned she had another abortion. She didn't even know who the father was. She had changed a lot, and it took getting married and having a son, before she calmed down.

I know now, Camellia suffered from post-abortion stress. She exhibited a lot of the symptoms. Drinking, depression, promiscuity, drug use, to name a few. I also noticed after her second abortion Camellia never was without two dogs. If one died, she immediately replaced it. I recognized this as her substitutions for her babies. When I was finally able to deal with my own abortions, and received healing, I shared this observation with her, and she believed there was credence to it. But she didn't want to deal with the pain of remembering. She didn't realize she dealt with it every day of her life.

Camellia also had rejection issues with her parents. Never feeling good enough. Never feeling she could compete with her brothers for her mom and dad's attention. This compelled her to look for love and acceptance in all the wrong places. Just like me. We were destined to find each other because our similar histories drew us to each other like a radar.

Camellia became everything she said she never wanted to be as a parent. Her parents were constant screamers, name callers, and were condemning of most everything she did. So, she ended up doing the same with her son, and as he got older, he did the same to her, his girlfriend, and his son. The generations repeating themselves. I can't remember hearing her parents say anything nice to her. But I also can't remember them saying anything nice to each other. It was their norm. It was also what they passed down to Camellia. This is a common theme in all the female players I will introduce to you. In one way or another, we all felt emotionally orphaned. Yep, our radars were up, and we found each other. And we helped each other make lots of deposits in our personal trauma banks.

And to add one more piece to Camellia's generational trauma story, her dad and his family had been prisoners in Auschwitz during World War II. He and his brother escaped with the help of a group trying to rescue as many as they could. His parents were not so fortunate. He and his brother were sent to the USA by the Allies. What he saw at the age of 12, what he experienced, was horrific. That type of trauma is unspeakable. There is research about the possible effect this has on the genes of the next generation. This is known as *epigenetics*, which is the study of how behaviors and environment can cause changes that affect the way our genes work, and can be passed to the next generation. It doesn't actually change the DNA sequence, but can change how the body reads the sequence. These can be reversible with proper therapeutic intervention. According to *Psychology Today* author, Milton Brown, Ph.D., a clinical psychologist, from his research of epigenetics, "Compared to boys, girls more often develop emotional disorders when their fathers have had post-traumatic stress disorder." (2022). Here is yet another parallel between Camellia and me.

I witnessed to Camellia for the last twenty years of her life. Sharing what Jesus had done in my life, and the faith I had now, was hard for her comprehend. Her parents were devout Jews, and this "Jesus-guy" just didn't fit for her. Camellia didn't practice the religion of being Jewish, but she clung to her Jewish heritage. Ironically, she often mentioned how much I had changed, and made efforts to listen to everything I said, went to church with me when we visited each other, and even talked with a rabbi who was a Messianic Jew. I took her to see *The Nativity Story* and *The Passion of the Christ*, hoping both movies would speak to her in ways I couldn't. She seemed moved by both. One of the memories that blessed my heart is remembering a discussion we had with her mom about Christianity. Her mother said, "How can anyone believe a virgin could get pregnant! It's ludicrous!" To which Camellia replied, "It's no more ludicrous, than you believing God parted the Red Sea!" Bam!

In her resistance, Camellia always promised me when she was on her death bed, she would remember my words, and ask Jesus into her heart. When cancer took her, I can only hope she did that. When she died, it left a huge void. She was one of the last connections to my past life. A life no one would have ever wanted to live, but a life that taught me so much that I now use to help others. That's what God does. He gives you back what Satan has stolen. And He helps you discover the person He always meant for you to be.

Lilly

Lilly and John were very close friends with my parents. I would venture, out of all the officer's wives my mother knew, Lilly was her best friend. She and John were very strong Christians and didn't hide it, not even in front of my dad. Lilly encouraged my mom a lot. They may have been one of the few couples who saw through the façade that made up my family.

Lilly was also very kind to me. She reminded me a lot of Carly in how she treated me—protective and with love. For that reason, when I wanted to plan something special for my parents, I turned to her, and I knew she would help me.

My dad's forty-fifth birthday was coming up and I wanted to throw him a surprise party with all his NOAA friends. I was only 15 years old, and we had only been living in this house for three months. I didn't feel equipped to plan something this big, so I called Lilly, and she was thrilled to help me. I told Mom what I was doing, and she wanted to help as well. We got together one weekend and wrote the invitations. Lilly had some ideas on how to make it fun with games and music. I just loved her enthusiasm!

We set the date of the party on Dad's birthday, and decided to have everyone gather in our basement level, since this was where Dad's bar was, and it had a decent stereo system. It would also be a great place to hide people. Mom was going to have Dad help her with some things in our garden in the back yard, while I directed everyone to the basement. Lilly and John would help guide the parking.

The day finally came, and Mom and I had picked up the cake and hidden it in the basement. She recruited Dad's help around 4 p.m. and everyone was to arrive around 6. Lilly and I rushed to get the room decorated, and the food put out. It was mid-September, and it was a cool night. Everyone arrived on time and were hiding quietly in the basement. I went out to get Dad, with the pretense I needed him to find a tool for me in his workshop, which was next to the basement. He was very resistant to come in, and so Mom stopped working and said she was tired, encouraging him to help me. He seemed a bit peeved because the work they had started was not complete, but finally came in the house.

He stopped in the kitchen and was about to make a sandwich, when I said, "Dad, I really need this tool to finish a project in my room" to which he replied I would have to wait. We went back and forth a few times, with me getting more persistent and him getting more resistant. He finally blew a fuse and started cussing me for my lack of patience. He cussed the whole way downstairs saying things I can't repeat. I followed him, and when he turned on the basement light, still letting me have it, everyone yelled, "Surprise!"

The look on his face was one of complete humiliation and he quickly attempted to cover it up by thanking everyone with smiles that looked more like grimaces to me. Someone handed him a drink and then Lilly told him the whole thing had been my idea. He looked at me, raising his glass as if to thank me. He then excused himself to change because he was wearing shorts and a T-shirt. I followed him upstairs expecting to get a big hug and a thank you, but that didn't happen. Instead, I got, "Of all the stupid, asinine things you have ever done, this tops them all. I can't believe you embarrassed me like that!"

I was speechless, and instead of going back down to join the party, I got my brother, made him some dinner, and gave him his bath. He always went to bed easily, and after reading him a story, I knew he was in for the night. Then I went to my room. I was crushed. I thought I had done such a great thing for my dad. I got into my pajamas, laid on my bed and listened to music.

There was a knock at my door, and it was Lilly. She looked surprised to see me in bed. "I have been looking for you. Aren't you coming down for cake?" She said everyone was having such a great time, and people had been asking for me. I didn't tell her what had occurred with Dad when he went up to change. Apparently, he had fooled everyone into believing this was the best thing that had ever happened to him. I told Lilly I didn't feel well and was just going to stay in my room. She kissed my head and left, but was back within a few minutes with cake for me. "You're a special young lady, Karin. Your parents should be very proud of you." I hugged her and she left.

That night, Dad got ripped, and he and Mom got into an argument. I checked on my brother, shut his door, and then went back to my room. I was sure in the morning everything would be either really good or really bad. It was a little of both. No one mentioned the party, and Mom wasn't talking. Dad finished the work out in the garden, and that was the end of that.

The following summer was the family trip to New Hampshire. I had done a lot of swimming in the lake at the Copeland's and came home with an earache. It wasn't too bad at first, and Dad just called it "swimmer's ear." I used some "sweet oil" that he got at the store, but I felt it getting worse. I had complained for about a week, and soon I was having a hard time hearing, and the swelling in my neck was getting worse. The pain had become almost unbearable, and I had started to feel like I had a fever.

The big July 4th NOAA picnic was the next day, and Dad was traditionally the anchor man for the annual rope pull, and he couldn't miss it. That night, Mom finally checked my temperature, and it was 102. Dad gave me Tylenol, and told me to take a couple of them every four hours. I went to bed early but was awakened because the pain was excruciating, and I could barely handle holding my head up. Dad had some cough syrup with codeine, so he gave some to me, and I slept the rest of the night. The next morning, he gave me more of it, and then piled us all in the car to go to the picnic. We had a big Pontiac station wagon, and I felt so bad, I laid down in the back.

It was about a half-hour ride to the picnic site, and most everyone we knew was there. I attempted to join the festivities, but the codeine had made my stomach upset and when I tried to eat a hamburger, the pain in my jaws from the swelling was too much. Lilly saw me and asked if I was ok, touching the area just under my ears. I winced and told her I had an ear infection, and thought I would just go lay down in the car. I slept for a little while but woke up completely soaked in sweat. It was pushing ninety degrees, and the car was hot. The codeine had worn off and the pain was out of control. I laid there and sobbed. I didn't know what to do because the rope pull was at the end of the picnic and there would be no way Dad was leaving till after that. I just had to grin and bear it.

After a while, I felt like I was in a dream or something. Things felt like they were floating, and nothing seemed real. I heard someone calling my name and it was Lilly. She had opened the door to the car and was feeling my forehead. I heard her say, "You are burning up" and then she left. Within a few minutes, she came back with someone I didn't know, but who was a nurse, and she told Lilly I needed to be taken to the hospital right away. Lilly said something inaudible to her, and the other woman went away. When she came back, Dad was with her, and started asking me what was wrong. The nurse told him how serious my condition was, and he denied any knowledge of it. He actually asked me why I hadn't told him. *What???* He was kind of chewing me out for keeping him in the dark. The other lady left, and Lilly lit into him. He was making some sort of excuse about the rope pull, and Lilly said, "To heck with the rope pull! Get her to the hospital."

I so wished Lilly had come with us because I knew what would happen—and it did. Mom stayed at the picnic with my brother, and Dad did not stop telling me how I had ruined his day until we drove into the ER entrance of Bethesda Naval Hospital. Then he was suddenly the concerned father again. When the ER doc said I had a bad case of mumps, Dad seemed relieved, and they handed him a prescription for pain meds to help me. The fever was blown off as a symptom of the mumps. So, Dad drove me home and left me there with my pain pills, and went back to the picnic.

I took the prescribed amount of the meds, and waited for them to work. I tried the heating pad Mom had given me. Nothing was working. After an hour, the pain was untouched, so I took two more of the pills. I ended up taking six altogether, and never did get any relief. By that evening, after everyone had come home, I was screaming in pain. I couldn't lay still any longer, and I was now completely deaf. I could hear nothing at all.

When Dad came upstairs, I was pounding the mattress. He gave me two more pills and told me if I wasn't better in the morning, he would take me back to the hospital. I finally got knocked out but was screaming again by 6 a.m. Dad took me back to the hospital, but this time he was dressed in his Admiral's uniform. The ER doc I had seen the night before was there, but the other doc, who seemed to outrank him, told him, "Get the chief of ENT down here STAT!"

My temp was 105 and I couldn't stop screaming. The chief of ENT arrived, and I saw he was a captain. He greeted my dad and then came to look at me. Dad told him about the mumps diagnosis, and he lost it. He was yelling something. His anger was tangible, but he handled the immediate issues first. I could see him shouting orders at the nurses, but I couldn't hear anything. They put an IV in my arm, and gave me a shot in my butt. I don't know what they gave me in the IV, but I was flying high. Higher than any pot I had smoked. Higher than the Quaaludes I had done with Karen. I was pain free for the first time in weeks.

They took me upstairs to the ENT unit, and the doctor tried to tell me what they were going to do, but I was unable to understand. The nurses put me in an exam chair, and the doc attempted to look into my ear with an otoscope. That wasn't happening. I screamed like a banshee. The pain was indescribable. I saw him tell the nurse something and she left. He was patting my hand and saying something to my dad. I don't know what it was, but I knew my dad well enough that it wasn't good. The nurse came back with leather belts that looked like something I didn't want placed on me. But on me they went. They attached one to each arm, and restrained me to the chair arms. She then brought another needle in, and put something in my IV. Within seconds, I was in LaLa land again.

The doctor tried to tell me something, but it was hopeless. The two nurses got on either side of me and held my head tightly. Then the doctor placed a pair of needle nose forceps in my ear and opened my ear canal. It was apparently completely swollen shut. I am certain they heard me screaming all the way down in the ER. But I could partially hear myself now. I then saw him put a piece of cloth in my ear, easing it in with a pair of tweezers. He then put some liquid on the cloth and had the nurses tilt my head so the liquid could drain into my ear. It was almost instant relief. He placed a bunch of other liquid in my ear, and waited several minutes. Though the other side was still racked with pain, this side was so much better.

I heard the doc tell me he was going to do the same to the other ear. I told him I was going to scream, and he laughed, and made the "ok" sign with his hand. The pain was as bad as the last time, but I knew the intense pain meant relief was on the way. They repeated the same process again. And the relief I felt was incredible. They took the restraints off my arms, and I could barely hear the doctor telling my dad how strict the regimen had to be with the meds for my ear. He said something else so softly, I couldn't hear it, but the look on Dad's face told the story. Guilt was written all over him.

The captain walked us down to the ER and before he let us leave, he called in the doc I had seen the day before, who told me I had mumps. He introduced him to my dad who, in his uniform, demanded a different reaction from lower-ranked officers. They briefly went into a small office, and I don't know what was said, but the ER doc walked out, with a red face.

The trip home was very different than the one the day before. Dad apologized profusely, and couldn't do enough for me after we got home. He and Mom stayed on top of the drops in my ears, and the antibiotic pills I had been given. They also made sure I had my codeine every four hours. I slept well for the first time in weeks.

When dad took me back to the doc, the swelling had gone down completely. I had not had any further temp and the pain had pretty much subsided. I could still barely hear, but I thought it was from the cloth strips, or "wicks," as the doctor called them. He gently removed them, and I still couldn't hear. I was getting a little paranoid something serious had happened to my hearing. He had me lie on a table and used the same forceps he had before to open my ear canal. He then reached for the needle nose forceps, and as he maneuvered them into my ear, I could feel something weird happening. It felt like suction as he seemed to be pulling something out. And then, just like that, I could hear out of that ear! It actually made me a little dizzy as he asked me to turn over to do the other side.

He repeated the same steps, and boom! I had my hearing back! I tried to sit up, but was extremely dizzy and off balance. He told me to lie back down and wait a few minutes. He explained it was normal and it would only last a short time. He then placed the two things he had pulled from my ear on a gauze pad. They looked like two giant ticks. He then took a scalpel and cut each of them open. It was so gross! There was blood, puss, and a bunch of green stuff. He told me algae had taken up residence in my ear and that was what caused the severe infection.

He then told me how fortunate I was to have not lost my hearing. He looked up at Dad and repeated it. Dad immediately looked down at the floor, then shyly responded with a nod of his head. I had to continue my drops and my pills for another week.

Lilly came to visit me several times during this time of healing. I thanked her for taking care of me at the picnic, and encouraging Dad to get me to the hospital. She just hugged me and told me to call her "ANYTIME," if I needed her. She made a point to enunciate the anytime part. It gave me very warm fuzzies to know she cared so much.

During my senior year of high school, my dad got his orders that he would be moving back to Seattle. He had been assigned as Director of the Pacific Marine Center. I wanted to throw a surprise party for my parents' twenty-fifth wedding anniversary, so I again called Lilly and asked her to help me plan the party. She immediately agreed and offered to do it at her house. The one thing I knew about Lilly, was she would help me. I told her who I wanted to invite, most all their friends in NOAA, and helped her plan the menu and decor. I told Aunt Ruby about it and asked her to help me convince Mom to come. She had become more and more resistant to go to anything relating to a party.

And as I feared, on the day of the party, she told Dad she didn't want to go. Both Aunt Ruby and I nagged at her until she became angry and said some pretty nasty things to me. Aunt Ruby told her she was going to eat crow that night, to which Mom gave her an odd look. Aunt Ruby said Lilly would be disappointed if she didn't go to the party.

I left home as soon as I was convinced she was going, and early enough to help Lilly with setting up. We were both excited as the guests arrived—about forty in all. When Mom and Dad walked in, and everyone yelled "Surprise!" Mom looked anything but pleased. She offered a wan smile, and walked over to me, and said, "So this is what you nagged me to go out for? I can't stand you!" Lilly was standing next to me, and said some things to Mom, none of which I could hear. I had a tornado of feelings circling inside me, and began to cry. I hugged Lilly and left. Dad thanked me the next morning, but nothing came from Mom.

The next day, Lilly came over. I don't think Mom knew she was coming, and after they talked, Mom seemed upset and went to her room. Aunt Ruby and I were in the kitchen, and she offered Lilly a cup of coffee, but she declined and asked for tea. She sat at the kitchen table with us, and she and Aunt Ruby talked awhile. Then Aunt Ruby left the kitchen and Lilly put both her hands over mine. "Your parents are leaving soon, but I want you to know, if you need anything, I am here for you. Anything you need, John or I will help you. You are a special girl, and we love you, and God loves you." And then she kissed me on the forehead and left.

I never knew what she and Mom talked about. I just knew she was a person who made me feel very safe. I found myself wishing for the umpteenth time in my life that I had someone like this as a mother.

I didn't take Lilly up on her offer. I didn't think my parents would like it. By this time, my inner voice spoke very clearly that I was the black sheep in the family, and so I shouldn't do anything else to embarrass my parents further. I often think of Lilly, and I now know she was yet another mystery, another person God placed in my path to give me love—and to reveal His love. I will never forget her.

24

Rose

Supporting Role

I met Rose in my sophomore year. She was in a few of my classes, and always reminded me of Janis Joplin, not only in her style of dress, but also in her mannerisms and attitude. She had long, dark brown hair down to her waist and I was so jealous of it. I had tried in vain to grow mine that long, but it never got past my bra. She carried a little extra weight, so we had that in common, but she also had a bad acne problem, and I think she was embarrassed about it. I never asked, and she didn't volunteer, but I was pretty convinced she had a bad situation at home, also.

Rose was one of the people I hung out with the least, mostly because she couldn't spend the night or go on any of our weekends with Ivy. But she did like to go to concerts, and hitchhike with me. We found quite a few parties on quite a few occasions and the people who picked us up were mostly friendly. We only had one sketchy ride, who threatened to take us to Florida. I had not liked the way he looked before we got in, and tried to tell Rose, but she felt he looked okay, so we took it. He wasn't ok. He didn't hurt us, but he scared us. So, after that, if a car stopped and I thought he looked questionable, I acted like we really weren't looking for a ride, but just wanted to ask what time it was. Obviously, this annoyed people, and we usually got some angry words thrown at us, and a few middle fingers, but that was better than taking a chance.

Rose liked to do weird stuff like use a British accent when we got in a car. We used to practice for hours before we would go out and we sounded legit. One time we got nailed because one of the guys knew his European geography and asked her where she hailed from, and that was the end of the game. Pretty humiliating.

She almost always had weed and loved to drink Boone's Farm. She wasn't into the Quaaludes like Camellia, or any downers really. Mostly she liked to do speed, like black beauties. I was not into pot because it made me paranoid and sleepy. I wasn't into the speed either, so mostly we drank together. When she drank, the persona I mentioned earlier was exaggerated. She talked tough and acted tough. She came onto guys, to the point it made me uncomfortable. She was blatantly sexual. Because of some comments she made about them, combined with the knowledge I have now, I suspect her father or older brother may have abused her sexually. So, both of us were the perfect storm for what we were about to encounter.

In March of 1971, Steppenwolf was performing at the University of Maryland in College Park. We loved their music, and decided to go. We figured if we left right after school, and started hitchhiking we could probably make the 7 p.m. show. So that's what we did. We got quick rides that day, and made it all the way to the Kenilworth Avenue exit on the beltway. We walked a while to get off the exit and then started hitching again. Three cars had stopped, and I didn't like the way they looked. And they were not much interested in giving us the time. So, I tolerated the language that was directed at us. But Rose was getting frustrated and told me the next car that stopped was our ride. Period.

The next car was a dark green VW bug. There were three guys in it, and they all had long hair, and beards. When I leaned over to get a better look, there was an American flag attached to the ceiling of the car. That seemed a good sign they might be hippies, and so they would probably be safe. They asked where we were going, and when we told them, the driver said they would take us as far as University Blvd. Perfect!

The guy in the passenger seat stepped out, and tilted his seat forward. He was huge. Very tall and stocky. I remember thinking he was a tight fit for the bug. He had a long beard and long blondish-brown hair that looked like it hadn't seen shampoo in a while. The driver had long dark hair and a goatee, and was small and skinny. They both had jean vests on. The guy in the back was thin and wiry, had short brown hair and a short beard. He was wearing a white muscle shirt and no vest.

Rose climbed in first and I followed. She had taken a pint of vodka from her house and had been drinking it, so she was being her loud and boisterous self. She was doing all the talking, leaning forward between the two seats. She apparently saw a patch on the driver's jeans, near the crotch, and put her hand on his leg and asked him what it said. His grin and his answer immediately made my gut hurt. Something didn't feel right, and I told Rose to sit back and shut up. She did and then tried to talk to the guy beside her, but he was saying nothing.

We drove only a short distance, and suddenly the driver made a right turn, and Rose asked where he was going. No answer. I told the driver he could just drop us off here because we could walk the rest of the way. No answer. Rose asked again, louder this time, where he was going. No answer. My heart was in my throat. I could feel it pounding. I tried again, pleading for them to let us out. No answer.

They turned left off the road we were on, and I realized we were in a park—like a state or national park. It had a lot of empty parking spaces as we drove through. He pulled into a space in front of some woods. There was not a single soul in site. No cars. No people. In front of us, back into the trees a bit, was a building that looked like it could have been used for storage—like a shed, where park rangers might store their shovels and tools. I looked all around us, and there was nowhere we could try to run. The driver turned the car off, turned to the big guy in front of me and asked which one he wanted first. My heart felt like it hit the floor. Rose yelled at them, asking what they were talking about, and to just take us back to the highway. The driver told her to shut up.

I was terrified and started crying. I don't know what I was thinking or what possessed me to say it, and I immediately regretted it. But I blurted out, "Please don't do this, I am a virgin!"

All talking ceased in the front seat, and then the driver spoke, "That settles it! I haven't popped a cherry in years. Let's get her in there." He started to get out of the car, and suddenly Rose lost it. She grabbed him and started pounding him in the face, and then swung on the big guy. That was a mistake. He backhanded her so hard, all I saw was hair flying as she hit the back seat. He turned around, and in one quick move, grabbed her by the throat. I was paralyzed with terror. Rose's face was getting red, and I realized she couldn't breathe. And I couldn't move.

"You're the one going in there first. Now get out of the car!" He almost whispered it to her. His face was contorted with anger, and letting go of her neck, he grabbed both arms and pulled her over his seat like she weighed two pounds. By this time, the driver was next to him, and when she gained her balance, they both grabbed her arms and dragged her to the shed. As they walked away, I noticed they had stitching on the back of their vests with a name above it. The name of an infamous motorcycle gang. I had heard about them and none of it was good. In the easiest description to offer, these guys were the East Coast Hell's Angels.

I was scrunched as close to the side of the car as I could get. The muscle shirt guy was watching me intently, and the terror I felt was mounting. There was no way to escape without having to climb over the seat. I just sat there and trembled. I was too scared to even cry. I don't know how long we sat there, but it felt like hours. At some point, I must have moved in a way that made him think I was going to try and get out, because he grabbed my left arm, and squeezed so tightly, I yelped.

"I think I need to show you something." He let go of my arm and reached behind the seat to the storage compartment in the back. There was a blanket there and he pulled it back. Under it was a sawed-off shotgun. I had only seen one in a movie, but it was identical to this one. "Don't think for one minute, I am afraid to use it. DO YOU BELIEVE ME?" His voice had raised several octaves, and I nodded my head. In that second, I thought I would wet my pants. I could see my heart beating under my shirt.

I heard a noise out at the shed. The big guy came out first, and had his arm under Rose's armpit, and then the second guy came out supporting her other arm. She was unconscious because they were partially carrying her, with her feet dragging behind. My breath caught in my throat as I realized her pants were down around her shoes, and blood on her legs. Her left eye was swollen shut and there was blood around her mouth. I had to force myself to take a breath. I felt like something was sitting on my chest preventing me from breathing on my own. They laid her across the front of the VW, and the little guy leaned in from the driver's side with a disgusting grin on his face, "You're next."

The big guy had come to my side of the car and opened the door. He pulled the seat forward and waited for me to get out. In that second, I remembered the prayers I prayed every night. And I threw one up, "God, I know I always pray for my family, but please help *me* today." I heard the big guy tell me again to get out. I wanted to run, but I couldn't leave Rose, and I couldn't outrun that shotgun. My legs felt like rubber, but I was finally out of the car, and standing in front of him. He was even bigger than I thought. The skinny guy was standing behind Rose. She had started to move a little.

Some weird thing came over me, and it wasn't anything I had felt before. I reached up and grabbed the front of his vest with each hand and said, "Please don't do this! I will do anything you ask, but please don't do this." His eyes were black, like a shark's eyes. Nothing there at all. Just darkness. Then he shut his eyes, and I instinctively ducked. My dad did that eye-shutting thing just before the slap came, so I was preparing myself for the blow.

"What's wrong? Why are you acting like that?" Bewildered because his voice sounded so concerned, I opened my eyes. His eyes had changed! They looked blue, and gentler. I was confused. Shocked. Still terrified, because this change in his voice, and his eyes, make no sense. "If you kiss me, I will let you go. I will let you and your friend go."

Immediately the little guy came around the car to where we were and started yelling at him, "You promised me the cherry! You can't let them go until I get the cherry!" In an instant, the big guy punched him so hard, he left the ground, landing a few feet from the car. He said nothing else. The big guy turned to me.

My brain was in overdrive. Was this guy for real? Why would he do something so kind? The reputation of this gang was well earned. I knew there wasn't a lot of conscience that would be guiding their behavior—at least that was what I had heard, and had clearly witnessed this day. But here I was faced with two choices, and both were bad. And one was much worse than the other. "Are you serious? You will really let us go?" For the first time, I studied his face in detail. He looked hard, like he had seen a few things in his life. His skin was sun-worn, and his beard was gross, stained with what I guess was chaw. Clearly no time recently had it been washed. All of this took a fraction of a second. I was still shaking and scared. I waited for him to respond.

"Yes, I promise you, I will let you go." So, I stood on my tip toes, and I kissed him. To this day I could not tell you what it felt like, or what it tasted like; I have blocked that from my memory. But I did it, and as soon as I did, he told me to take my friend and go. The guy in the back seat asked if he was sure about this. He was told "yes."

I went to Rose who had recovered and was pulling up her pants. Her face was much worse than I first thought. I told her we could leave, and she said nothing. I waited for her to adjust her clothes, and then placed my arm under hers and tried to help her walk. She was in a lot of pain, and as I passed the big guy, I heard the driver cussing. At that moment I started to feel unsure about all this, and I leaned close to Rose and whispered, "They have a shotgun, and they will use it. Can you run?" She grunted she would try and when we got past the car a few feet, we both started running. I listened for the gunshot, but it never came.

We ran into the woods at the end of the parking lot, and followed a tall chain-linked fence for what seemed like forever. Eventually, the fence came out at the beltway, and we found a loose part in the fence, and climbed through it. We walked till we saw one of the emergency phones that were every few miles along the highway. I called Ivy and told her the mile marker where she could find us, and we waited. When she arrived, I unloaded everything that had happened. Rose was silent. Ivy wanted to take her the hospital, but she was adamant she couldn't go, because her father would "kill" her. Ivy explained the chance of pregnancy, disease, and other serious damage they may have done to her. Rose wasn't concerned, she just wanted to go home.

We drove in silence for a while and then Ivy asked Rose if she would share what had happened to her, but she wouldn't talk. She then asked me if I was ok, and I said I was, but felt sick for what had happened to Rose. She stayed silent the rest of the way to her house. Ivy suggested we stop before we got there to clean her up and maybe put some make-up on her face. We did the best we could, and when we got to her house, she just got out of the car and went in. No goodbyes or anything.

This was the spring of my sophomore year. Nothing seemed real after that. I felt like I walked around in a daze for the next few days. I never told my parents, and Ivy suggested I shouldn't. The whole incident must have only consumed about an hour because we had gone to hitchhike right after school, got two rides right away, so it was probably around 4 p.m. when we got the ride in the VW. And now I was getting home at 7 p.m. Mom was cooking dinner, Dad was drinking his Manhattan, and my brother was watching TV. Life as usual. I could imagine telling them the whole story, and then getting chewed out for hitchhiking. It was easier to swallow it. I knew how to do that.

Rose and I were never close after that. We didn't do anything together unless we were doing stuff with a whole group. We didn't talk about it, with each other or anyone else. I have often wondered what happened to Rose. What I know now about abuse, sexual assault, and trauma, makes me pray that she was smarter than me, and didn't wait for decades to deal with that event. I pray that whatever was going on at home, she got away from it and dealt with that pain as well. I pray she found peace.

I remember the first time I shared that event with my counselor, decades later. She asked if I had any emotion attached to it. I had no tears. No anxiety. Nothing. I was just telling a story—as if it happened to someone else. I didn't know what she meant by her question. It was the first time I had spoken about it since the day it happened. Was I supposed to be feeling something? I hadn't allowed myself to feel anything.

We worked on that until I was able to reconnect with the pain, the terror, and the parts I had hidden so successfully over the years. Well, the truth is, I had not been successful at all in hiding it. It was in every drink I took. Every drug with which I experimented, and every risk-taking behavior I adopted.

The definition of insanity? Doing the same thing over and over and expecting a different outcome. Yes, I hitchhiked again.

***

Author's note: Not long after writing this chapter, I found myself in the DC area, and decided to look for where this may have occurred. Coming off Kenilworth Avenue, the scene played back like a video, and as I drove in the direction we had been taken, sure enough, on the right, was a park—Greenbelt National Park. And as I took the right and ventured in, I felt my pulse quicken, and my heart pound. It may not look exactly as it did fifty-three years ago, but I found the spot, and I found the fence we followed to escape as it ran parallel to the beltway.

It was surreal. . . and it was closure.

25

Heather

Leading Role

Beautiful Heather. Heather was one of those people who was as beautiful on the inside as she was on the outside. I clearly remember feeling privileged that she had become my friend. She was the friend in my sophomore year who I wanted to be the most like. I wanted to do my make-up like she did, I wanted to dress like she did, and ironically most everyone outside our school, thought we were sisters. I learned a lot of really good things from Heather. But like me, she had parents who were not well trained in the parenting department. And over the years, the beautiful girl on the inside became a woman I didn't know. Our lives paralleled in that way. Trauma does that.

We had a small gang of friends in high school that consisted of Heather and me, along with Willow, Rose, Don, and Ethan. Ethan and Don were best friends, and they lived close to each other, and both of them lived close to me as well. When we weren't hanging at Don's house, we would hang at Ethan's. Pretty innocent stuff, just listening to music or watching TV. Just before Christmas, a relationship sparked between Heather and Ethan, and consequently, this increased the time she spent at my house. And that was fine with me. They dated for a few months, and during that time Heather and I became closer friends.

Heather was one of the first to bring to my attention how badly my parents treated me. One of the first times she came over, we were sitting in the living room, listening to my dad's stereo. When he came home, he casually reminded me I wasn't allowed to sit on the living room furniture. I thought nothing of it because I had been banned from sitting on it since we moved to this house.

Heather thought it was awful that my parents treated me like that. She was also appalled that my dad took me to see *Last Tango in Paris*, a very sexually provocative movie that was originally rated "X" and which included an intense sodomy/rape scene. She thought it was "obscene" that he would take me to a movie like that. Obscene was the word Heather used for anything she found disgusting. She used it frequently and it was quite unique to her.

I want to elaborate on a couple things here. The furniture Dad had banned me from, was Scandinavian and it was expensive. It was their new stuff, and Dad felt I was too heavy to sit on it. At that time, I was five feet, ten inches tall and weighed 185 pounds. Now, I knew this was well made furniture, so I should have realized how ridiculous this rule was. Telling me it would not support my weight, when so many of his friends were larger than me, was just cruel. But thinking I could defend myself did not occur to me back then. I just accepted it. Well, I should say I accepted the ban. I didn't accept the message. My bulimic episodes became more frequent.

Heather only hitchhiked with me a couple times. She didn't think it was safe, which is why she also didn't participate in any of Ivy's jaunts. So, we mostly went to a teen club called *The Garish Grape* on Friday nights. They sometimes had bands, and always had good music. There were parents there to chaperone and that was the only reason Heather's mom and dad allowed her to go. Her parents seemed nice but very strict. Heather was the oldest of the three kids, and as she became more rebellious with their stringent rules, she soon became the identified person (IP) in her family. Like Willow was. And like I was. You may have noticed this is a common theme with all my friends. Each of us was the "reason" the family had problems. We were the scapegoats, and ironically, the most emotionally honest in the family. When people don't want to hear truth, they just make you out to be the crazy one . . . the troublemaker . . . the one who needs to be silenced. So, we became the target of our parent's vitriolic words. Words to crush us. Words to silence us. The other siblings either had shut down in fear or had given up trying to be heard.

Heather met a guy at the Garish Grape who she grew to like a lot. His name was Brad, and he was 21 years old, and was there acting as a DJ. He was very respectful of her, and she reveled in his positive attention. They soon began to date, but it was on the sly. We discovered he only lived a few miles from my house, and my mom was cool with Brad coming over and watching TV with us on the weekends when Heather stayed over. Heather really liked him, and it wasn't long before she started using the "L" word when she talked about him.

So far, her parents knew nothing, but she was petrified of them finding out because of the age difference. She said they would never accept him. I really liked him too, and hoped, for her sake, her parents would eventually feel the same. Heather would be turning 15 years old in December, so though we were in the same grade, she was almost a year younger than me. This made their age difference even more grievous in her eyes. And then a bomb dropped.

We were in math class, when Heather told me her dad had accepted a new position, and they were moving out of state—at the end of the school year—and only five months away. She was crying and could barely control herself. We decided to skip out of school that day, and Heather asked if Ivy could pick us up. She did, and we hung with her until Brad got off work, and then we went to his house. Heather told him her news, and he assured her things would be fine because it was only going to be an hour away. But she was not consolable, believing they would never see each other again. He just held her gently, and allowed her to cry. It was a beautiful thing to see.

Eventually, Heather was all cried out, and Brad's mom invited us to eat with them. His parents were very friendly, and they cooked burgers on the grill for us, and we ate on their deck. Afterwards, Brad asked if we wanted to listen to some music, so we went to his room. He lived in the basement of his parents' house, and he had a quadrophonic stereo system. I will never forget how awesome the Pink Floyd, *Dark Side of the Moon*, album sounded in quad! Heather was calmer now, but I wondered how this was all going to play out.

Heather was still spending some weekends with me but had started asking me to cover for her so she could see Brad. He would pick her up after my parents went to bed, and they would go back to his place and stay till dawn, and then he would bring her back. She was always apologetic for leaving me, but felt she and Brad had to spend as much time as possible together before she moved. And it wasn't long before she confessed, she had lost her virginity and they were having sex most nights. I asked if she was on birth control, but she said they were being careful.

One Saturday, Heather and I had gone into a Dart Drug, and were looking at some makeup. There was a paperback book stand next to the makeup aisle and Heather was looking at one called *Everything You Always Wanted to Know About Sex * but were afraid to ask*. She said she felt so inexperienced with Brad and wanted to learn more about sex. I agreed and thought it might teach her some stuff about birth control as well, so I told her she should get it. We didn't have enough money for the book, and since Ivy had been training me, I made the brilliant choice to do a five-finger-discount. Bad idea. I got caught. My parents were called. Dad came to pick me up. I was mortified that he saw me with that book. He apologized to the manager, drove Heather to her house, and warned me it wasn't going to be good when I got home. That was a major understatement.

When I got home, I heard Mom upstairs screaming about how embarrassed she was. How her dad had been a sheriff and how I had destroyed the family name and how he would be turning over in his grave in humiliation. Of course, this had become all about her and her reputation that I had ruined. When I got to my room, she had cut up all my jeans and all my "cool" shirts, broken many of my records, and torn my posters off the walls. I had nothing left in my closet except some polyester pants and shirts, things I would wear if I went out with them for dinner. I was crying hysterically and begging her to stop. I could think of nothing except what a fool I would look like wearing those clothes to school. Dad finally came upstairs and told her enough was enough which started a fight between them. I sat on the floor and cried, and wished with every fiber in me, I was dead.

Mom finally went downstairs, and Dad was left standing in my doorway. He said he was sorry for what she had done. And then he said something I could hardly wrap my head around. "Karin, I think you should find somewhere to go for a few days until she calms down. I don't care where you go, just go somewhere until things cool off." I sat there in shock. Where was I going to go? Who was going to take me in? It was February and we had snow on the ground. I couldn't even sleep outside. I didn't know what I was going to do. Dad gave me $10 and apologized again. So, I packed some of my polyester things in my book bag, found my warmest coat, scarf, hat and gloves, and walked out of my house.

Hmm. No offer to put me up in a hotel. No offer to talk to anyone's parents for me. Just get out. You're on your own. Kind of a "you made your bed, now lie in it." But it was said with such concern—as if he was recommending this to help me—as my compassionate and loving caretaker. Unbelievable. As an adult, and after having my own children, this memory just floored me. It still does.

I walked to the closest shopping center and bought a burger so I could get change. I called Heather. She had a private phone line, and I was glad. She was so sorry about what had happened, and blaming herself. I told her my situation, and she started crying. She told me to wait till it got dark, and come to her bedroom window. She also had a basement bedroom, so it was easy to hide out by the window till her parents went to bed. I snuck in her window, and spent the night on her floor. The next morning, I got out just before she left to grab the bus, and took the bus with her. I told her bus driver I was staying with her a few days while my parents were out of town, and he was cool with it.

Going to school, while wearing those clothes, was about the most humiliating thing I had experienced thus far in my life. The looks I got, and the comments, were unbearable. But I had a really cool art teacher named Miss Bowser, and when I got to her class, she saw the shame written all over me. She pulled me aside and asked me what was going on. The tears came, and then she took me into her office, and I told her everything. Miss Bowser was very young, and this was only her second year of teaching. She just shook her head, but held her tongue. She asked me to meet her after school, described her car and made me promise to wait for her. I promised I would. I didn't know what to expect, but I had nothing better to do.

When she got to the car, she asked if I was hungry, so we went to Shakey's, a popular pizza place. Afterward, she took me shopping for clothes. I was adamantly opposed to her doing this, but in her sarcastic, but harmless way, she asked me if I really wanted to go to school the next day, looking like I did now. I chuckled, and quickly agreed. I don't know what she spent, but I got three pairs of jeans and some shirts and sweaters. I was so grateful. It had started snowing, so when we got to Heather's street, we sat and talked until we saw the upstairs lights go off at her house. I thanked her profusely, put on all my warm clothes, and wrapped up tightly. It was frigid, and I hoped I didn't have to stay outside long.

When I tapped on Heather's window, she jerked open the curtains, hushing me. Apparently, her mom was getting clothes from the dryer, and had decided to fold every one of them before heading back upstairs. I had covered up as much of my face as I could, but the wind was like tiny knives cutting into my skin. Finally, I saw the basement light go off, and then saw her mom stop at Heather's door and ask why she was still awake. She proceeded to lecture her on her need for sleep to do her best in school. Heather patiently listened and at last, her mother took the clothes basket and went upstairs. As soon as Heather was sure her mom was out of hearing range, she opened the window. I could hardly climb in; I was so stiff from the cold. I slept hard that night.

The next day, my dad picked me up at the end of the school day and told me I could come home. I don't know what happened, but I wondered if Miss Bowser had anything to do with it. Of course, Mom wasn't speaking to me, and no one seemed to notice my new clothes. I went to my room and found it as I left it. I spent the next few hours cleaning up the broken record shards and poster pieces. I was unsure what the next few days would bring.

Surprisingly, Heather's parents asked if Heather could stay with us a few days while they went house hunting. My mom was completely agreeable—and just like that—things were back to normal. Brad came to visit on a couple of the evenings, and Mom joined us in playing cards together. It was as if nothing had ever happened, and it was never discussed. *Have you noticed how often you hear about this behavior?*

Heather's parents were successful in finding a new home, and this brought on more despair for Heather. In April, they invited me to ride with them to see their new house. It was a new development, and the house was still under construction, but it was probably three times the size of their old home and nestled in the back of a cul-de-sac with woods behind it. It was beautiful. Heather said she finally had a house as big as mine, but the joy quicky left her face, as the reality of the move settled in. Her parents took us to dinner, and on the ride home Heather was silent. Her mother asked if she was okay, but Heather said she felt sick to her stomach. She asked her dad to pull over, and almost didn't get the car door open in time to lose her dinner. Her mom asked again if she was okay, and felt her forehead. Heather didn't have a temperature. But she was very pale. They dropped me off at home, and I told Heather to feel better.

The next day in school, Heather got sick again. We were in math class, and she looked terrible. She asked to use the bathroom, and the teacher gave me permission to go with her. I held her hair, while she threw up, and I remembered going through this with another friend. I asked her if there was any chance, she could be pregnant, and she said no, but I wasn't convinced. I told her about the place Camellia went, Planned Parenthood, and we decided to try and get a ride there. It took a few days, but Ivy took us after school, and the next bomb dropped.

Ivy dropped us off at Brad's and we waited for him to get home from work. Heather seemed in shock. She wasn't crying, but wouldn't talk either. When Brad got there, she literally fell into his arms. He was so understanding, holding her, and caressing her hair. He told her not to worry, they would get married. She seemed relieved and asked Brad how they should handle it with her parents. After all, they would need parental permission because she was underage.

They both decided to keep the pregnancy a secret until Brad could afford a ring, and they would tell her parents together. He said it could take a few months, but by June, he should have the money. Brad went upstairs to tell his parents, and I completely felt ready for the sky to fall, but instead he came down and got Heather. They both went upstairs and talked to his parents, who told them it wasn't going to be easy, but they could do it, and welcomed them to stay in the basement until Brad could afford to get a place of their own. I was stunned. Brad was one lucky guy to have parents like this.

Time ticked on. I didn't see as much of Heather because they had started packing their house. I was dreading her leaving as much as she was. I still did things with my other friends and Ivy, but Heather had been special in my life. Like a sister. I wondered what it would be like not having her close by. Plus, we learned we wouldn't even be able to talk on the phone very much because it would be long distance. It was depressing.

They moved in June and Heather invited me to come stay with her one weekend, and help her decorate her new room. My dad drove me there, and we had a great time hanging her posters and unpacking her things. She showed me how her belly had started getting bigger and worried her parents would notice. I told her to keep wearing all her big, blousy peasant shirts, and it probably wouldn't show. She said she thought she had felt the baby move, and it felt like a "swishing" in her tummy. It was exciting for us, and scary at the same time. Neither of us knew how her parents were going to react to the confession when it came, but Heather could hardly wait.

She didn't have to wait long. Brad had saved his money and gotten her an engagement ring. Heather called me and told me he was coming the following weekend and she was hoping all was going to go well. I assured her I thought it would. I couldn't have been more wrong. Two days later, Heather showed up at my house. Brad had dropped her off, and she was hoping my mom would let her stay with us. I was completely in the dark as to what was going on, and when the whole sad story came out, I felt certain Mom would not turn her away. And she didn't.

Brad had shown up at Heather's house, dressed in suit and tie, and with flowers in hand. Of course, Heather's parents didn't know who he was and when he asked for Heather, they had called her downstairs, quite bemused. When she came down, she asked if they could all sit in the living room because she had something to tell them. She and Brad had decided to tell them about the engagement first, and save the news about the baby until after they got their blessing. Heather and Brad had sat together, and he had pulled out the ring and asked permission to marry their daughter. Heather said that was the last nice thing she remembered happening.

Both parents were livid, and asked how long this relationship had been going on. Heather told them it had been several months, and begged them to understand how much they loved each other, and they didn't want to wait to marry. That wasn't going very far, so as a last-ditch effort, Brad blurted out she was pregnant.

Heather said the whole room went silent and then her father ordered Brad out of the house. Her mother screamed at her to go to her room. Brad tried to show them the ring, and explain how much they loved each other, and how he had plans in motion to take care of her and the baby. No one was listening. She said her dad asked him how old he was, and when Brad told him, he said he was having him arrested for statutory rape, and he better get out of the house before he called the police. Brad had walked toward the door and Heather had gone after him, but was stopped by her parents. She said she kept begging them to listen to their plan, and then her mother dropped her own bombshell. Holding Heather back from the door, she looked at Brad, and said, "She will never have your baby. It will be gone by next week."

She said Brad's face had turned pale, then they slammed the door in his face. Heather was crying as she told this story, and my heart hurt for her. I asked her what her mom meant by the "baby being gone by next week" and Heather said they were going to force her to have an abortion. I remember thinking she had felt the baby moving, so it was too far along to have an abortion, but what did I know. Heather asked my mom if she could stay at our house until she and Brad found a way to get married. My mom said yes, and it was one of those times in my life when I was really proud she was my mom. She told me to keep all this from my dad. That wouldn't be a problem.

The next day, Brad came over and gave us more bad news. Somehow, Heather's parents had found out his name and where he lived. They had contacted his parents, and told them if Heather wasn't returned home right away, they were going to have Brad arrested. His parents had assured them Heather was not at their house, but the threats were bad enough that Brad's parents felt we should know. Brad and Heather sat on our family room couch, holding each other. I felt so helpless. There seemed to be no good solution to help them. Brad kept saying they could run and hide somewhere until she turned 16, and then they could get married. But that was another six months. She was going to have the baby before she turned 16. We talked about how hard it would be for her to go to a hospital to have the baby, as an underage kid. Too many questions would be asked, and Brad could be arrested for kidnapping.

Heather cried a long time. When she calmed down enough to talk, she told Brad she couldn't stand the thought of him going to jail, so she would go back home. She felt things would work out, and when she turned 16, they could be married. No one could stop them after that. I saw the concern on Brad's face, but she hugged him and told him she was sure it would be okay. She believed when she told her parents how far along she was, and that she had felt the baby moving, they would never make her hurt it. She wasn't the first kid who believed she could trust her parents to do the right thing.

Brad took Heather home the next day and I heard nothing else. Heather was not allowed to call any of her friends in Rockville, and she was cut off from most everyone else for several months. So, I didn't hear the rest of the story for a quite a while. When we finally saw each other again she had gotten her license, bought a car and had come to Maryland to visit her friends for the weekend. She had asked about spending the night and I was thrilled since I had not seen her in so long. We had spoken by phone on a few occasions, but she said her parents were always close by, so this would be the first time we could really talk. I was surprised her parents let her go away for the whole weekend, but it had been a year since everything went down. Sitting in my room, she shared what had happened.

Brad had taken her to her parents' house while they were at work. Heather wanted him to leave before they got home, and they hugged promising to talk again soon. That was the last time they ever saw each other. Three days later Heather was taken to a doctor. She was five months pregnant. The doctor told her and her mother they would have to do the procedure in a hospital because it would require an overnight stay. Heather had begged for her baby's life, but her mother's mind was made up.

The following week she was taken into the hospital and on the first day, they had put something inside her to make her body ready for the abortion. The next morning, they put her to sleep and performed the procedure. She said she had awakened and found a nurse next to her bed. Heather said the woman was not very kind, and said nothing to her as she checked her vital signs every half hour. When Heather needed to get up to use the bathroom, she saw a basin on the floor next to her bed, and the baby was in it. Heather said she got sick, and the nurse apologized and said she didn't mean to leave it there, and took it away. But it occurred to Heather that if that was true, she would have removed it during the many times she had come in to check her.

Heather shared this story with me as if she was talking about it happening in a dream or something. She was emotionless and had no inflections in her voice. I was crying, but she just said, "Its done. Nothing I can do about it now. I just need to forget it." She then asked me if I could sneak some booze from my father's bar. This was a new one for Heather. Of all my friends, she was the one who had not been a drinker. But I obliged, more because I needed something myself after hearing her story. I got a large glass of vodka knowing this was what Dad would miss the least, and brought it to my room. Then I went to get some mixers for us. When I got back to my room, she had polished off the whole glass. Straight down. And she asked if I could get some more. I knew that wasn't a good idea, so I made a phone call. Ivy to the rescue.

We went over to her house, and everyone was asleep, so she made a pitcher of her famous martinis, and we sat in her family room and talked. Ivy expressed her sorrow for the abortion, but Heather waved her off. Almost with disinterest. Something was different, but I couldn't discern what it was at first. A coolness. No, a coldness. Lack of emotion. Even when she shared that horrendous story with Ivy. I was sitting there hating her parents, and she sounded like she was discussing the weather. We all got blitzed and somehow Heather and I made it back into my house without waking anyone up.

She left the next morning. And I didn't see her for a very long time. It was years later, before we reconnected, when she was planning her wedding. I was so excited to see her again, but when we got together, I didn't recognize who this was. Yes, she looked the same, but that was all.

I have realized in recent years, the last time I saw the real Heather—the Heather that was so beautiful inside and out, the Heather I adored as my dearest friend—was the night she and Brad sat on the couch together, in my family room, and planned their future. Planned their wedding. Planned their family. Planned their life together, a life based on the love that had created their baby. That was the last time I saw her. Because when she was taken to that hospital, it wasn't just her baby that died. Trauma comes in many colors. Wears many faces. And damages in ruthless ways. Heather was my second friend who had an abortion and had experienced what I now know to be called Post-Abortion Stress (PAS), a form of PTSD. Both my friends had changed drastically. And my time was coming . . . because I didn't learn from them.

Heather got married and she and I stayed friends for as long as I could handle where life had taken her. The alcohol and the cocaine had gotten out of control, and even she recognized it. When her marriage ended, she went to Oregon to seek something new. A new beginning. A new life. But the surreptitious character of trauma is—it follows you. The more you try to cover it up, numb it, or hide from it, the more it sucks you in. And it will bury you unless you face it. Head on. In all its ugliness.

I pray for Heather every day. I have heard she has kicked the substance abuse, but takes many meds to keep her anxiety and depression at bay. I touched base with her a few years ago, and realized quickly, the demons from her past were still there. She had been victorious over the drugs and alcohol, but the battle with her memories—her trauma—was ever present.

I tried to talk with her about it. I shared my own story of redemption from the devastation of abortion. How the abortions had piled on more PTSD triggers to my already existing mountain of trauma symptoms. Most of all I shared with her the story of the One who took my guilt and shame, and who forgave me of all my mess. The One who healed me of all the traumatic luggage I had carried since I was a kid. I assured her Jesus would do the same in her life.

But her anger was tangible. She blamed God for what happened to her, and for everything since. "How can there be so much pain and horror in the world if there is a God who loves us? If He loves us, why doesn't He stop it?" *Oh, how Satan does like to use that one to keep people in their chains.* My explanations of man's free will, and the knowledge that Satan wants us to stay stuck in our pain, fell on deaf ears. She wanted nothing to do with God or His son.

So, I will continue to pray for Heather. Pray someone crosses her path who can help her see the truth. Help her find hope, healing and the Truth that will set her free. Because if there's anyone who deserves the love of the Savior, it's Heather.

26

Willow

Supporting Role

Willow was an interesting person. She had a great sense of humor, but was also somewhat sarcastic. She was in a couple of my classes, and was very quick with her responses to being reprimanded by a teacher—comments that made the whole class laugh, at the expense of the teacher. She had very short brown hair and was quite slim. We became fast friends once we shared our home lives with each other. Her parents were the opposite of mine. They were vigilant with everything she did. But only when it was to show her how poorly they felt her decision making was, which increased her rebellion. Her father was a psychiatrist, and she believed being the younger of three kids, she had been set up by her two older brothers. They were perfect in every way possible, and now Willow was paying for it. She could do nothing right. She liked the fact that my parents were oblivious, and so she spent a lot of time at my house.

Because she and Rose were friends, she learned about our hitchhiking to find parties. Neither Rose nor I ever told anyone about the green VW, so Willow didn't realize there could be any danger. She was more cautious than I was, and only went with me a few times, but when we did, she was a party animal. She was very open, almost like Rose, but without the need for alcohol to lose her inhibitions. When she liked someone, she told them, and they often responded to her assertiveness. I longed to be more like that, but it wasn't in me.

One of the few times we hitchhiked, a van stopped to pick us up. There were three guys, two in the front and one in the back and they were all friendly. The one in the back where we were sitting, was kind of quiet. Willow was trying to talk with him, and he seemed nervous. They had given us some beer, and I asked him if he wanted one also. He just shook his head, and asked the driver to pull over. He got out of the car, and was gone for almost ten minutes. When he came back, he seemed calmer. The driver asked him if he was alright, and he said he was much better. He laid back against the side of the van, and almost went to sleep. I asked the driver if he was okay, and he said he just needed a "boost." Whatever that was.

We spent a lot of time with them that night, and the guy in the back seemed sweet, once he woke up. I guess Willow made an impression on him because she gave him her number. They started dating, and I found out what a boost was—it was when he shot up heroin. That didn't sit well with me, but when we would hang out with them, they were all so nice, it was hard to not be glad we met them. Until the weekend my parents went away.

Ivy had told my parents I could stay with her while they went to a wedding, but she thought they should leave her a key, "just in case" I needed anything. Of course, that was a rouse for using my house to party while they were gone. My dad had talked with Willow's parents as well because we thought it would be fun for her to stay at Ivy's also. Her parents called Ivy and did the usual drill about everything. Ivy was very convincing, so it was approved.

As soon as my parents left, Willow called our friends and Ivy picked up some vodka and let us into my house. The guys showed up soon after, and Ivy stayed for a while as well. She set up the bar in the family room and the party commenced. All was well until I came upstairs and found Willow's boyfriend passed out on the living room couch, with a needle still in his arm. His color was off, very pale, even his lips looked white. I screamed for Ivy, and everyone came running upstairs. One of the guys said, Man, he's done it again!" I asked what "again" meant and he said OD'd. I was horrified! Was he dead? The same guy felt for a pulse, and said he could feel it, but it was weak. I ran for the phone and called for an ambulance before anyone could stop me. When I announced what I had done, I got barraged with how stupid I was, how much trouble he would get in, and even Ivy said someone would report to my parents they had seen an ambulance in front of the house I wasn't supposed to be in.

I thought I had done the right thing, but now I felt like an idiot. Ivy told his two friends we had to get him moved to her house right away. She rushed home and sent JD on a grocery run, and told all the girls to go to bed. When she came back, they were wrapping him in a sheet to carry him over. The ambulance arrived at my house, and Ivy told them the address was wrong, and led them to her house. I was amazed at her ability to lie so convincingly. His friends said he had overdosed, and the paramedic gave him Narcan and he woke immediately. He looked around asking where he was, and Ivy told him, and then asked him and his friends to leave. Willow said nothing. None of us did. That was the end of hitchhiking for Willow. But not our friendship. She apologized profusely for causing all the problems that night. We spent the rest of the weekend with Ivy.

During my sophomore year, I had made friends with a senior, Tim, who was in my French class. He was very nice and as we got to know each other, we soon talked about sneaking out at night just to ride around and talk. I would sneak out and he would pick me up just down the street and we would ride around a few hours. When I told Willow about this, she thought it would be fun to join us. We started picking her up, and we would drive for a while, then just sit and talk. Nothing more. We did this for several months. Our game was up when Willow's parents discovered she was missing, and waited for her to come home. During the interrogation, she told them who Tim was, but didn't mention me. Because Tim was 18, and Willow was 15, Willow's dad called Tim's parents, threatening to charge Tim with statutory rape if it ever happened again. It didn't.

In June of my sophomore year, Mom and Dad announced we were going on a camping trip to New Hampshire to visit family and friends in New England. This was going to include visiting the Copeland's, who had a cabin on a lake. (You may remember the Copelands as the people we went horseback riding with back in Wheaton.) I asked if I could please have a friend come with me, and Dad approved of Willow coming. He rented a camper, and we did some additional camping along the way. When we got to the Copeland's, Dad set the camper up in the driveway next to the cabin. Willow and I slept in it. It was so beautiful there. I thought how lucky this family was.

The Copeland's had four kids, three boys and a girl. The oldest boy, Andrew, was my age and I had had a crush on him since we were young. This is also the family I stayed with a few weeks after Mom's accident. Andrew and I had done everything together at that time. I had really liked him. And nothing had changed for me. I still liked him. And I had the feeling it was mutual.

They had a boat, so we did a lot of water skiing. Well, they did a lot. I think I got up one time. Andrew was great and would slalom right off the boat dock. I thought that was the coolest thing. About the third day, it was obvious Andrew's younger brother was interested in Willow. He was two years younger than Andrew and me, but only a year younger than Willow. We went for walks around the lake and hung out in the camper, playing cards and board games. It was a blast.

One day, Dad took us into the local town to get some groceries. Willow and I found a small store that had a café, and we got milkshakes. There were six guys there, sitting at the table next to us; some of them were kind of smallish. Of course, Willow started talking to them, and there was one in particular whom she talked with the most. It turned out they worked at the local race-track, two of them were jockeys and the rest were trainers and stable hands. The one Willow liked, Josh, was a trainer. It wasn't long before Dad came to get us, but not before they had exchanged phone numbers. Every chance Willow got to be near a pay phone, she would call Josh. On the last day we were there, she said she was going to meet him, and asked me to cover for her.

That evening, Andrew asked me to go out on the boat with him. Just the two of us. Didn't need to ask me twice. Parents approved and we were on the water. Andrew had driven the boat out to the middle of the lake, and then it started sputtering. He said, "Uh, oh. We're out of gas. Not sure what we are going to do." He was wearing a smug grin, so I didn't know what to think, but I relaxed, and we just floated, and talked. And talked. And talked. It was won-derful. We watched the sun set from the middle of the lake, and I thought I had never experienced anything more special—having Andrew there was pretty cool, too. When the sun went down, he went back to the front of the boat, and it started right up. He smiled, and I knew then, he had been joking about running out of gas. I had warm fuzzies all over. When we got back, the parents were playing bridge, so no one even asked about Willow. Andrew and I went into the kitchen and played some games, until Willow came back.

Our parents played well into the night. Andrew's brother had joined us, so we stayed up as well. It was past 2 a.m. when the parents told us to go back to the camper and go to bed, and for Rick and Andrew to go to bed too. Willow had lots to tell me about her date. She really liked this guy and wanted to figure a way to get back up here to see him. I couldn't think about anything except Andrew.

Early the next morning, Mom and Dad were packing up, and Mom want-ed us out of her way. My brother was helping Dad, so Willow and I went into the cabin, and she fell asleep in the recliner, and I laid down on the couch. I was so tired; I fell asleep right away. Something woke me, and when I opened my eyes, Andrew was sitting in the rocking chair beside me, and I immediately started apologizing for falling asleep, but he assured me it was no problem. "I was just looking at you." We talked a long time, and the warm fuzzies I had felt the night before, were even fuzzier now. I'm not sure my feet touched the ground when I got up, but I was flying high. I woke Willow, and we helped finish packing down the camper. Saying goodbye was so hard. I had no idea if or when I might see him again. I knew it wouldn't be soon enough. And that ended our trip to New Hampshire. Well, at least for that week.

After a lengthy time of listening to Willow whine about how much she wanted to see Josh again, we decided to ask Ivy if she would take us back up there. I told Willow she had to do the asking. I didn't like making requests for anything because Ivy already did so much for me. So, Willow asked, Ivy said yes, and the plans were made. She would call both sets of parents, and explain we were going to her family's summer beach cottage in New Jersey, and we would be gone five days. Everyone was cool with the plans and after she made excuses to JD and the girls, we were set to leave in a couple weeks. She had even talked JD into letting her drive his Impala convertible instead of the station wagon. Very cool!

Willow had told Josh we were coming, and filled him in about Ivy. He suggested a motel where we could stay, and he would invite some of his friends. It was a twelve-hour trip and when we arrived, I was exhausted but also was psyched at the idea of possibly seeing Andrew again. We checked into the motel, and Willow immediately called Josh, and when he arrived, two other guys were with him. Ivy had brought a lot of booze, including beer and wine, so the partying commenced. I wasn't in a party mood; my mind was set on seeing Andrew. The guys stayed until 2 a.m. and I could finally sleep.

The next day, we went to the track where the guys worked, and we were introduced to a lot of Josh's friends. A couple of them were older, and Ivy didn't miss a beat inviting them to our next party. I had no interest in any of these guys. Right now, my attention was on seeing the horses! There were so many of them, and they were all very well kept. When we had toured all the stables, Ivy was ready to leave. Willow wanted to stay. I wanted to call Andrew. So, we left Willow at the stables, and Ivy and I split.

We found a nice place and got lunch, and I found a pay phone. Andrew's mom answered and was very friendly, and thought I was calling from home. She asked if she could speak to my mom after Andrew and I talked. Ugh! I lied and said Mom was out. I don't know why I didn't say I was in NJ. I guess when you start lying, it's just easier to keep going. When Andrew got on the phone, he sounded glad to hear from me, and just talking to him made my heart pound in my chest. I told him I was back in New Hampshire and asked if we could get together. He asked about the details, and when I told him, he said we better plan it when his parents were out. They were to play Bridge the following night with some friends, and he said I could come to the cabin. I couldn't wait.

Ivy and I did some shopping and then went back to pick up Willow. One of the older guys Ivy was interested in asked if he could follow us, and she had no hesitations. Also, a guy from the night before, who seemed to like me, asked if he could come too. And there was a jockey who also followed. We got to the motel, and no one wasted any time in getting smashed. The guy Ivy was with had brought some weed, as well, so they were all lit. I did some drinking, but not much. I didn't like the other two guys who were there, and just wanted them to leave.

I wasn't much interested in what Ivy and Willow did. My focus was on the next night. Ivy and her guy had gone for a ride, and Willow and Josh were out walking, so I turned on the TV, and asked the two remaining guys what they wanted to watch. The jockey sneered and left, and the other guy, the one who liked me, said anything I wanted to watch. Wherever he sat, I sat somewhere else, and he finally got the hint. He ordered pizzas, so we just ate, drank, and watched TV until everyone came back and Ivy's buddy took everyone back to the stables. Willow laid on her bed and confessed her love for Josh, ad nauseum. I told them about my plans to see Andrew, so Ivy said she would drive me to the cabin the next day. I was counting the hours.

The next day we went out to the stables and spent the afternoon on a lake which was just down the road from the track. The guys made a delicious picnic lunch, and filled a cooler with Hop'n Gator—the only beer/ale I liked. It was a cool, sunny day and we had a great time. Because I was seeing Andrew, I took it easy on the ale. By late afternoon, we wrapped it up.

Everyone at the picnic followed us back to the motel, and then Ivy took me to meet Andrew. Willow wanted me to invite him to join us, but I didn't think that was the best idea. When I got to the cabin, Andrew was sitting on the porch waiting for me. We couldn't take out the boat, so we went for a walk. It was a cool evening and all the nervousness I felt began to dissipate. I liked him so much and found it unbelievable that he might like me also. After our walk, we sat on the porch facing the lake. It was beautiful. He asked how long I was staying, and I told him, but it didn't seem there was a possibility of seeing each other again.

Ivy came to get me at 11p.m. and saying goodbye was even harder than last time. I asked him not to tell his mom about my visit, since my parents thought I was in NJ. He promised he wouldn't. We hugged and said goodbye. I had hoped for a kiss, but it didn't happen, and that felt like rejection. It didn't take much for me to jump on that train. Going back to the motel was difficult, and I talked myself into believing there could never be anything between us since we lived so far apart. Their home was in Seattle, and that was 3,000 miles away. I also didn't think I was attractive enough for him. I mean, he would have kissed me if I was pretty. Right? So many negative messages swirled in my head on the ride back. I drank a lot that night, and was ready to go home.

The next twenty-four hours was a blur, and Ivy drank herself into oblivion. I didn't think I had ever seen her that buzzed. The guy she liked didn't show on our last night there, so she substituted the alcohol for him. But that was her MO. Willow was in her own oblivion—the "I am so in love!" euphoria. I just felt depressed and rejected. So, when Willow said Josh was coming back with us, I didn't even care. That would be Willow's obsession for the next several weeks, till he moved on, or she did.

When we told her the next morning, Ivy didn't care about the extra person. She wasn't caring about much at all. She was so hung over, she asked me to drive. This was a huge clue that she was seriously in bad shape. Me, drive JD's precious convertible?!? I hoped he never found out. I'd only had my license for about eight months.

We packed up, and headed out. By the time we hit I-95, I was the only one awake. Lots of thoughts were going through my head, none of them making me feel any better. I had never been good enough, and I never would be. No matter how hard I tried, I was always going to get the short end of the stick. Why was I even born? As these thoughts simmered to a full boil, I looked down and saw the speedometer needle was hovering over 110 mph. I had a quick but scary thought that I would take it all the way to 120, and see what happened. I look back on that now and it seems surreal. Speeding down I-95, I wanted to see how fast that car could go. *Or was it something else?* What little common sense I had left, stopped me, and I slowed back to the speed limit. After another ten miles, I realized my whole body was trembling uncontrollably. Major adrenalin rush. A feeling that was familiar to me, but was still overwhelming. I almost stopped the car; I was shaking so badly, but pushed through. Swallowed that one. I still can't believe I didn't get pulled over. Another mystery.

Years later, when I realized what my true intentions were in this incident, it haunted me how dangerously close I came to being successful. Suicidal ideation was not part of my conscious thinking, but it was present. This was another step in my risk-taking behaviors.

Josh hung around for about six weeks, and then he told Willow he was going to Baltimore to try and get a job at Pimlico. Apparently, Ivy had told him that was where she and JD went every week, and she had offered to give him a ride. Willow was not happy, but since she was 16 years old and he was 24, her opinion didn't matter much. The night before he left, we all went out to Lake Frank, built a fire, and got lit. He seemed like a nice guy, but there was nothing for him in Rockville. He was a horse person, and he wanted a job where he could work with them. So, the next day he was gone.

We were a few months into our junior year, when Willow had met some older girls who liked to party, and they would come pick us up anytime we wanted. They always seemed to know where to find a party, so on the weekends when they worked late, we either had to sneak out or not go. So, we snuck out. It was always from my house because of the incident with Tim. We were not going to take any more chances with her parents. We got away with this for a while but eventually we got too slack, and I guess we woke up Dad when we left on this particular night.

Of course, we had no way of knowing this and unbeknownst to us, he had tied a string to his wrist, and then to the washroom door, so when we snuck back in, and opened the door, the string would yank his hand and awaken him. It did. He had staked us out. He screamed like a man possessed, no words, just screamed. I think the purpose may have been to scare us, and he was successful. He told us to sit down while he called Willow's parents. After they picked her up, Mom came down to the family room, too, and Dad lost control. He was yelling, and hitting me, then threw me on the floor. Mom brought him a pair of scissors and told Dad to cut off all my hair because "she thinks she is so beautiful!" I begged Dad not to do it, and though he didn't, the slaps and punches followed me to my room that night. I was grounded a long time, and as far as our parents were concerned, the days of Willow and I being friends were over.

Willow's parents were convinced her behavior was the result of some form of mental illness, and had her admitted to the Psychiatric Institute of Washington, DC. There was one much closer in Montgomery County, but I guess they didn't want the proximity of her friends to be an issue. It didn't matter to us, we found a way to go visit, and I still don't know how we got away with it, but we did. A car full of us went to visit her a handful of times while she was there before we were barred. She was so drugged up; she didn't seem like Willow. The second time we visited she told us she was on suicide watch, and that's why we had to be searched when we came in. It was hard for me to believe Willow would ever think of checking-out. But heck, I had. And more than once.

I don't know what happened to Willow. I don't know how long she was in the hospital. And I don't know what happened to her after she got out. She didn't come back to school and her private phone was disconnected. She is one I have thought about a lot. In her family she was the IP, or "identified person." The one on whom the family blames all their problems. Willow was no different than me. She just wanted to be loved and accepted for who she was. She was never able to live up to her parents' standards—and like myself, she quit trying. She rebelled. I know nothing about her family history, so I can't speak to that, but I saw a lot of parallels in our behaviors.

My self-talk after leaving Andrew that night was not unlike hers after Josh left. Andrew had done nothing wrong. I just assumed the worst because that's all I had known. I had "black and white" thinking. Either everything was all good or it was all bad. Also known as crisis thinking—it keeps you in a constant state of anxiety and stress. It's the adrenalin rush I mentioned earlier. Willow had the same reactions.

I know we were out of control, but it wasn't because we were bad kids, it was because we never felt accepted. Never felt good enough. We felt ignored. Allow me to reiterate a very important truth. When asked, "What is the opposite of love?" most everyone answers—hate. But it takes energy to hate someone. That's why a lot of kids push their parents by misbehaving—so they can get some form of attention—even if it's negative attention. At least you know you exist when someone puts out the energy to yell at you, or spank you.

No, the opposite of love is being disregarded. Rejected. Neglected. Abandoned. Ignored. And Willow and I were very familiar with these.

Isn't it interesting that those are the words many orphans have used to describe their feelings?

27

Tim

Supporting Role

Tim is someone I remembered as I started writing this book. He played a very positive role in my life, and one that will be presented a bit differently because he served as my memory in some places that were missing. He was a senior when I was a sophomore, and the memories I had of him were of a person who rescued me when I was in trouble. Usually that trouble centered around having had too much to drink, or hitchhiking somewhere and needing a ride. And Tim would pick me up from wherever I was, feed me coffee until I was sober, and then take me home. Otherwise, I probably would have hitchhiked in that condition, and I guess Tim tried to prevent the possible repercussions of that mess.

The other memories I had of Tim were of sneaking out at night, and just hanging with him. I addressed some of this when I shared Willow's story, but not in full detail. We did quite a bit of this late-night rendezvousing before Willow joined us. What I remembered the most about Tim was him being one of the few safe places I had. And the crux of that, I now realize, was his faith in God. Though he tried to share that faith with me, I was absolutely resistant to hear it. But something within me convinced me he was a safe person.

I mentioned earlier, after the event with Rose, it seemed my ability to remember a lot of my sophomore year had been wiped out—most likely due to a dissociative trauma response. So, when Tim's name came to mind, the things I shared above were all I had in my memory bank. But I was interested in knowing if he would be able to fill in some gaps for me, and so I began to search for him. I had a Facebook site I used to keep up on our high school happenings, so I posted a note that I was searching for Tim, and I got a lead, and an email address. Tim did not remember my name, but when I sent a picture, he recognized me, and he was able to fill in some lost time for me.

To help the reader understand, trauma can cause many different responses in our psyche. The most protective, as I shared about earlier regarding children, is a complete loss of time, known as dissociation. It's an involuntary detachment from reality and a defense mechanism that allows you to continue surviving after a painful, traumatic experience. It's a component of the flight or fight response, and when you can do neither of those, you freeze—and you disconnect. For me, this happened after the traumatic event with Rose. There are just huge pieces of time missing from that year, and re-connecting with Tim, helped me to remember many of them.

Tim filled me in on all the events I shared in Willow's story. Those memories were not in my bank. He was the senior I referred to, and he reminded me we had met in French class. I had no memories of us getting caught, but maybe that was because Willow didn't disclose my name to her parents, so it wasn't as huge for me as it was for Tim. I found it remarkable, as I received the information from Tim, how these memories were triggered to return. It was like getting a piece of my life back—a piece that was good . . . and fun . . . and safe. One story he shared with me made me laugh out loud! It was the story about how he accomplished this whole sneaking out business. So well planned. So meticulous. So humorous. It made me remember how important those high school relationships were to us. Here is how it went:

"My dad had a Chevy Nova and somehow, I found out I could disconnect the odometer so the mileage wouldn't change. This was important because my dad kept meticulous records of gas and mileage. So, I would disconnect the odometer, put the car in reverse, and roll it down the driveway. We lived on a cul-de-sac at the top of a small hill. So, all I had to do was get the car into the road and gravity would start it rolling down the hill. I'd wait until I got to the bottom before turning the car and headlights on. I'd drive to your place, pick you up, then we'd drive over to the other girl's place and pick her up. Then we'd drive around for a while and eventually park some place and hang out together and just talk."

The extent kids will go to hang out together! These were very fond memories, and I am so grateful to Tim for giving them back to me. I had few places in my life then where I felt completely safe, and this was one of them. But there was a bigger reason I felt safe with Tim. One I didn't appreciate at the time because of my father's anti-God beliefs, and my mom's on-again, off-again church attendance. Tim constantly told me how much God loved me and how much He cared for me. Tim told me he prayed for me and wanted to see me in safer places doing safer things. I had shared my hitch-hiking "fun" with him and even some of the experiences I had. Tim didn't judge me, he prayed for me. He didn't dump me because I lived a different lifestyle than he did in his home. He witnessed to me instead.

Tim was also one of the first people I can remember who really complimented me on my good qualities. When he was brought to my mind at the inception of this book, I looked him up in my high school yearbook, and found a beautiful and encouraging message from him, telling me I was a "warm and kind person and there should be more like you." This led me to begin to read what others had said as well. As I shared, my memories of my sophomore year were not only few, but what I did remember, were not pleasant. However, what I discovered was shocking. The kinds of things Tim had shared in his note, were repeated by almost every person who signed my yearbook. Dozens of entries of kids telling me how funny and sweet I was and how much they enjoyed my company. I even found several teachers sharing the same compliments.

This was yet another reminder of the damage trauma can do to the brain. I had blanked out all the good, and only recalled the negative and the painful. Negative bias. I could imagine myself reading those notes at the time they were written, and completely dissing them as false. My low self-esteem and feelings of worthlessness were primary to my self-image and my self-talk. It hurts to even remember I was like that.

As I write about Tim, I realize the gratitude I have for him and how he has given me back some of my missing pieces. Some fun pieces. I have gratitude for how this book was first initiated and why, and how sovereign our God is to hear our prayers and answer them. Not always in the way we expect, and not always without walking through some fire. But always knowing Jesus is about to do something miraculous as He walks us further down that hard road of healing. Healing all those places that never should have been wounded. Most of all I have gratitude for the love shown to me by a loving and compassionate God, my Daddy, who through his desire to give me back all the enemy has stolen, included pieces of my memory that encompassed the good times, the fun times, and the times where He had strategically placed a person in my life to speak life into my mess. To speak truth into my heart. Tim was another of the "mysteries" being revealed to me throughout my life.

28

Marty

Supporting Role

During the summer before my junior year, I met a girl at the community pool, Darla, and we became fast friends. She lived close to the pool, so I would go to her house a lot. And the added bonus for me was her cute younger brother. She was a year older than me, and he was a year younger. Some chemistry started between us, and after several months of hanging at their house, one night he walked me out to my car and kissed me good night. That was the beginning of my first real "love" interest. I had stayed true to my mother's teaching that a girl should remain a virgin till she was married. Through all the stuff with my friends, all the parties, all the drugs and alcohol, and all of Ivy's hotel weekends, I had stayed true to that belief. But I had also longed desperately to feel loved. To feel wanted. To feel safe in someone's arms. I thought Marty could fill all those roles. So, I hoped.

I had just turned 17, and talking to my parents about boyfriends was a conversation that was never going to happen, so I turned to Ivy. And her answer to my quandary was to have sex so I could see what "real love" felt like. She said that was what love was all about. I found this interesting since Dad had inferred a similar belief.

When I was 16, Dad came up to my room with two books. One book was for women, *The Sensuous Woman* by J, a book that taught you how to please men sexually, and the other was for men, *The Sensuous Man* by M, a book showing men how to please women. He told me if I memorized all these things, I would never be without a man in my life. So, love and sex became synonymous for me. If I wanted to be loved, all I had to do was perform well in the sack. This would promise me not just a man, but happiness, love, and, at some point, marriage. So, Ivy's suggestion lined up perfectly with what Dad had instilled in me.

As Marty and I got more involved, my former boundaries were going by the wayside. I longed to feel the love she talked about. And Marty had said he loved me, and I believed him. He was also a virgin, and seemed committed to me. I had no birth control and already had two friends who had gone through abortion last year, so I didn't want that to happen to me. But I had no one to turn to except Ivy. And she said she was going to set me up. And she did,

She supplied the place—her bedroom. She supplied the ambience—incense and candles. She supplied the relaxation—the Asti Spumante. She also supplied the sexual stimulation—the pornographic movie. And she left me the key to get into her house while everyone was gone. So, I picked up Marty and we entered the devil's den. We drank the wine. Watched only a few minutes of the movie, and just like that—I wasn't a virgin anymore. Ivy let us use her house a lot for our trysts. And the basement of my house became a regular rendezvous spot, as well. It didn't stay that way. Dad came down to the basement one day, while we were on the couch, under a blanket. He told me to get up and I wouldn't, so he just went back upstairs. We settled on Ivy's house after that.

Here is another place where a "mystery" dogged me for so many years. Looking back, I could never understand why I didn't get pregnant. We didn't use any protection. And we were sexually active for over six months. I was as regular as clockwork, and on only one occasion was I late. Really late. And I was scared. I had tried to talk to Ivy, but she had no ideas to help me, and zero spiritual advice.

Now, I had not met Jesus yet, and it would be another sixteen years before that would happen, but I had been praying every night since I had moved to Rockville. No idea why. I just got on my knees and each night, I prayed this prayer,

"God, please bless Mom, Dad, Aunt Ruby, and my brother and don't let anything happen to them. And please forgive me for any commandments I have broken or any sins I have committed. Thank you. Amen."

Where I learned that, or why I started praying it, is another "mystery." But it started when we moved there, and it didn't stop, all through high school. So, because I was late, I took myself, with my prayer, to the Methodist church I had attended with my mom on Easter. No one was there. I just walked in, sat at a pew, and prayed that I would not be pregnant. I cried, begged, and pleaded that I would start my period. I went home and prayed again that night it would come. And the next day, it did.

Marty and I had lots of fun together. We went on a lot of picnics and sometimes we would even travel up to the mountains in Thurmont, MD, and visit

Cunningham Falls to have a picnic. I have always loved nature, and having a picnic next to a waterfall, with the person I thought I loved, just couldn't get any better. We also packed picnics and went to DC to the National Zoo, and a few times to the National Mall and saw all the museums. It felt like we enjoyed our time together.

I lived and breathed to spend time with Marty. When we were not together, I felt lost. Of course, I didn't realize these were early warning signs of codependency showing themselves. And I wouldn't know that for twenty more years. But I am sure after a while it became suffocating for him. I didn't want him to do anything with anyone except me, and all my friends had taken a backseat as well. So, when things became increasingly uncomfortable, and I started to feel as if he was pulling away, the fear of losing him was terrifying. To have someone to hold and to be held, to feel wanted and loved, and to have someone to share life with was incredible, and I couldn't lose it. But I would.

As in most times I was happy, I should have expected, this too would end, or be taken from me. Darla had become very jealous of my relationship with her brother, and the time we spent together. In my codependent stupor, I had abandoned all my friends to spend every waking moment with Marty. She decided to break us up and started inviting Marty to join she and another friend, Kathleen, when they went out. And he went. And they started to hit it off. He started making more and more excuses to not get together with me. I learned through the grapevine he was hanging out with Kathleen a lot. I think worse for me, I had her in a lot of my classes. It was torture to see her. I couldn't take responsibility for my part in the breakup. I didn't even recognize I had a problem.

When Marty started to make the break with me, to say I fell apart would be a misnomer. I was completely devastated. When this relationship had started, we had used a pin to carve each other's initials in our hands. Every time I looked at mine, I cried. When he finally told me he was breaking up with me, I couldn't accept it. A few days later, I even faked an assault, making superficial cuts in my back. I called and told him I had to see him, so I could tell him what had happened to me. I fabricated a wild story of being assaulted in a parking lot. He wasn't impressed. I made statements like I couldn't live without him, and I would rather die than lose him. Nothing worked. It was over, and I needed to accept it. But I didn't know how I could. So, I started drinking again.

Just reading my words above is embarrassing. Well, maybe embarrassing is the wrong word. It's more of a capsule in time where I can see how far I have come. How very unhealthy I was then. How desperate I was for attention. For love. These are some of the signs and symptoms being played out from my prior traumas. Some of these could appear histrionic, and then I could throw in some borderline symptoms. A lot of drama, and a lot of neediness and control. Around this same time, I also remember exhibiting some obsessive-compulsive disorder (OCD) symptoms. I couldn't leave my room in the morning without flipping my light switch seven times. I was certain if I didn't perform that ritual, something bad would happen to me. I was in desperate need of professional help. But I didn't know how to get it, and my parents were not interested in it.

And the breakup with Marty was about to throw open the floodgates.

29

Shang

"I keep fighting voices in my mind that say I'm not enough,
Every single lie that tells me I will never measure up,
Am I more than just the sum of every high and every low?
Remind me once again just who I am, because I need to know."
Lauren Daigle

Leading Role

During the fall of my senior year, I really worked to keep my grades up, and was succeeding. On the weekends, Camellia and I still went hitchhiking. One Saturday night, a guy pulled over and offered us a ride. He looked middle eastern, and had an accent, and was really cute. He was driving a pale-yellow VW bug, so Camellia and I had to decide who was riding shotgun, and I got that spot. He introduced himself as Shang, and then asked us our names. I couldn't discern his accent, so I asked where he was from, and he said Persia, but I thought he said Paris. Camellia said his accent didn't sound French, and he said, "No, I am from Persia—or Iran." So that cleared up his appearance and his accent.

Driving down Rockville Pike, he stopped at McDonald's and bought us dinner, and then asked where we were going. I was embarrassed to say we were just looking for a party, so I lied and said we were going to White Flint Mall. He drove us there, talkative the whole time. He seemed like a really nice guy. When he dropped us off, he asked me for my phone number, and I gave it to him. He then wrote down his, and handing it to me, asked if he could take me out sometime. I said sure, and told hm to give me a call.

I really didn't expect him to call, but he did, and we went out and had an enjoyable time. We went to dinner and a movie and then back to my house. Sitting in front of my house, we talked for close to an hour. I really liked him, so when he leaned in for a goodnight kiss, it was a no brainer. Coming into the house, my dad asked where I had been. I told him I had been on a date, but there were no questions about with who, how we met, or a request to meet him. Just this, "Hope you had a good time." A protective and invested father would have saved me so much pain.

Our relationship escalated exponentially within a few weeks. We had not had sex, but we were together whenever he wasn't working or in classes. I knew he was older because he was taking classes at Montgomery College, but the discussion of age had not come up yet. I finally asked and he said he was 27. His birthday was in January like mine, so he was almost exactly ten years older than me. I was okay with that since he was so nice. Plus, he was such a hunk, I didn't really care how old he was. When he met my parents, my mother acted like a blushing teenager, and after he left, she went on incessantly about how handsome he was. "He looks like a really nice guy, Karin! And so handsome! Don't do anything to mess it up!" Yep, my mother, the cheerleader.

When we celebrated two months together, he took me out for dinner, and afterwards bought some champagne. I told my parents I was spending the night with Camellia, and went to his apartment. It was the first night we were intimate, and I finally felt loved again since Marty and I had broken up. *This love/sex thing had become knitted together in my mind. Like they were inseparable.* There was a major hiccough that night, however. Why I answered his question the way I did is unbeknownst to me. My best guess was my fear of losing him, so when he asked me if I was a virgin, I said "yes." It seemed to be very important to him, and I did what I felt I had to do to maintain the relationship. This was in the top ten bad choices I had made up to this point in my life.

Shang knew how much I loved dogs and so had promised to get me one. He took me to a pet shop in a little strip mall in Twinbrook. I looked at all the puppies, but really didn't see any I was drawn to. Just outside, in the parking lot was a young boy with a laundry basket, and there were three little puppies in it. I stopped to look, and he explained they were six weeks old, and if he didn't get rid of them, his dad was going to drown them. That was all I needed to hear! I played with all three of them and asked what breed they were. He explained their female German shepherd had been in heat, and a fox got to her. That explained some of the coloring. The two bigger puppies looked more like the shepherd, but the small one was all red. He told me she was the runt, and his favorite because she liked to snuggle. So, I took her home.

My dad said there was no way we were having a dog. Mom overruled, and she found an old wardrobe box from our move and helped me set it up in my room. Shang saw little white spot under her chin, and said it looked like a beard, and suggested Reesh as her name—which means "beard" in Persian. So Reesh it was, or Reesh-ie as I called her. She may have been the best dog I ever had. That year, I had inherited my dad's VW convertible which he had totaled. He had fixed it up enough for me to drive, and she would stay in my

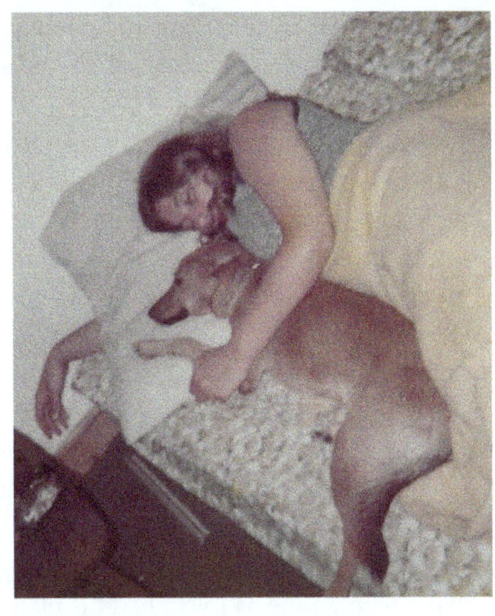

car, with the top down, no matter how long I was gone. Never had a single accident in the house—even as a puppy. She loved me as much as I loved her. We were attached! If you saw me, Reesh was close behind.

Shang and I also did everything together. He didn't want me to hang with my friends if we could be together. So, as with Marty, my friends took a back seat. We doubled on a few occasions with Camellia and her boyfriend from Delaware, who came down to visit a few times each month. We would go dancing wherever there was a good band. When we were at these places, Shang always walked me to and from the bathroom. He must love me so much.

In the spring, we went to a large celebration at the Iranian Embassy for one of their holidays. Shang wasn't Muslim, he was raised in the Baha'i faith, but he told me this celebration was a Muslim holiday, and since he had worked in the palace for the Shah, he had received an invitation. My mother made my dress, and it was beautiful! It was a long gown. I felt like a princess. The event was over the top. There were all kinds of food, and some of the various khoresh dishes Shang had already taught me how to make. Khoresh is like a stew, usually has a type of meat, lots of spices and veggies. It felt good to be familiar with so many of the recipes.

It was a lovely evening, and I felt very special in my new dress. He told me many people had shared with him how beautiful I was. Of course, they were speaking Persian so I didn't understand, but after they walked away, he would tell me. I noticed how vigilant he was in keeping me close to him. It was the first time I realized Shang acting possessively. He didn't want me to talk to anyone else unless he was with me, even accusing me of flirting with someone there. He seemed to accept my apology, and nothing else was said. But this was my first warning sign.

When his summer semester ended, he and two of his friends were going to Iran for at least six weeks. I couldn't imagine how I was going to live without seeing him every day. I was a mess. He warned me about hanging with my friends. I had hardly done any drinking since I had been with him, but he knew when I hung with Camellia and her boyfriend, we got ripped. I promised I would be on my best behavior.

I went to the airport with him, crying the whole time as I watched his plane take off. That night I called Camellia, and she invited me to spend the night. Yep, we

drank. She told me about a friend of ours, Greg, who had bought a horse and suggested we go see it. I was on that like white on rice.

Greg had bought this beautiful chestnut mare, a quarter horse, but didn't know how to ride yet. I would go with him after school and groom her, and then ride. I helped him learn how to use a curry comb and brush her out, put on her saddle and bridle, and eventually he rode her. We had a great time, and I spent many days with them. The weather was starting to turn cooler, and I explained to Greg how frisky horses can be in the winter, and to ride her as often as he could.

One afternoon, after Greg and I finished riding, it began to rain, so we left early. I was driving my parents' Pontiac and going the speed limit, but when rounding a corner, the car hydroplaned, and crashed into a huge oak tree. These were the days before seatbelts, and we hit with such force, my face bounced off the steering wheel. Greg was holding his arm, but said he was ok. I opened my mouth to say something, and blood poured down my chin. Apparently, my lip had gone over the steering wheel and my teeth under it, and the inside of my upper lip had split all the way up beneath my nose. Looking in the mirror, I touched my nose, and the whole thing moved in a way it shouldn't. Like it wasn't attached to my face anymore. Someone had called an ambulance, and Greg was taken to one hospital, and I was taken to Bethesda Naval Hospital.

The plastic surgeon who saw me explained to me all the damages, and explained it would take a lot of time to heal. No stitches needed. When Dad came, he was with Ivy. I wasn't surprised Mom didn't come. He told Dad what had happened and what the prognosis was. He wanted to see me back in two weeks.

Mom took me to that appointment, and when he finished examining me, said I was good to go unless he could help me with anything else. I asked if I could get my nose fixed. He asked me what I wanted done and I explained my dad had always said my nose looked like a parrot's. (In truth, I had my mom's nose.) He made a weird face and repeated what I had just said, and asked if my dad had really said that. It didn't seem unusual to me, but he just shook his head, rolling his eyes. He examined me and said he could help me, but I would need to do a lot of healing first. We scheduled my surgery for January. Just ahead of my 18th birthday. I visited Ivy, and told her about the surgery, and she took some pics of my profile and said she thought I would be happy with a new nose. All I cared about was that maybe Dad would finally think I was attractive.

Mom had been giving me quite the cold shoulder since I had totaled her car. She said I destroyed their plans for their annual Ocean City vacation. Going in our VW ruined their plans in her opinion. I admitted it would be really crowded and the friends we went with would probably have to take some of our things in their station wagon. She was not interested in hearing any of this. She had one goal—to make me feel guilty—and it was getting old. By the third week of listening to this, I had had enough.

We were in the hallway between Dad's office and their bedroom, and she started in on me again. I felt the heat rising in my face. I surely didn't plan the accident, and I had certainly paid dearly with my face. My voice was rising, and I asked her why the car was more important to her than what had happened to me. Suddenly Dad came out of their bedroom and backhanded me. It felt like my nose exploded and the evidence of that was the blood on the hallway wall. All the healing that had been accomplished inside my mouth, was now wide open again. I couldn't believe he had done that. No one said anything.

I ran upstairs to my room, got my dog, and walked back down. I stopped to see if either of them had anything to say. An apology. "Are you ok?" "Should I take you to the doctor?" Anything to show they cared. But there was only silence. I went down the next set of steps to the front door, and walked out. I heard, as the door was closing behind me, "Where are you going?" but I didn't miss a step. I was out of there. *Should I really have expected anything different? This had been the norm my whole life.*

I went to Ivy, and asked her to drive me to the best beltway ramp, which was Georgia Avenue. She gave me ice for my face and offered to let me stay with her, but I just wanted to get away from everyone. She drove Reeshie and

I to the ramp, and dropped us off. I didn't know how much luck I would have, but I had intentions on making it to Crisfield. So, I stuck out my thumb. I certainly was no stranger to it.

It only took about ten minutes before a pick-up truck pulled over. I asked him if it was ok for my dog to get in his cab, and then told him she was a fierce protector, so I was just giving him a heads-up. He smiled, and leaned over to let me in. He tried to talk to me, but I just looked out the window. When he asked what happened to my face, I said I had run into a wall. He didn't buy it and I didn't care. He drove me to the Route 50 East exit off 495.

The next ride came almost immediately. It was an 18-wheeler, and I confess, I was scared when he pulled up next to me. He opened the passenger side door and asked me where I was going. I told him Crisfield, and then did my song and dance about how dangerous Reeshie was. He laughed out loud and said he wasn't going to do anything to upset my dog, and for me to get in. I climbed into the cab, and was surprised at how big it was. He had a cross stuck to the front of the cab with a "Jesus Freak" sticker. There was a full-size bed behind the seats. He noticed me looking, and assured me I was safe, then told me about his own kids. He made no mention of my face, and I was glad. I felt tense until he dropped me off in Easton.

The next ride was a green VW bug. *Yes, I seemed to attract them.* The guy was young and seemed nice. I immediately noticed he also had a cross hanging from his mirror, and quite a few stickers about Jesus inside his car. He asked me what happened to my face, and I lied again. He said he didn't believe me, but if I didn't want to talk about it, he understood. He informed me he was a student at the Salisbury State College (now known as Salisbury University), so he was headed that far. He asked where I was headed, and I told him. We didn't talk much, and he played a tape with songs about Jesus. The stress of the day suddenly overwhelmed me, and before I knew it, I was out. I awoke with him shaking me, asking where I was going in Crisfield. When I looked out the window, we were already there! I was so grateful, and then directed him to Aunt Ruby's house.

When we pulled into the driveway, he jumped out and rushed to the front door before I was even able to get out of the car. Aunt Ruby came out, and he was talking with her when I walked up. She was shocked to see my face, and I slipped by her into the house. She invited him in, and offered him something to drink, but he refused and said he just wanted to be sure I was safe. She thanked him, and said, "You're an angel for helping her!" *Truer words may have never been spoken . . . we may have been entertaining an angel.*

I told Aunt Ruby about the accident and what happened to my face, and she was hot. It was one of the few times in my life I had heard her cuss. She called Mom and Dad. I guess Dad answered, and she laid him out. I was not privy to what was said on his side, but Aunt Ruby said I would stay with her for as long as I wanted to. I spent a week with her, and Shang ended up coming to get me. He had come home from Iran, and Mom and Dad told him where to find me. When I got home, nothing was ever mentioned. No apologies were made. No questions about how I got to Crisfield. Just life as usual.

My grades suffered a lot after my surgery. I was spending most of my waking hours with Shang. I missed quite a few days immediately after the operation, and when I did go back to school, it was embarrassing because the swelling was bad, and my face looked deformed. I kept skipping, and if Shang was available, he would pick me up from home or school, and we would hang out. I was 18 now, so I could make my own choices, and the choice ended up being to drop out and take the GED. Shang had become so possessive; he was fine with that.

Camellia and her Delaware boyfriend, Pat, were going to the prom, and she wanted us to go with them. Even though I had dropped out, they still let me buy tickets. Camellia and I were excited to pick out our dresses. Pat was bringing his tux with him, and Shang ordered his as well. We counted down the days.

Prom night arrived, but Pat didn't. Camellia tried and tried to reach him with no response. She had cried most of the day, and told us to go without her. I told Camellia she had her beautiful new dress, and she shouldn't let him ruin her senior prom. So, the three of us got dressed up and headed down to the Mayflower Hotel in Washington, DC. When Shang pulled up to the front door in his VW, Camellia and I had second thoughts. The couples were all arriving in limos and the girls' dresses were far fancier than what we had. See, neither Camellia's parents nor mine had any investment in our prom. There was no taking us shopping to pick out our dresses, no photos taken, no help getting a boutonniere. I would not have even known it was a big deal, if Camellia had not told me. Same with Homecoming, and Senior Banquet. Both of us were ignored during these special events in our lives. Orphaned emotionally. We didn't go to the prom. We went to a bar and went dancing instead.

Driving home that night, I felt so grateful that I had a boyfriend who didn't abandon me—like Pat had abandoned Camellia—I started to feel guilty that I lied to him about being a virgin. It came over me like a wave. I needed to tell the truth. He loved me, and he would understand. So, when we pulled up to my house, I told him. And I totally did not get the reaction I expected. He called me awful names, and ordered me out of his car. Stunned, I started crying, and kept apologizing, but he was adamant. I reached out to hug him, and he smacked me. Right across the face. I was speechless. He called me a few more names, and I finally got out of the car. He drove away before I had even closed the door. Numb, I went into the house, but I had no parents asking how my prom night went or how I was. Just, "Did you lock the front door?" I laid on my bed, in my beautiful dress, wishing I hadn't told him the truth. And still in disbelief that he had hit me. I couldn't lose him. I was so in love, and believed he loved me, too.

I cried most of the night, and in the morning, when my parents finally asked how my night was, I lied. My heart was sick with grief and loneliness. I couldn't function at all. Then he called. He picked me up, and explained how hurt he was by the lie. He said he would stay with me, but I better never cheat on him. I promised him I wouldn't, and then asked him to promise me he would never hit me again. He promised. He wasn't the first liar I had known in my young life.

Shang had moved to a new townhouse that same week of the prom, and he allowed me to bring Reeshie when I came to visit. On this occasion, he wasn't home yet, and he left the back door open for me. He was working nights at a restaurant in DC, and I found a pack of matches from there on his dining room table. Inside was a phone number with a girl's name—Angie. My heart was trip-hammering. I panicked and called the number. I asked the woman who answered if Angie was home. She explained Angie had left that morning to return to England. Apparently, Angie had been their "Au Pair" for the summer and was now going back home. I couldn't speak. My heart felt like it would jump out of my chest. After a brief pause, I asked if I could come talk with her. What was I thinking? I wasn't.

They lived in a very ritzy section of Potomac, and I spent an hour hearing how much this girl was in love with Shang. Apparently, they had spent a few days and nights together. How had I been so oblivious? I thanked her and apologized for intruding, and she dismissed it as "no problem." But it was a big problem. And I needed answers. Though we were still together, things had changed. I could feel it. I just didn't realize how much I would *feel* it.

I went back to Shang's that night and tried to pretend nothing was wrong, but the day's epiphany was too much to keep hidden. He was appalled when I questioned him, and then admitted he had taken Angie to the airport that morning. When I asked how he could do this to us, he told me I got what I deserved for lying to him. Somehow, it didn't feel like equal justice. It felt like betrayal. But I had betrayed his trust as well. So, I swallowed it, and made dinner for us. While we were eating, he started complaining about the food. I apologized, and said I could make something else, but it wasn't the food that was the issue.

He started hitting me, with his fist this time, I dove under the dining room table and crawled to the corner to get away from him. He got as close as he could to me and took off his heavy work shoe, and began beating me in the head with it. Because I was in the corner, I couldn't get away from him. I don't know how many times he hit me, but it stopped when Reeshie attacked him. He turned and started to hit her, but she was fast, and so he went after her. Afraid he would hurt her, I jumped out, and ran to the back door, calling her. She came right away, and I was able to get to my car and get out. He didn't come after me.

The next morning, I was sitting at our kitchen table, eating cereal, while Mom was making lunch for my brother. Our neighbor from across the street, Mrs. Riddle, came over to have coffee with Mom. She was a super sweet lady, and had six kids of her own. She always hugged me, and this time was no different. She came up behind me and hugged my shoulders, and asked me how I was. She could see I was sad, and started rubbing my head asking me what was wrong. She stopped in mid-sentence, and gasped. "What happened to your head, honey? You have lumps all over it! What did you do?" She then asked my mom what happened. Mom looked at me with an inquiring face.

"Shang did it. With a shoe." I wanted Mom to run to me, take me in her arms and tell me how sorry she was this had happened to me. Instead, she turned around and kept cooking. Mrs. Riddle was shocked and asked her if she was going to do anything about "this horrible deed" done to me.

My mom's response? "He is a nice man. She must have done something to make him angry." Mrs. Riddle gasped, and I got up from the table and ran up to my room. I laid on my bed and thought about what Mom had said. Maybe she was right. She probably was. I had lied to him, questioned him, and then didn't make a good dinner. He had done a lot for me, and I probably did deserve it. I didn't want to be alone, and I didn't want to get out of the relationship. So, the cycle continued. I would make him angry, he would teach me a lesson, and afterwards, he would be sorry, and for a time, it was bliss. A honeymoon. Until I did something else to make him angry. So, I lived for the fantasy.

And this began the downward spiral into a domestic violence relationship. With all its twists and turns. The signs had been there long before my "virgin" confession, but I was ignorant to them. I believed his jealousy was an expression of his love for me. He wanted me all to himself. And I certainly wanted to feel loved and desired. No matter the cost. I was so afraid of being alone again, I would get panic attacks. My codependency was peaking. The feelings of abandonment and rejection, that had permeated my formative years, were now setting me up for very poor choices as a person getting ready to face adulthood. The little girl inside me who was scared, terrified, and needing to feel attached to something or someone needed to be given a voice. But instead, was shut down even further. And I swallowed it all.

Four years of my life, I stayed with this man, I even accepted an engagement ring and called him my fiancé. I lived in the domestic violence cycle from set-up to honeymoon. I put up with his infidelities, just like Mom put up with Dad's. I was pressured to accompany him to stripper bars, where he felt I should witness what a "truly sexy woman looks like," while Dad's words about men hating fat women rang in my ears the whole time I watched the show. And I stayed because I thought I deserved it. My parents had not protected me nor had they role-modeled how I should protect myself. No relationship advice. No communication. No help.

Mom had told me the beatings were my fault, and Dad, if he knew of them, certainly didn't go after him. It was understood that this was what I deserved. Those four years became so much more trauma for me. Things that would change the trajectory of my life. And after him would come other men whom I trusted and thought I loved. And they, too, would treat me in ways that are hard to write about. The years of unhealed trauma were catching up to me.

With the knowledge I have now, I realize my mom and her family had experienced domestic violence. Without someone to help them understand it wasn't their fault—to reframe their perspective—they had remained stuck in the cycle. It was an open and gaping wound. It is completely possible Aunt Ruby was a player who helped my mom believe she needed to stay in her first marriage, and put up with the beatings. After all, she had warned her "not to start anything." The inference was if you did, you got what you deserved for rocking the boat. I have wondered if someone had given Aunt Ruby the same message—to stay in her abusive relationship—and not make waves. It would make sense in this tale of generational pain.

My mom did have the advantage of a father who, when he found out the truth, took care of the problem for her. But how unfortunate that Mom never knew he did. She believed the man just left her. So, her insecurities and false thinking remained. How wonderful it would have been for her to know her father was her protector.

My dad never felt protected either. His abandonment and rejection issues started the day his mom died, and they didn't stop, I would venture to say, for his whole life. He wasn't going to protect anyone because no one protected him. He didn't even know what it looked like.

There is a void a girl feels when she does not have her father's approval. His attention. His love. This was the beginning of a long search for what my heart needed. What my heart desired, and what I had been created to receive. God had never intended for me to be hurt. He had never intended for me to feel unloved, unwanted, or rejected. He had created me for much more than this. But it took me a long time to understand that. To unpack that. Years of attempting to undo the condemnation I had lived under in my young life. From one generation to the next, I was passed the baton. And I took it and ran with it.

It would take someone special to help me untangle that mess. To finally hear the truth my spirit thirsted for. *Truth.* Something I was only vaguely familiar with. I needed a knight in shining armor. And he was coming. The rest of THAT story will be told under separate cover, but for now, this is where I lived . . .

"There is a place, deep inside every little girl's heart that longs to be loved and protected by her father. She desires to be adored, to hear loving endearments, to feel precious. She wants to be the twinkle in her daddy's eye. When those things are absent, she develops a void. Add to that, abuse of any form—physical, emotional, mental, or sexual—and the void grows. She desperately tries to fill it with substitutes that she hopes will make her feel less empty inside. Less meaningless. Less hopeless.

Substances—or even people— that allow her to say and do things that she will regret.

With each failure, she becomes needier and more desperate. She thinks if she just has a man who can fill the void, maybe she will be happy. So, she often jumps from one relationship to another in the hope of getting some relief. She rejects the men who are kind to her because they don't fill her need to suffer, to be the victim.

She chooses the ones who treat her as her father did, hoping maybe she can correct that failed relationship. But these, too, are failures because they don't perform the needed exorcism from her bondage. She allows the name-calling, the beatings, and the infidelities because there is an internal message that says she deserves what she gets. And when the man of the hour gets tired of her desperation, he leaves, and she replaces him with another who will do the same. Each man fails because no one can succeed in filling the role of her father. No man can. So, her search continues..."

Forgiven Much, Leslie T. Dean

30

"The Fruit Don't Fall Far from the Tree"

"I will not leave you as orphans. I will come to you." John 14:18

So, I write this last chapter to hopefully help you, the reader, to understand the deep, dark hole generational trauma can dig, and how very hard it is to get yourself out . . . if you continue to ignore the symptoms. And it's even more challenging to help those whom you have unwittingly taken with you. Because when you heal and experience how good it feels, you want those you love to experience the same freedom.

With all I had learned, I had a grand goal for my own kids. This generational mess was going to end! My motto became, "The buck stops here!" A phrase made famous by President Harry S. Truman. Meaning? I am taking responsibility for what has been done so far, and I am not expecting anyone else to be accountable for it. And my grand plan was to get everyone into counseling, and nip all the potential problems in the bud. Too much damage had already been done with my poor choices in men. Men who should have been guiding, leading, and protecting, but instead they rejected, abandoned, and abused. A lot had to be unpacked, undone, and healed.

Here's the part I didn't realize. All those wonderful goals I had were dependent on the people in question wanting to heal. Knowing they needed to heal. And not being afraid to walk the painful road to get there. Those are tall orders when the adults in their lives—the ones who were to be their role models—had not been good examples of healthy behaviors. Tall orders to ask them to tell the truth about situations when fear had controlled most of their thinking and reactions to situations as they were growing up.

So, they didn't talk. Just like I didn't. Because the message has been made clear, *it might not be safe to tell.* I had been an amazing example of how to pretend "all is well." Someone asks, "How are you?" And with a quick smile, my response was, "I am fine. No problems here," I had role-modeled for them what "family secrets" looked like. I had set the example of what victim mentality looked like. And my mother had been that same role model for me. I have shared examples of terrible things happening in our family, and then . . . they were just dropped. As if they had not happened at all.

It's funny when I think about my kids growing up, and how they thought I was so "anal" or overly protective about everything they did. Calling to talk to their friend's parents. Checking up on activities and times. Who was attending the event with them. What an event included. When I could pick them up, or who would be driving them home. And at home—what they watched on TV, what movies they wanted to see, putting parental protection on the computer—all of these were viewed by them as overkill. And maybe sometimes it was. Though the argument I often heard was, "You don't trust me!"—what they didn't understand was—it had nothing to do with them. It had everything to do with me knowing, quite personally, what evil was out there in the world, and how easy it was to invite it into your life. Unknowingly. Unwittingly. And more importantly—regrettably.

They never realized, my one and only objective was to protect them. Protect them from all that I had experienced. The bad choices in my high school years that led to even more trauma that would affect me the rest of my life. I wanted to be everything for them that I had never experienced. I wanted them to know how much I loved them, and so I wanted to be involved in every aspect of their life. The counseling I had received helped me see the areas that had been so unhealthy, and then plan out how to be the best mom I could as I healed from my own wounds.

As a single mom, it wasn't easy, but I loved every minute of it. Being abandoned by their father took its toll on all of us, but I was determined to do my best to be both mom and dad to them. Taking them camping, on picnics, and day trips to the beach (I even took a blow-up pool for the youngest so he wouldn't feel left out of the fun.) We would have "camp-out" every Friday night which consisted of lighting a fire in the family room fireplace, cooking hot dogs, and making s'mores while we watched a movie.

I loved playing with them at every chance, especially wrestling with them on the floor and playing "helicopter." I tried to get them into every sport they wanted to play—baseball, soccer, football, lacrosse. I loved letting them cook with me at every meal—even sitting on the counter when they were too short to reach. Every night I sang worship songs to them and then we all prayed together before saying goodnight. These were the best times of my life.

I did a pretty good job at all of this—for a time. But, as I said before, there was one thing in my life I was so ashamed of, and with which I carried so much guilt, I didn't share it—even with my counselor. So, this left me with unhealed places, which left me open to make another devastating choice. You see, as long as I had no man in my life, I could keep it at bay. But it was there. Waiting for the right moment to raise its ugly head once again. Waiting for the triggers to ignite all the pain afresh. A wound, only superficially healed with a temporary covering that could easily be ripped off to expose the corroded infection below. It had kept me captive—unbeknownst to me. And this new choice was going to bring even more trauma. A choice that would lead both me and my kids down an ugly road. And consequently, it would inject them into this curse of generational trauma. The one thing I had tried so hard to prevent.

When I first read the story of King David and the rape of his daughter, by her half-brother, I thought how much it sounded like my family.

"Her brother Absalom saw her and asked, 'Is it true that Amnon has been with you? Well, my sister, keep quiet for now, since he's your brother. Don't you worry about it.' So, Tamar lived as a desolate woman in her brother Absalom's house. When King David heard what had happened, he was very angry. And though Absalom never spoke to Amnon about this, he hated Amnon deeply because of what he had done to his sister" (New International Version Bible, 1973/2011, 2 Samuel 13:20-22).

All three of these are players in David's story. And remember, David was a "man after God's own heart." But he was a failure as a father. If we apply the generational trauma piece, you will see how he was treated disrespectfully by his father and brothers. Of all the brothers presented to Samuel, he was the only who was not called by his father to be there when Samuel was seeking to anoint the next king of Israel. He was left in the field with the sheep. And in another situation, his brothers made fun of him when he wanted to challenge Goliath. They didn't even want him around when he brought them food from home. He was rejected by his family—and all the baggage that goes with it. So, he didn't learn how to parent. And in this traumatic scene with his sons and daughter, you can witness the generational consequences.

Though angry, David didn't discipline Amnon. According to the law. he should have been stoned for the rape, but the Bible does not share that anything was done. *Family secrets*. And carrying it further, David clearly did not model talking about family issues or crises, because it states Absalom told his sister to keep quiet and forget about it. And Absalom never spoke to Amnon about the rape, but then later in the chapter he has Amnon killed. Yes, the generational mess was now working its way into a third generation, and it didn't stop there. David's children had known nothing else.

And mine hadn't either. They didn't understand the future consequences of keeping silent. Of keeping it inside. They didn't know what I knew. The counselors I took them to, who tried to talk with them, confirmed repeatedly, "there is nothing that can be done until they are willing to talk." No matter how much I wanted them to get well. No matter how much I wanted them to forgive me. No matter how much I tried to offer restitution for my failures, it wasn't going to happen until they were ready. And it was their choice. And it remains their choice.

***

Many people have asked me why I would want to share such private and intimate moments in a book for just anyone to read. I guess my best and most candid answer is, I didn't. I didn't share these things for decades. In fact, the first part of this book I had pretty much never shared. The story of Karin, my younger self, was buried deep in my trauma hiding place, because it hurt too much to think about it, much less talk about it. As I wrote her story, I realized I had only told the stories of the older Leslie—the person who had gone out into the world with a plethora of unhealthy thinking, feelings, and behaviors. I had never addressed the origin of those detrimental symptoms. In retrospect, I am still amazed that I survived.

However, it was a good thing I shared those stories of my later life because they were what my counselors were able to use to begin my journey to heal. And with each stop along the way, as we healed a new place we had discovered, I became more open to hearing truth, and began to have my faulty thinking reframed with facts. These were very significant parts of my life because a lot more happened after high school. A lot more trauma that set me up for making even more unhealthy choices for my future.

For you the reader, to understand the rest of my story, I will share those significant parts again. But they will be told in another book. A book about an orphan looking to belong to anyone who would smile or act like they cared about her. Who settled for things no one should ever allow, in hopes of eventually being loved.

Until she meets her Prince. Her Knight in Shining Armor. The author of all the "mysteries" I have mentioned in this book. The One who was present during the good . . . and the bad. The One who performed miracle after miracle attempting to guide me to Himself. The One who provided a *way* of escape in times of danger, and the One who provided a voice of *truth* and hope when I needed to hear it. The One who gave me back the *life* I was created to have from the beginning. The One who is the Way, the Truth, and the Life.

I realized writing Karin's story, her part of me, was finally allowing her to grow up. She was finally given a voice. A voice hushed even by me. My family's generational traumatic damage had been passed to her, so it started with her, and her story needed to be told . . . because it didn't end with her. Showing what she lived through laid the groundwork for teaching me much about intergenerational trauma, and how insidious it is in families. Because no one realizes there is problem.

The lies—often in the form of gaslighting, and at times during triangulation—have been accepted by the victim, and often the whole family, as truth. A great example of that is in the story of Willow where she was identified as the *IP*- the *identified person*. These are the people who see what is wrong, try to tell, but no one listens to them. This is because they are seen as trying to change the fabric of the family where everyone else feels "comfortable." So, they become the target—the "crazy" one—and the family keeps its unhealthy homeostasis. And when someone tries to help the victim untangle that nasty web—to re-frame the wrong perspectives that were bought—the impression is more gaslighting. Getting to the truth is an arduous journey. Misplaced perceptions practiced for generation after generation are accepted as the norm. I pray the truth I have shared in this book will bring many more to a place of recognizing their own need for re-framing false perceptions, and dig into it, so they too can make the "buck stop here."

So, why would I share such intimate pieces of my life? Because if there is anything I have learned about healing, it's that a person needs hope. Hope in a God who loves us so extravagantly, His mercy and grace are poured out on us like rain. How do you gain that level of hope? For me, it was discovering I wasn't alone. I wasn't unique. I wasn't the only person this stuff had happened to. I witnessed others whose lives had been horrible but were now redeemed because they believed there was a Savior named Jesus who died so they didn't have to carry their burden any longer. People who had seen a Savior reach down into their mess and yank them out of a life where they believed words like "worthless," "crazy," and "rejected" are what defined them. Living as an orphaned child, and believing they were so unlovable, that accepting whatever attention they could grab onto was better than nothing—no matter how much it hurt.

I shared my story, in all its ugliness, because I was one of those people. But I don't live there anymore. My prayer is that anyone who picks up this book, and relates to a few of these stories, will find the hope I found. Will believe, "He did it for her, maybe He will do it for me." Because He will. There is no hierarchy in God's family. We are all His children. We are all his sons and daughters, and no matter where we have been, or what we have done, we are still within the reach of His strong right arm.

He will chase you down and rescue you.

He will love on you as the Savior who died so you could be free.

And He will adopt you into His Kingdom, to be his child . . . for an eternity.

Epilogue

This has been the second book I had no plans to write. When I wrote my first book, *Forgiven Much*, it was only after seven years of feeling the Holy Spirit push me. I finally gave in after becoming disabled at work, and crying out to God, "What am I going to do now?"

To which there was a quick and loud directive, "Write the book." So, I did.

For this second book, it was in February of 2020, just after the Covid lockdown began, and I was alone in my house, missing my kids. Some were local, and some further away. I missed hanging with them, and hearing about their lives. I really just missed being a full-time mom. Living alone was way too quiet. I knew things were not as they should be, because most of my relationships with them felt superficial. I also knew there was unhealed baggage from them having shared life with my two ex-husbands. And there was what remained of my own trauma. I had received counseling for the damage done to me, but they had resisted help for themselves. I will say it again: It's hard to recognize there is a problem, until someone points it out. And then you must want to do something about it.

So, as I sat there alone, I prayed and cried out to God about all of this, and how desperately I missed them, and wanted things to be as they should be. I repeated over and over, "Why, God, why?" I was crying and wanted answers. And I wanted to understand how these kids who I loved with my whole heart could feel so estranged from me.

And He answered me but not in the words I wanted to hear. "You orphaned them. What do you think they should feel?"

"What??? I orphaned my kids? That's not true! I never left them. I did everything with them because I didn't want them to ever feel the way I had felt growing up. I wanted them to know I was invested in them, in everything they did. I don't know what you mean, God?"

"You did all those things so they would not feel like you did. You didn't want them to feel the rejection and abandonment you felt. Because you were orphaned, too. Your mother checked out with each of your dad's infidelities, his control, and his gaslighting. Your mom modeled all her unhealthy reactions, and you unwittingly adopted them. When those same things happened to you, you reacted in the same way. You didn't want to, you didn't plan to, but it's what you knew.

And you are not alone. Your mom was not alone. And so many others need to know they are not alone. Your dad had his own issues passed to him—and many he passed to you as well. This is a generational issue, daughter, and I want you to write about it. I want you to tell your story, your whole story, and I want your story to give hope, not only to your kids, but many, many families who suffer with this issue."

So that is how this book got started. I dug into all I could find on intergenerational trauma, and discovered so very much of what I had experienced as a child, set me up for shutting down— instead of standing up. I had done a lot of healing over the years, but there were parts of me who had not had that opportunity. When I shared my stories of trauma with my counselors, I only shared the parts about my teen years and older—the Leslie years. I didn't talk about the young me. I didn't talk about Karin. And I learned that is where it all began.

In God's faithful love for me and His desire to make all things new, He laid out this work, so I could finally recognize the little girl who had not grown up yet. Who had not been given a voice, and who was still blaming herself for all the downfalls, bad choices, and mistakes. A little girl who needed to tell her story. Because that is what opened my eyes to the trauma my parents experienced. And that discovery helped me immensely in viewing them with different eyesight. This is what I have referred to as "re-framing one's perspective." It's where truth enters in, instead of hanging onto a perception based in trauma and pain.

A perfect example of this was when my mom said to me, on the day my dad first left on the ship, "All the tears in the world will not make any difference. You're wasting your time." I took that as meaning she thought my tears were an act, and she was being cruel, but what she really meant was, "Honey, I have cried all those tears, begging him not to leave, but they didn't make him stay." This colored my mom in a different light. One of empathy, and not sarcasm. I am sure there were many more examples, but because I expected the worst, I painted it that way. And many other victims do as well.

It is the deepest desire of my heart for my kids to re-frame some things as well. For them to know none of what happened was ever intentional. That if it were possible, I would wipe out all the wrongs they experienced. And we could live the rest of my days with the love I always intended for them to know and feel. And that is my prayer for everyone who picks up this book.

For some of you, this may have been a difficult read. Maybe because you find it hard to believe these things happen to people. Or maybe because similar things may have happened to you.

If you have related to my story, and are still dealing with the aftermath of trauma, seek help. It could be about those things that happened as a child, completely beyond your control. It could be about the choices you made because you were acting out the trauma you experienced. Whichever, seek help. You don't have to live there. I have included some resources for those who would like to do more searching. These are books that have not only helped me, but have helped many to whom I have recommended them. These are excellent resources to help you begin your healing journey.

If you do nothing else in your life, don't carry this with you. Learn to confront your anger, and look at the cold, hard truth about who has hurt you. Remember what I said at the beginning—it's not disrespecting your parents to admit they made mistakes, but it is disrespecting the young parts of you who need to tell their story. Find a counselor with whom you can connect and let them help you unload all that pain—feel it, experience it, and finally—let it go. That's when you will be free to forgive those who have hurt you, and, if need be, learn how to forgive yourself. Jesus wants you free, and He holds His hand out to you. Take it.

Tell your story.

End

References

Henry, T. (2013). *Atlas of sexual violence.* St. Louis, MO: Mosby

Keffer, S. (2018). *Intimate deception.* Grand Rapids, MI: Revell

New International Version. (2011). Zondervan. (Original work published 1973)

Resources

Love is a Choice: The definitive book on letting go of unhealthy relationships
by Robert Hemfelt, Frank Minirth, and Paul Meier (1989)

There is no joy in doing everything for another and calling it love. Even if you believe you are making intelligent choices. *It's simpler to do it myself! He needs my help! I the just want to keep the peace! If I don't do it, no one will!* The burden of codependency will cause untold misery in your life and in the lives of your family members. Is codependency at root of your unhappiness? Let the doctors Of the Meier New Life Clinic and The Minirth Clinic walk you through their ten proven stages to recovery from codependency, introducing a new dimension: the important stage of seeing God's unconditional love as the answer to your deepest emotional needs and your hunger for love.

The Betrayal Bond: Breaking free of exploitive relationships
by Patrick J. Carnes (1997)

For seventeen years *The Betrayal Bond* has been the primary source for therapists and patients wrestling the effects of emotional pain and harm caused by exploitation from someone they trusted. Divorce, litigation, incest and child abuse, domestic violence, kidnapping, professional exploitation and religious abuse are all areas of trauma bonding. These are situations and relationships of incredible intensity or importance lend themselves more easily to an exploitation of trust or power. In *The Betrayal Bond*, Dr. Carnes presents an in-depth study of these relationships; why they form, who is most susceptible, and how they become so powerful. Dr. Carnes also gives a clear explanation of the bond that compels people to tolerate the intolerable, and for the first time, maps out the brain connection that makes being with hurtful people comparable to 'a drug of choice.' Most importantly, Carnes provides practical steps to identify compulsive attachment patterns and ultimately to change or end them for good.

Intimate Deception: Healing the wounds of sexual betrayal
by Sheri Keffer (2018)

Nothing destroys trust like sexual betrayal. Beyond broken vows, a woman who discovers that the man she loves has been viewing pornography or having an affair must deal with devastating blows to her self-image and self-worth. She must grapple with the fact that the man she thought she knew has lied and deceived her. She may even bear the brunt of shame and judgment when the people around her find out. Drawing from her experience both as a marriage and family therapist and a woman who personally experienced the devastation of sexual betrayal, Dr. Sheri Keffer walks women impacted by betrayal through the pain and toward recovery. She explains how the trauma of betrayal affects our minds, bodies, spirits, and sexuality. She offers practical tools for dealing with emotional triggers and helps women understand the realities of sexual addiction. And she shows women how to practice self-care, develop healthy boundaries, protect themselves from abuse or manipulation, and find freedom from the burden of shame and guilt.

Boundaries: When to say yes, how to say no to take control of your life
by Henry Cloud, John Townsend (1992)

Does your life feel like it's out of control? Perhaps you feel like you have to say yes to everyone's requests. Maybe you find yourself readily taking responsibility for others' feelings and problems. Or perhaps you focus so much on being loving and unselfish that you've forgotten your own limits and limitations. Or maybe it's all of the above. In this bestseller Drs. Henry Cloud and John Townsend help you learn when to say yes and know how to say no in order to take control of your life and set healthy, biblical boundaries with your spouse, children, friends, parents, co-workers, and even yourself.

Into Abba's Arms: Finding the acceptance you've always wanted
by Sandra D. Wilson

Wilson leads readers on a personal journey toward healing by helping them to hear God's voice inviting them to find ultimate acceptance and safety in a deep relationship with him.

Forgiven Much
by Leslie T. Dean

This is a love story between one who is forgiven much and one who loves much. A woman's painful search for love and approval begins as a young girl in Rome-occupied Israel. Her repeated failures to please her parents leave her longing for acceptance. She crosses paths with an extraordinary family who offer her the love she has been seeking, albeit short-lived. When they mysteriously disappear, her hope goes with them, and she is left feeling abandoned and rejected. Subsequently, her life's choices lead her in a downward spiral that culminate in the face-to-face meeting with the lover of her soul . . . and the forgiver of her sins. Her struggles with unworthiness and guilt are keenly revealed when God's unconditional love penetrates her heart. This transforming love of God changes her life forever and proves those who have been forgiven little, love little, but if you have been forgiven much . . .

Healing is a Choice: 10 decisions that will transform your life and 10 lies that can prevent you from making them
by Stephen Arterburn

DO YOU WANT TO GET WELL? The power to heal—physically, mentally, emotionally, spiritually—is in God's hands. But the choice to be healed is yours. Everyone, at some level, needs healing. You may have prayed for healing many times, for many years. Perhaps you have lived with your brokenness so long that you have become accustomed to it. Maybe you wonder just when God is going to take all the hurt away. He can. But you also must choose to let the hurt go and let the healing begin.

Unraveled Roots: Exposing the hidden causes of damaging behaviors
by Karen Barbito, Melinda Means, and Lisa Rowe

Are you weary of finding yourself in the same painful cycles no matter how hard you try to break free? Do you long for life to be different? There are reasons why you find yourself in the same places of hurt and struggle time and time again. Today's damaging behaviors and choices are often tied to yesterday's childhood pain and other traumas that lie beneath the surface. Until we recognize this, we will continue to make the same poor choices. We need intervention to begin to forge a new, more positive path. Karin, Melinda, and Lisa are living proof that change and freedom is possible.

The Wounded Heart: Hope for adult victims of childhood sexual abuse
by Dan B. Allender

For those who have experienced childhood sexual abuse and those who love and care for them, *The Wounded Heart* offers a tender, compassionate window into the psychological effects of abuse and the theological foundations for healing. Thirty years ago, with great courage and vision, Dan Allender brought Christians to the table to acknowledge, understand, and help victims heal from their experience of the evil of sexual abuse. His work continues to help victims and those who love them to honestly acknowledge their abuse, understand the unique challenge of repentance for victims of abuse, and learn to love boldly in defiance of their trauma. Ultimately Dan offers the bold assurance to sexual abuse victims that even they can find their way to joy and hope in the comforting embrace of a good God.

Unlocking Your Family Patterns: Finding freedom from a hurtful past
by Henry Cloud, John Townsend, Dave Carder, Earl Henslin
In this honest and forthright look at families of all shapes and sizes will help you down the path of healing (whether you know you need it or whether you're just not sure). *Unlocking Your Family Patterns* combines decades worth of counseling wisdom and pastoral care insights into this one practical resource. Your past may hurt, and your family's patterns may have left emotional scars, but your future has not been laid in stone yet. There is hope for healing, there are lessons to learn, and there are paths toward family health. Using clinical, biblical, and practical examples to help you uncover the patterns your family has lived in, this book might lead you toward the family U-turn you've been looking for.

www.ingramcontent.com/pod-product-compliance
Lightning Source LLC
Chambersburg PA
CBHW061243120726
48001CB00001B/118